Walking Away from Terrorism

This accessible new book looks at how and why individuals leave terrorist movements, and considers the lessons and implications that emerge from this process.

Focusing on the tipping points for disengagement from groups such as Al Qaeda, the IRA and the UVF, this volume is informed by the dramatic and sometimes extraordinary accounts that the terrorists themselves offered to the author about why they left terrorism behind.

The book examines three major issues:

- what we currently know about de-radicalisation and disengagement;
- how discussions with terrorists about their experiences of disengagement can show how exit routes come about, and how they then fare as 'ex-terrorists' away from the structures that protected them;
- what the implications of these findings are for law-enforcement officers, policymakers and civil society on a global scale.

Concluding with a series of thought-provoking yet controversial suggestions for future efforts at controlling terrorist behaviour, *Walking Away from Terrorism* provides an comprehensive introduction to disengagement and de-radicalisation and offers policymakers a series of considerations for the development of counter-radicalisation and de-radicalisation processes.

This book will be essential reading for students of terrorism and political violence, war and conflict studies, security studies and political psychology.

John Horgan is Director of the International Center for the Study of Terrorism at the Pennsylvania State University. He is one of the world's leading experts on terrorist psychology, and has authored over 50 publications in this field; recent books include the *The Psychology of Terrorism* (Routledge 2005) and *Leaving Terrorism Behind* (co-edited, Routledge 2009).

Series: Political Violence
Series Editors: Paul Wilkinson and David Rapoport

This book series contains sober, thoughtful and authoritative academic accounts of terrorism and political violence. Its aim is to produce a useful taxonomy of terror and violence through comparative and historical analysis in both national and international spheres. Each book discusses origins, organisational dynamics and outcomes of particular forms and expressions of political violence.

Aviation Terrorism and Security
Edited by Paul Wilkinson and Brian M. Jenkins

Counter-Terrorist Law and Emergency Powers in the United Kingdom, 1922–2000
Laura K. Donohue

The Democratic Experience and Political Violence
Edited by David C. Rapoport and Leonard Weinberg

Inside Terrorist Organizations
Edited by David C. Rapoport

The Future of Terrorism
Edited by Max Taylor and John Horgan

The IRA, 1968–2000
An Analysis of a Secret Army
J. Bowyer Bell

Millennial Violence
Past, Present and Future
Edited by Jeffrey Kaplan

Right-Wing Extremism in the Twenty-First Century
Edited by Peter H. Merkl and Leonard Weinberg

Terrorism Today
Christopher C. Harmon

Combating Terrorism in Northern Ireland
Edited by James Dingley

Leaving Terrorism Behind
Individual and Collective Disengagement
Edited by Tore Bjørgo and John Horgan

Unconventional Weapons and International Terrorism
Challenges and New Approaches
Edited by Magnus Ranstorp and Magnus Normark

International Aviation and Terrorism
Evolving Threats, Evolving Security
John Harrison

Walking Away from Terrorism
Accounts of Disengagement from Radical and Extremist Movements
John Horgan

Walking Away from Terrorism

Accounts of disengagement from radical and extremist movements

John Horgan

Routledge
Taylor & Francis Group

LONDON AND NEW YORK

First published 2009
by Routledge
2 Park Square, Milton Park, Abingdon, Oxon OX14 4RN

Simultaneously published in the USA and Canada
by Routledge
270 Madison Ave, New York, NY 10016

*Routledge is an imprint of the Taylor & Francis Group,
an informa business*

© 2009 John Horgan

Typeset in Times by
RefineCatch Limited, Bungay, Suffolk
Printed and bound in Great Britain by
TJ International Ltd, Padstow, Cornwall

British Library Cataloguing in Publication Data
A catalogue record for this book is available from the British Library

Library of Congress Cataloging-in-Publication Data
Horgan, John, 1974–
Walking away from terrorism: accounts of disengagement from radical
and extremist movements / John Horgan.
    p. cm.
  includes bibliographical references.
  1. Terrorists—Psychology 2. Terrorism—Psychological aspects—
3. Terrorism—Prevention. 4. Terrorists—Psychology—Case studies.
5. Terrorism—Psychological aspects—Case studies. 6. Terrorism—
Prevention—Case studies. I. Title.
  HV6431.H668 2009
  363.325—dc22   2009001053

ISBN10: 0–415–43943–4 (hbk)
ISBN10: 0–415–43944–2 (pbk)
ISBN10: 0–203–87473–8 (ebk)

ISBN13: 978–0–415–43943–5 (hbk)
ISBN13: 978–0–415–43944–2 (pbk)
ISBN13: 978–0–203–87473–8 (ebk)

This book is dedicated to my grandfather, Martin Hewitt

Contents

Foreword

Understanding the Radical Mind

Jerrold M. Post, M.D. [1]

In order to optimally counter terrorists, it is imperative to have a clear understanding of their psychology. John Horgan and I both believe that in order to find out 'what makes terrorists tick', we have to ask them. John won his 'bones' with his pioneering research on the IRA, but in recent years has been leading an important research effort exploring radicalisation, de-radicalisation and disengagement internationally. In this preface to Horgan's initial book on this major multi-year effort, I would like to share some thoughts on the entrance into the path of radicalisation that very much complement John Horgan's work, and suggest some of the challenges for counter-terrorism these understandings raise.

In a major interview study of 35 Middle East terrorists, including 14 secular nationalist terrorists and 21 radical Islamist terrorists, incarcerated in Israeli and Palestinian prisons (Post, Sprinzak and Denny, 2003),[2] a finding for both the secular nationalist terrorists and for the Islamist fundamentalist terrorists was that the subjects revealed how they were exposed, early in life and usually in the mosque, to the stories of how 'they' (Israelis) stole the land from their parents and grandparents. And also very early, they were taught that the only way to become a 'man' was to join the revolution and fight to regain those lands. They were not being trained to be terrorists but to be soldiers in a revolution. Over 80% of the secular group members reported growing up in communities that were radically involved and slightly more than 75% of the Islamist members report a similar experience. Thus there was a generational transmission of hatred – a hatred 'bred in the bone'.

A vivid example of this generational transmission of hatred was provided by Mohammad Rezaq, an Abu Nidal terrorist tried in federal court in Washington, D.C. for his role in the skyjacking of an Egypt-Air airliner over Malta.[3] During the botched special forces team attack on this plane in Malta, 55 passengers lost their lives. I served as an expert witness for the Department of Justice and had the opportunity of interviewing Rezaq over a three-day period. His mother was eight years old in 1948, living in Jaffa, an Arab suburb of Tel Aviv, when the 1948 war occurred (called the *War of Independence* by the Israelis, the *Catastrophe* by the Palestinians). They were forced to flee, and ended up in her grandfather's farm on the West Bank.

There they lived an idyllic life until 1967 when the terrorist to be, Mohammad Rezaq, was eight years old, when the 1967 war occurred, and they were again forced to flee, this time ending up in a refugee camp in Jordan. On the way to the camp, the mother said to her son, bitterly, 'This is the second time this has happened to me, where they have forced us to leave our homes, our land.'

In the camp, with UNESCO funding, Rezaq went to school. He recalled vividly being told by his teacher, a member of the PLO that the only way to become a man was to join the revolution and regain the lands stolen from his parents and grandparents. They had reading, writing, and arithmetic in the morning, and in the afternoon were taught paramilitary techniques, training on obstacle courses, how to devise booby traps, weapons and explosives handling. When he played a lead role in the skyjacking of the Egypt-Air plane, it was one of the proudest moments of his life. Rezaq was at last fulfilling his destiny.

At the major International Summit on Democracy, Terrorism and Security held in Madrid, Spain on the first anniversary of the Madrid train station bombing, I had the challenge of recruiting a committee of experts on the psychology of terrorism to develop a consensus statement on the psychological causes of terrorism. John Horgan, whose *Psychology of Terrorism*[4] provided a model of rigorous social science research applied to the phases in the life cycle of terrorists was a key member of the committee. Among the conclusions were that:

- Explanations at the level of individual psychology are insufficient. It is not going too far to assert that terrorists are psychologically 'normal' in the sense of not being clinically psychotic. They are neither depressed, severely emotionally disturbed, nor are they crazed fanatics. In fact, terrorist groups and organisations regularly screen out emotionally unstable individuals. They represent, after all, a security risk.
- A clear consensus exists that it is not individual psychology, but group, organisational and social psychology that provide the greatest analytic power in understanding this complex phenomenon. Terrorists have subordinated their individual identity, to the collective identity, so that which serves the group, organisation or network is of primary importance.[5]

Both for nationalist-separatist groups *and* religious fundamentalist terrorist groups, the pathway to terrorism is entered early. There are pictures of infants with toy suicide bomb belts on; parents lead their young children onto the path of martyrdom early. But what is it that leads these children initially on the path of extremism and radicalisation and finally to become engaged in terrorist violence? And, what is it that leads them to become disengaged? Of critical importance here, John Horgan distinguishes between de-radicalisation and disengagement from terrorist violence.

Finally, if one truly accepts the premise that terrorism is a vicious species of psychological warfare, waged through the media, then countering this psychological warfare is imperative. I would suggest four principles, all of which are based on a nuanced understanding of the psychology of terrorism:

- inhibit potential terrorists from entering the group in the first place
- produce dissension in the group
- facilitate exit from the group, and
- reduce support for the group and delegitimise the leader.[6]

To implement such a program requires optimal understanding of the psychology of terrorism. And this can only be developed by intensive interviewing, as exemplified by the pioneering work of John Horgan.

Preface

A personal reflection on fieldwork

My flight landed at Rafic Hariri International Airport, Beirut, just after 5:00am on 10 September 2007. Already over an hour late because of a delayed departure from Heathrow, I was able to proceed quickly through immigration because Irish citizens do not require a visa. The immigration official checked my passport and asked: 'Hulk Hogan?' 'No, *Horgan*,' I smiled. I wondered if I should remind him that he had made the same joke to me six weeks earlier when I came to Lebanon with my Danish colleagues Michael Taarnby and Lars Hallundbaek for research on *Fatah al Islam*.[1] Exhausted because of the hour, I opted not to. He stamped my passport and I was on my way.

One of my former students at St Andrews once asked me if I ever felt in danger during the interviews for this book. I answered that the danger did not necessarily come from doing interviews, but from actually getting to one. In this case, I was once again playing the Russian roulette that is riding in a Beirut taxi. Despite being only 6:00am and with no traffic on the road, the driver hurtled towards downtown Beirut at breakneck speed. My pidgin Arabic was enough to enliven him, and once he understood I was Irish he became even more animated.

It was 6:25 when we arrived at the hotel in Beirut's *Al Hamra* district. I was excited to be back and did not waste any time in stepping out onto my balcony. The whole city was visible from where I stood. The pock-marked buildings to the west bore the tell-tale scars of the trauma that has plagued this beautiful country. The shiny new office buildings to the east bore tales of a different kind. Commercial property in Beirut was developing at an impressive pace. Downstairs, I practised more Arabic with the hotel receptionist: 'Where can I find the nearest ATM?' (trans. 'wain al bank?'), to which she replied in English – a clear indication of just how elementary my Arabic was. After getting cash, I approached a nearby taxi stand and asked the first driver to take me to Tripoli. I haggled down the price from 70 to 50 US dollars and felt proud of my negotiation skills as I settled in for the 125-kilometre trip.

Once clear of the chaotic traffic in Beirut, the taxi's speedometer rarely dipped below 160 kilometres per hour (kph). Only once on the main highway did we slow down, to 110kph, to peer out at the latest casualty. A brand new

BMW was turned completely over on its side and had rolled into a deep ditch. A small band of soldiers stopped to help, but before I had time to look for the vehicle's occupants, my taxi driver sped up, and off we went in the direction of Tripoli. Minutes later, a ragged jeep carrying half a dozen soldiers appeared. The taxi driver tailgated them, honking his horn impatiently for them to let us pass. With their rifles resting across their knees, the soldiers did not bat an eyelid. They did not even look irritated as we overtook them, missing them by mere inches.

Before I knew it we were only 15 kilometres outside of Tripoli, and slowly approaching an army checkpoint. I wondered if the ease with which we passed through the checkpoint was a reflection of the previous weekend's events at Nar El Bared, the Palestinian refugee camp the Lebanese army 'liberated' with heavy bombardment. I leaned towards the driver: 'I want to go to the city centre, to the clock tower.' He duly obliged and dropped me off.

Downtown Tripoli is overwhelming. Nestled in a small corner of northern Lebanon, it assaults the senses: intense, noisy, claustrophobic, and bursting with so much activity one does not know where to look. There are people everywhere, walking in every conceivable direction. Traffic horns blare, brakes screech, and voices shout. In the background, the *muezzin* blared over the loudspeaker, calling all Muslims to prayer. A few weeks earlier, in Dublin, I had lunch with an Irish Army officer who warned me against wandering off the beaten track in Tripoli. The Jihadists of *Fatah Al Islam* had been active in certain pockets of the city (the *Abu Samra* district was out of bounds for now) and walking around Tripoli I recalled the details of my meeting in Dublin. I stuck out like a sore thumb. While I had been to Tripoli with Michael and Lars a few weeks earlier, I now missed their company. Now, I felt like I was the only foreigner in the whole city.

I had been instructed to go to the local McDonald's on the corner of Spenny's supermarket, a well-known meeting place. I asked a local taxi driver to take me there, and we arrived within five minutes. I found a bench outside the main entrance to the supermarket and sat down to phone my interviewee. I dialled his number. No answer. I waited two minutes and tried again. Still nothing. I wrote a short email message from my BlackBerry: 'Dear Sheikh, I have arrived, and am outside Spenny's. Tried to call you.' Fifteen minutes later, he called me: 'John, where are you?' I told him. He replied, 'I'll be there in a few minutes.' Waiting around, watching the cars pull up to the McDonald's, the midday sun was intense. Although I sat in the shade, I roasted in what felt like 110 degrees.

A few more minutes passed, and in anticipation of my interviewee's arrival to pick me up, I started to pace. I looked inside the supermarket to see half a dozen staff milling around, doing nothing but staring back out at me. Ten minutes passed. Then 20, 30, 40 minutes. *Something's wrong. Why is he not here? Maybe another interviewer is keeping him? Surely he wouldn't let me come all this way and say nothing?* By now, I was out of water and went to go into the supermarket to get more. As I did, the heat and anxiety about the meeting combined such that I convinced myself that he had changed his mind.

I had been in situations like this before. Years earlier, while doing my PhD at University College, Cork, I began my fieldwork under the direction of my mentor Max Taylor. On many occasions, I had sat in hotels and bars in tiny little towns, scattered around the border counties of Ireland. I would spend what in hindsight felt like endless hours, watching and waiting for interviewees from the Irish Republican Army, or one of its sister groups, to walk through the door. For the most part, people turn up and are cooperative, granting interviews to academics like myself. But sometimes, despite having agreed to an interview, they would not show up. And of course, there is nothing one can do about it but accept it and try again, either with the same person or someone else. In those days, it was sometimes the case that I would get a call, and someone would apologise for running late. Other times, they would contact me a day later, and sometimes (though rare) I would hear nothing at all. Once I even found out from a colleague in the field months later that one of my interviewees (whom he had since met) did not want to meet me because of a suspicion I was too closely linked to the security services. But despite the variety of considerations and issues to be worked through in interviewing those involved in terrorism, the reality of fieldwork is not the constant 'knife-edge' experience that some terrorism experts falsely claim. The reality involves a lot of work, with careful planning and meticulous communications with potential interviewees well in advance of the actual meeting. This kind of research also requires having extraordinary levels of patience in the lead-up to an interview, finding something constructive to do while the hours pass, all the while avoiding the creeping suspicion that you may be about to face crushing disappointment – having come all that way, engaged in weeks of study, research and preparation, to face the possibility that your interviewee had changed his or her mind. Back in Beirut six weeks earlier, a member of Hezbollah had pulled out of an interview at the last minute and I worried that this was about to happen all over again in Tripoli.

I left Spenny's and walked back outside, resigned to the fact that my interviewee was not coming. I started to think about my options for returning to Beirut. As I wondered about how best to proceed, I glanced at the boy guarding the entrance of the supermarket car park. *How does he stand this heat?* He had barely moved an inch the whole time I waited. As I was about to dial the Sheikh one last time, a black Nissan SUV sped towards me, the driver waving enthusiastically. He gestured for me to come around to the passenger side, and before I could even get in, he was already apologising: 'John, I'm so sorry. I went to leave but my phone kept ringing. I'm sorry you had to stay out in the heat.' I shook hands with Omar Bakri Fostok, better known as Omar Bakri Muhammad. Expelled from the United Kingdom, Omar Bakri was the one-time leader of *Al Muhajiroun*, a major Islamist movement. But Omar Bakri was more than that. He is also allegedly an Al Qaeda 'spiritual guide'. Having begun his political life in the Syrian Muslim Brotherhood, Omar Bakri was closely connected to Al Qaeda. In August 1998, he prepared and issued a series of statements on behalf of Osama Bin Laden shortly after the bombings of the US embassies in Kenya and Tanzania. Omar Bakri was now living in exile. A few weeks after our initial encounter while in the region with Michael and Lars, I returned to Lebanon to interview him about what I described in my emails as the processes of radicalisation and de-radicalisation. In our original meetings, Omar Bakri not only criticised the use of the term radicalisation, but described Al Qaeda as 'legend . . . because you never see them coming'.

Omar Bakri was one of the final interviewees I spent time with for this book and the larger project of which this book is part. Thus my experiences with him are memorable in a personal sense. However, I chose to begin this book by recalling an experience from the field for reasons that will soon become apparent. I decided early in the writing process that the preface would see both the beginning and end of my offering personal reflections on the meetings with those interviewed for this book. At the same time I wanted to challenge some of the lingering myths surrounding interviews with terrorists. The reason for this arose from experiences I had throughout 2007. I encountered some unexpected reactions to a series of presentations and public lectures on the subject of disengagement and de-radicalisation from terrorism. Audience members were more intrigued by the fieldwork and would ask more questions about the practical aspects of my research than substantive issues of my findings: they seemed more interested in *me* than in understanding political violence. Time and time again, questions focused on what fieldwork was like, if there was danger involved, if I feared for my life, and more generally about how and why terrorists and former terrorists meet with academics.

I understand and appreciate the curiosity that surrounds such issues. Terrorist movements are, above all, secretive, and it follows that in order to gain access to those who participate in terrorism, there must be some special, equally secretive process. But, experiences from many field researchers have shown that this is rarely the case. The overwhelming majority of the time, the reality of fieldwork on terrorism does not involve being bundled into cars, or being held at gunpoint. With the appropriate preparations, one can arrange meetings, and interview participants in what would otherwise appear like perfectly normal and mundane circumstances. In the mountains outside Tripoli, I interviewed Omar Bakri for four hours that day without interruption save for the glances and whispers of other diners looking over at our table.

In any research that involves meeting with people who have engaged in violence, there is a temptation to place oneself at the centre of the narrative. The temptation is to present an insider account of what it was like to come 'face to face with an *actual* terrorist'. While exciting to some, such accounts from academics run the risk of presenting what is at best a personal or journalistic account, and at worst an unfettered ego trip. Often what is written about terrorism tends to be opinion presented as if it is based on expertise. Stylistically, of course, while the former might appeal to a much broader audience, the latter may not, and both rigour and substance may be compromised as a result of an accessible text. Writing about the challenges inherent in researching terrorism, Marc Sageman[2] has often made the observation that data is not the plural of anecdote, yet we are still slow to accept this in much of the work on terrorism.

This book is not about my personal opinions, or what regard I have for the subject matter or those I interviewed. Instead it is presented with the principal regard for evidence and analysis in challenging and unusual research circumstances. It is an attempt to engage questions about the psychology of terrorist behaviour through scientific reasoning and rigorous scrutiny. It is not about my experiences, but the experiences of those who allowed me to interview them about being involved in terrorism, and about leaving it behind. This book is an attempt to contribute to our knowledge of these people and the processes involved, and to describe the significance of the qualities and meaning of the accounts offered by them.

The background to this book lay with my previous volume, *The Psychology of Terrorism*. In that book, I wrote about terrorists by providing the basis for a micro-model for understanding and explaining how and why people became involved in terrorism, what involvement entailed, and giving a sense of what kinds of factors influence how and why people leave. I did this without providing much by way of the personal accounts of who these individuals were, and how they themselves constructed meaning around their acts. From my previous interviews with both active and former terrorists in Ireland, I knew a great deal about this, but it emerged that those who read the book did not. Therefore, I wanted to take a different approach to illustrating these arguments. In recent years, several books about the 'root causes' of terrorism identified and addressed the broad social and political conditions necessary to inspire and give rise to terrorist violence. And while much has been written about the terrorist from an individual perspective, there are far fewer accounts based on interviews with former terrorists about their experiences, let alone allowing them to speak in their own words. Convinced that a book detailing the accounts of how someone becomes (and remains) involved in terrorism would be useful, I came to the realisation that the academic community had ignored almost everything to do with *disengagement* from terrorism. Related to this, with almost everyone writing about radicalisation, why was there virtually nothing about *de-radicalisation*? In fact, was the notion of de-radicalisation realistic? Perhaps de-radicalisation was not even something that necessarily followed disengagement? To paraphrase my good friend and colleague Dipak Gupta, why did we not consider the qualities of the pathways *out* of the collective madness into terrorism in the first place? And so I decided to make my plans for the interviews that appear in these pages.

In addition, the focus on my work to date was on individual terrorists. Terrorism researchers have long accepted that to understand terrorism, we need to appreciate that it operates at multiple levels – there is the individual terrorist, but there is also the group and broader network to which he or she belongs, the community being represented by the terrorist, and broader social, cultural and other issues that can impinge upon the individual terrorist at any time and at any phase of their involvement. To paraphrase a key concern of Walter Reich, attempting to understand terrorism from one single level of analysis is a recipe for failure.[3] But before attempting to achieve an integrated understanding of terrorism (i.e. by appreciating how the different levels interact) it is critical that we understand what an individual level of analysis actually means. It is not, nor has it ever been, a valid presumption that terrorism can be *explained* through individual factors. Instead, the individual level of analysis should be characterised as aspiring to achieve a sense of both what role exists in terrorism studies for features assumed characteristic of individual issues (e.g. decision-making, personality, demographics, intelligence, predisposing risk factors for involvement, etc.), and also where the relevance for those (and many other) issues can be situated within a broader, multi-level perspective – in other words, where and how does the identification of risk factors for involvement matter to the degree that knowing about such factors may be relevant to managing and controlling the problem? Nobody familiar with the literature would attempt to understand involvement in terrorism without looking at group and organisational dynamics. But we have become increasingly confused about how to understand the individual (and individual issues) within a multi-level analysis of terrorism. One objective of this book is to redress some of the recent faulty assumptions that have unfairly and incorrectly taken root in popular discussions of the topic.

Though this book is an exploratory reflection on the nature of involvement in terrorism, it has a specific concern about exploring one particular phase of involvement – *disengagement*. In thinking about this, there is not a lot of prior research. Martha Crenshaw wrote in the 1980s and 1990s about how terrorist movements decline and end. In the late 1980s, Alison Jamieson[4] interviewed Italian terrorists in prison. Her extraordinary meetings with *Brigate Rosse* member Adriana Faranda, detailed in Jamieson's *The Heart Attacked*, proved insightful and revealing. What emerged from Faranda's life history was a complex, gradual process of 'dissociation' from her involvement with the Red Brigades. The unexplored process of disengagement, and the decision-making behind the dissociation of Jamieson's interviewees, tantalisingly hinted at the existence of a process that *might* be just as complex as the initial radicalisation pathways that led to involvement in the first place. It also hinted that there were *many* potential ways out of terrorism, and that if we tried to identify them there might be implications for the development of policy initiatives.

These and a small few other exceptions aside, there was next to nothing about how and why individual terrorists decided to leave behind violent activity. Around 2004, I discussed with my colleague Tore Bjørgo issues of 'becoming an ex-' – Tore's work on right-wing extremists and gang members illustrated some of the issues around how and why people leave extremist groups. But I was not convinced that his findings would apply to terrorist movements and neither was he. Our collaboration led to the production, with several colleagues, of another book, *Leaving Terrorism Behind: Individual and Collective Disengagement*, an edited collection the findings of which I return to in Chapter 9 of this book.

With *The Psychology of Terrorism* finished, I had a unique opportunity: to explore the story of how and why men and women leave terrorist groups behind. One further challenge became apparent. In working on this area, I asked: why not go to the terrorists themselves to get their accounts, in their own words? It might be surprising to discover that terrorism researchers generally tend to ignore terrorist movements when they cease to exist. The dearth of research on individual disengagement might be explained by the implicit assumption that once terrorist movements cease to function they are irrelevant. This assumption is a grave error. It is when movements *cease* their activities that the greatest opportunities often exist for research on former participants more willing and better able to respond to interview requests from academics. While some former terrorists become minor celebrities, participating in high-profile media interviews, there are many former members willing to participate in serious research activity.[5]

Therefore, *Walking Away From Terrorism* represents an attempt to address a host of issues. It is an extension of my previous book in that it offers a more detailed treatise on the nature of involvement in terrorism, and provides illustrations of the kinds of data needed to develop the model presented in that book. It also explores and finds greater meaning for the individual perspective, and in doing so is supported by the cases that derived from a series of interviews conducted over an 18-month period of preliminary research from late 2006 to early 2008. During this time, I travelled around the world interviewing former terrorists in Belfast, Beirut, Oslo, London, Paris, Tripoli, Jakarta and elsewhere. I interviewed 29 former terrorists and accessed a broader pool comprising 52 people in total. The remaining 23 were supporters, family members and friends of those interviewees. Of the 29 former terrorists, my time spent with them varied from person to person and from location to location. I spent only a little amount of time with some. One interviewee stayed for 20 minutes – he arrived late and gave little more than a few words in answering my questions. He got up to leave early, and I never saw or heard from him again. Most of the interviewees spent about an hour with me (which seemed to become a standard unit of interview time), while others spent several hours. A small few allowed me to come and spend several days with them, and in one case I visited an interviewee over three weekends in one month. Consequently, and given that research on terrorism is still very much characterised by the pre-scientific description and the exploration of many basic concepts and ideas, the reader will see that some cases are necessarily more complete than others. Some chapters present loose sketches, while others contain complex, deep accounts that will warrant years of analysis.

I realised late into this project that, although the research was very much exploratory in nature, I could not present all of the cases here – while they are as complex as they are detailed, some are exceptionally long. My interactions with one former terrorist ran to 100 pages after I transcribed all the tapes. Attempts to reduce their size for editorial reasons can sometimes be worse than leaving them out altogether. Instead, I have presented what I feel to be a representative cross-section of accounts from a selection of different terrorist groups to illustrate the complexity, nuance and unique ways in which people come to be involved with, and ultimately disengage from, terrorism. Interestingly, that complexity is also appreciated by some of the former terrorists themselves. One of my interviewees with whom I spent a long time working through how and why he came to be, in his words, an 'effective' member of a terrorist movement (he became a commander who oversaw dozens of murders) was resigned to believing that there was nothing that could really 'explain' him: 'Honestly, I think it was being at the right place at the right time.' When I suggested to him that explanation might not actually ever be possible, that *description* might be the closest we get in providing insight into the development of 'an activist', he nodded in disappointment.

Another former terrorist, on learning that I am a psychologist, asked: 'So are you trying to get inside my head?' When I told him that I thought that might be very difficult to do, he repeated the enquiry twice more before the interview began. These sentiments epitomise not only the complexity and idiosyncrasies of the accounts presented here, but also represent the frustration some will experience from this book. I will make this very explicit from the outset – in understanding the terrorist, we have not yet found any reliable patterns, any discernible profiles, or any easy answers. In part, that is because there probably can never be a terrorist profile, just as there can never be a profile of 'criminals'. While the academic community is making steady progress in understanding these difficult issues, we have a long way to go, and while we might aspire to developing a *scientific* study of terrorist behaviour, exploration (let alone *description*) might be a more noble and realistic achievement than true explanation at this point. The nature of this exploration may be empirical, but it is important to accurately reflect on the scientific limitations of our enquiry, at whatever level we operate as academic researchers.

In *The Psychology of Terrorism*, I argued that if psychology was to offer the study of terrorism tangible ways of working towards more effective solutions, the discipline would have to move beyond thinking about a psychology of terrorism as something only concerned with trying to search for a terrorist personality. One of the greatest challenges for psychologists engaged in terrorism research is to show that really, the issue of finding a terrorist personality (and more broadly, a terrorist profile) does not really matter as much as we think it does. Furthermore, and maybe more importantly, accepting this fact will not prevent us from uncovering valuable practical lessons for responses. This will become clearer by the end of the book.

Additionally, we will discover that just as there is no root cause behind involvement in terrorism, there is equally no root cause that explains disengagement. Just like the process that characterises how people become involved, leaving terrorism behind involves a complex, socio-psychological process that does not look the same, or necessarily work in the same way, for everyone. The pathway to disengagement may be as non-linear and dynamic as initial involvement. Some of the pathways may be similar in terms of the qualities experienced by individuals, but they are not necessarily embarked upon in the same way or progressed through in terms of 'stages'. Furthermore, the routes into, through, and out of terrorism are not always the same even for members of the *same* network. The consequences of sustained involvement in terrorism are experienced differently from person to person, and the variation we see in terms of what it *means* to be involved will necessarily be a reflection of that.

That is not to say, however, that there are no meaningful psychological patterns to be identified – on the contrary, and as Chapter 9 will illustrate, we do have some tangible avenues for the development of strategies that might form the basis of interventions. This, I will argue, is relevant whether we are seeking to develop efforts aimed at the *prevention* or control of initial involvement, the *disruption* of subsequent engagement, or the *facilitation* or promotion of disengagement. I am optimistic that we can reliably develop these, but they will take time. In supporting this effort, we will need to find new and more innovative ways of providing the bedrock of empirical evidence needed to support and stand by the claims we make. One outcome of this book is an argument of how we can move closer to that objective. There is a case made for moving from analysis of profiles to *pathways*, and from roots (as in 'root causes') to *routes*, and that this will have valuable relevance for those seeking to develop informed policy.

I present here a total of *six* case studies from the overall sample. Some are leaders, and others are rank and file members. All of the leaders, however, were once followers who graduated from peripheral, apprenticeship roles into senior positions. A challenge was in deciding how many cases to include, but this number and the particular cases chosen for selection, represents a varied cross-section from which we might begin to develop an understanding of the issues inherent in the disengagement process. Given the enormous practical challenges inherent in such research, it will be clear that this is not a truly 'scientific' study. As above, though guided by empirical principles, it is more aligned with what I feel is the true state of terrorism studies today – pre-theoretic, pre-paradigmatic, exploratory and (at best) descriptive. The current field of terrorism studies is, in truth, very far from explanatory. However, this is neither a criticism of terrorism studies (though a reminder every now and again of our limitations is useful) nor is it a pessimistic evaluation of the study from which this book derives. Instead it is a reminder that we should ask the right questions, do more to embrace what tools we have at our disposal, and what we are currently able to do, safely and with the data we can collect. There is a creeping sense in which the theories we have at our disposal for understanding the terrorist are informed less and less by the reality of terrorism as illustrated in accounts from participants. Thus, we should embrace the richness of exploratory accounts, and not prematurely rush to seek some cause or explanation that is increasingly so broad as to be of little benefit to anyone.

However, those for whom this collection is not enough will find the remainder of the cases (as well as some of those included here) presented in a series of academic papers where the accounts (those presented here as well as the remaining cases) are subjected to detailed scientific analysis. What the reader can expect to find in the chapters that follow is data in a relatively raw format, not yet subjected to the rigours of contemporary social science methodology. While the academic or enthusiastic general reader will therefore be able to access the structured qualitative analyses separately, this book is not about that. Instead it presents the accounts, as they were specifically intended for this book – the terrorists' experiences in their own words. Some structure and context are provided to help make sense of the accounts (and a final major section is devoted to broader analysis), but the social scientist reader may find the accompanying case studies written as individual papers more suitable to his or her needs.

The project that gave rise to this book and the broader set of interviews was, in essence, an 18-month pilot study. The study remains technically open – I have begun what in time will be characterised as a longitudinal project with individual former terrorists. The pilot study will be extended in 2010 into a major systematic research programme and some of the individuals interviewed for this book will be re-interviewed and their continuing experiences documented in a database.

Chapter 1 provides an introduction to thinking about the terrorist. Here I discuss what is meant by involvement in terrorism and illustrate some of the basic tenets of terrorist psychology. I make a case for what I view as the 'individual perspective' in the study of terrorism. In doing so, I illustrate the complexity of involvement in terrorism without getting bogged down in unnecessarily academic arguments about the definition of terrorism (this was done in the earlier book). Additionally, I expand on some of the themes mentioned here and explain the challenges inherent in not only developing a psychology of terrorism, but also in the study of terrorist behaviour more generally. This chapter sets both the scene and tone for the individual cases to follow and also serves as a prelude to the analysis and lessons that emerge in the final sections.

While Chapter 1 presents a basic introduction to the issues being explored, Chapter 2 presents a more systematic exploration of the research literature and addresses how and why terrorist movements fall into decline. From this, I present a preliminary examination of how and why individuals might disengage from terrorism. The relevant literature to date is summarised before I develop some basic assertions as a prelude to what will follow, as well as the definitions I offer much later in Chapter 9. I make a number of critical distinctions throughout the book and a major one will be found here – the distinction between *disengagement* from terrorism and *de-radicalisation* from terrorism.

Chapter 3 presents the first of the six case studies. The book is structured in such a way that the reader can go directly into the interviews, but to gain an understanding and appreciation of the significance of the accounts, the reader is encouraged to read Chapters 3–8 in a linear format. The reason for this is explained at the end of Chapter 2.

As is probably evident by now, a major objective of this book is to consider themes that emerge from the qualities of the accounts that could be of relevance for policy. Put simply, what can we learn from individual experiences that can inform responses? Can we find ways of promoting disengagement from terrorism? In some contexts, this is thought of as 'flipping' or 'turning' terrorists. Taking this one step further, can we extend this to thinking about *anti-terrorism* and *counter-radicalisation*? Can the lessons learned from accounts of disengaged former terrorists be used in some way to help prevent others from becoming involved in terrorism in the first place? In the final sections, I present some reflections on the accounts from the interviews, and move towards presenting greater clarity around these issues. In addition, the final chapter is concerned with distinguishing disengagement from de-radicalisation in the context of the development of a psychological and behavioural contribution to counter-terrorism. Chapter 9 seeks to answer the inevitable questions that arise from a study of disengagement from terrorism: *why is it important and what can we do about it*?

John Horgan
Bellefonte, Pennsylvania
January 2009

Acknowledgements

The Airey Neave Trust saw fit to fund the research that led to this book and for that I am extremely grateful. This book is a testament to the extraordinary work of the trust and the efforts of, among others, Mrs Hannah Scott and Dame Veronica Sutherland.

The ideas for this book developed from discussions with a number of people. In particular, I benefited from long conversations with Dr Elizabeth Dunne at the Department of Applied Psychology, University College, Cork. I benefited more broadly from her wit, wisdom and friendship. She is greatly missed.

In Ireland, Jim Cusack's encyclopaedic brain on all affairs IRA-related proved, as always, invaluable. I am grateful to Michael and Lars for their support during our first field trip to Beirut, our meetings with the PLO and our experiences at the Beddawi camp. Comdt. Philip Brennan, Comdt. Conor Lynch and Colonel Con McNamara at the Defence Forces Training Centre, Co. Kildare, also helped with Lebanon. The ever-smiling Noor Huda Ismail helped in Jakarta, while Graham McKendry assisted with affairs in Troon. I am grateful to Shahid Bux and John Morrison during my time at St Andrews and since then for their assistance with research literature. Laurent is always a welcome guide in Paris, and I am grateful to Bob Lambert for his help in London.

Gillian McIlwaine at the Centre for the Study of Terrorism and Political Violence at the University of St Andrews helped with some of the difficult travel arrangements throughout the project, and I am very grateful to her and Julie Middleton for providing two sensible heads during my time in the field. It is difficult to overestimate the support of Paul Wilkinson for his encouragement throughout this research, and his unwavering support before and during my time at St Andrews. One of the founding fathers of terrorism research, I am proud to have worked with him during my time there. I also thank students from IR3008 International Terrorism, IR4526 Terrorism, Radicalism and Extremism and IR5007 Terrorism and Liberal Democracy at St Andrews whose enthusiasm has meant that I had perfect test audiences for some of the ideas presented here.

To take back a phrase originally stolen by Johnny Adair, Max Taylor is simply the best mentor I could have wished for. Depleted wine stocks in Crail could not match the value of our extensive late night discussions about the psychology of terrorism. I will always be grateful to him for giving me my first academic job and for his guidance and support ever since.

Lorraine Bowman helped with research assistance on communities of practice and Shadd Maruna graciously helped with some of the work on desistance. Su Chuen Foo and Kurt Braddock both helped with tracking down literature at Penn State and were generally helpful throughout.

Since moving to the United States, I have been fortunate to benefit from the support and encouragement of far too many people to list. Rick and Louise in Chicago, as always, lent a friendly and supportive voice throughout. The inimitable Marc Sageman lent his thoughts on some early ideas as this work unfolded. I am especially grateful for the support of my new colleagues at the Pennsylvania State University. In particular, I would like to acknowledge Graham Spanier, Susan Welch, Hank Foley, Peter Schiffer, Eva Pell, Rick and Jennifer Jacobs, Greg Eghigian, Mel Mark, David Hall, Sam Hunter, Jan Cleveland, Jake Graham, Frank Ritter, Jonathan Marks, Peter Forster and John Jordan. I reserve special thanks to Kevin Murphy, Susan Mira and my other colleagues at the International Center for the Study of Terrorism, Chris Woods at the College of the Liberal Arts, and to Machelle Seiner and Connie Moore at the Department of Psychology. I also want to thank Patrick Straub for his support and assistance in State College and Virginia.

The terrorism research community is a constantly developing and growing body. I have long benefited, however, from repeated interactions with a number of colleagues including Marc Sageman, Dipak Gupta, David Rapoport, Sir David Veness, Marcy Ribetti, Ariel Merari, Michael Taarnby, Jerrold Post, Victor Asal, Randy Borum, Gary LaFree and Leonard Weinberg.

Andrew Humphrys, Rebecca Brennan and all at Routledge deserve my thanks on this, our second major collaboration. I am especially grateful to them during the final stages when once again their patience knew no bounds.

In early 2007, my good friend and colleague Tore Bjørgo saved my life after our experience traversing the Norwegian ice and I cannot repay him for this.

I wish to thank all those interviewees who allowed me to ask them often uncomfortable and difficult questions. I met most of them in genuinely challenging circumstances. They each had their own reasons for agreeing to speak with me about what they knew would not always be easy if this book was to be done right. I will not say who they are (they know this, and those who requested anonymity will recognise themselves in this book, and in the papers to follow in the years ahead), but to each and every one of them – I am grateful. Some of them I will never meet again, but if I saw them on the street, I would cross the road to meet them.

Finally, to you Mia, for everything else.

1   Qualities are not causes

Introduction

In this chapter, we examine several issues for understanding the development of the terrorist. We look at how attempts to profile the terrorist have floundered and instead consider involvement in terrorism as a complex process. The difficulties associated with terrorist profiling are not new, yet our thinking about the terrorist is rooted in age-old assumptions which have proven unfounded, impractical and devoid of empirical support. Viewing involvement in terrorism as a process may, ironically, lead to the development of more practical benefits than current attempts to profile terrorists can offer. One of the main arguments of this chapter is that in understanding the terrorist, our focus ought to change from the pursuit of *profiles* to the mapping of *pathways*, and from the search for *root causes* to the identification of *route qualities*. This chapter presents an alternative to the profiling metaphor and sets the scene for a greater consideration of the model to follow.

From profiles to pathways

On the morning of 7 July 2005, four men travelled from England's West Yorkshire and Luton to the centre of London. Upon arrival, the men went their separate ways. Within 30 minutes all four were dead along with 52 civilians in the Al Qaeda movement's first strike on the United Kingdom. The coordinated suicide bombings of that day left a further 700 people seriously injured, wounds ranging from cuts by flying glass, to blindness and dismemberment.[1]

Though shocked, London's commuters had little choice in the aftermath of the attacks but to return to their normal routines. In the meantime, details of the four bombers captured public attention across the country. Mohammed Siddique Khan, Shehzad Tanweer, Germaine Lindsay and Hasib Hussain became household names. The media pored over every detail of the men's lives, from the jobs they held to the breakfast cereal one of them ate the morning of the bombings. And while a slew of terrorism experts offered their opinions on what drove these men to blow themselves up, a House of Commons Report[2] into the events of that day concluded:

> What we know ... shows that there is not a consistent profile to help identify who may be vulnerable to radicalisation. Of the 4 individuals here, 3 were second generation British citizens whose parents were of Pakistani origin and one whose parents were of Jamaican origin; Kamel Bourgass, convicted of the Ricin plot, was an Algerian failed asylum seeker; Richard Reid, the failed shoe bomber, had an English mother and Jamaican father. Others of interest have been white converts. Some have been well-educated, some less so. Some genuinely poor, some less so. Some apparently well integrated in the UK, others not. Most single, but some family men with children. Some previously law-abiding, others with a history of petty crime. In a few cases there is evidence of abuse or other trauma in early life, but in others their upbringing has been stable and loving. (p31)

The report captured the imagination of the public. Its narrative style was an attempt to calm an uneasy British audience by making sense of horror through *structure* – just like the 9/11 Commission Report, this report presented a beginning, middle and end.[3] Logical though that structure was, however, many questions remained unanswered. Implicit throughout was a sense of frustration – frustration that there was no clear profile, no obvious terrorist personality, no easy answers as to what the seemingly endless flow of recruits to Al Qaeda had in common. Though the frustration was understandable, the content and tone of the report hinted at something less obvious – that popular thinking about the terrorist was still rooted in age-old assumptions about terrorist psychology.[4] But, and perhaps no less frustrating to many who read the report and other accounts like it, was the fact that after 30 years of research, the social and behavioural sciences had not delivered a meaningful terrorist profile.

The issues that drive the search for the terrorist profile are clear. One issue relates to what terrorists *do*, and how that shapes the way in which we think about who they are and what they are like. The second issue relates to the fact that there are relatively *few* people who engage in terrorism.

To address these issues, we need to consider some of the defining qualities of terrorism and political violence. An inescapable feature of terrorism is its ability to shock. To instigate a climate of heightened psychological arousal, terrorists will engage in high-profile activity that results in death or injury to those who least expect it – civilians, passers-by and commuters on their way to work. The dramatic, immediate and longer-term consequences of terrorist activity force us to confront behaviour that both shocks and sickens us. Consequently, we could easily assume there is something special or different about those who perpetrate such vile acts. Bruce Hoffman[5] describes the first operation of the Black September organisation when, in November

1971, they shot Jordanian Prime Minister Wasfi al-Tal in the lobby of the Cairo Sheraton Hotel. As the Prime Minister lay on the ground dying, one of the members of Black September knelt down on the ground to lap up al-Tal's blood. That one image burned indelibly into the public consciousness, forever characterising the terrorist 'madman'. And such seemingly sadistic tendencies aside, to seek to *deliberately* kill apparently random strangers (through a car bombing for example) in the name of righteousness suggests delusion or abnormality on the part of those who partake in it: 'How could any normal person do this?' is a typical reaction.

A second feature of terrorism is that there are few terrorists. Despite the potentially enormous consequences of terrorism, it remains a disproportionately low-volume activity perpetrated by relatively small numbers of activists. There may be a larger network that contributes in some way to sustaining the terrorist individual, but it remains a low-volume activity. The drama that surrounds terrorism obscures this fact. Much of the social and political commentary in recent years has emphasised the need to consider the 'root causes' of terrorism – generally, calls to address the assumed broad social and political conditions that provide a pretext for involvement and engagement in terrorism.[6] These include poverty, lack of (or an abundance of) education, humiliation for some perceived wrongs, discrimination or a combination of these. But a difficult question arises: given the level at which these conditions become apparent, i.e. to so many people in society affected equally by such conditions, why do so relatively few people act upon those perceived grievances in *this* way?

These questions are both complex and challenging. Over the years, attempts to answer them have polarised many, even within the narrow field of long-term terrorism researchers. We know enough by now, at least, to realise that any answer is not going to satisfy everyone. In the past, researchers have tried to answer these questions with reference to micro-level explanations – in particular, psychologists and psychiatrists focused on the *individual* in an effort to uncover and map the kinds of presumed qualities that may be inherent in terrorists. A frequent temptation was to assume there might be some inherent qualities that characterise terrorists.[7] Perhaps, the argument goes, all terrorists are unified by distinct qualities? Or, maybe at least there are grounds to suggest that a terrorist might be different in some way to the rest of us who do not engage in terrorism?

These days, a popular trend in terrorism research is to stress that there is *no* such thing as a terrorist profile. This argument is often followed with assertions that terrorists are not mad, that they do not suffer from some pathological condition and that they are not abnormal at all. Aside from the fact that these three issues reflect three distinct questions, such claims are actually not entirely accurate. Unless we think about abnormality in a statistical sense (i.e. that terrorist events are rare), what constitutes abnormal is a matter of opinion. These aside, there is a little more agreement on what is meant by both profiling and the argument about whether terrorists are 'mad'.

More problematic is the fact that we do not definitively know if a terrorist profile at some level does not exist. As Ariel Merari argued, it is probably more correct to state that no terrorist profile has been found.[8] However, this is not necessarily negative – what if there is no profile to *be* found?

While it is easy to get bogged down in the complexity of terrorism, we have to anchor our starting points.[9] We should never allow the complexity of terrorism to deter us from searching for practical solutions to its management. Max Taylor has observed that efforts to pathologise the terrorist have resulted in simplistic explanations of terrorism that obscure its true complexity.[10] As a result, the nature of our responses inevitably echoes that simplicity. Taylor is correct, but a reason we do not know if any terrorist profile does exist is that we lack the necessary data to properly test this hypothesis. There is yet another problem. If we *were* able to construct data-driven terrorist profiles, we might question the practical contribution of such knowledge. Profiles tend to encourage one-size-fits-all approaches to management and response. It is doubtful that a profile could tell us anything meaningful about why or how someone seeks to become involved in terrorism in the first place. In fact, any terrorist profile would more likely be a reflection of what someone who has *become* a terrorist has *already* experienced through the process of violent radicalisation. Hannah Arendt,[11] in writing about the 'new militants' in *On Violence*, wrote: 'Their behavior has been blamed on all kinds of social and psychological factors ... A social common denominator seems out of the question, but it is true that psychologically this generation seems everywhere characterised by sheer courage, an astounding will to action, and by no less astounding confidence in the possibility of change. *But these qualities are not causes*' (pp15–16, emphasis added).

This argument is not new, yet its implications for terrorism studies are critical. For the most part, profiles tend to be guides for investigators, comprising a checklist of qualities assumed relatively static in perpetrators. The logic of the profile is that they will enable the investigator to predict what the next terrorist (or set of terrorists) is likely to look like. If reliable, this would assist in directing resources at specific persons or communities. However, it can be difficult to reconcile checklist qualities with the rapidly changing silhouette of terrorists as well as the process that characterises increasing radicalisation into a terrorist movement.

Adriana Faranda, a former member of the Italian Red Brigades, once said: 'When you remove yourself from society, even from the most ordinary things, ordinary ways of relaxing, you no longer share even the most basic emotions. You become abstracted, removed. In the long run you actually begin to feel different. Why? Because you are different.'[12] Faranda's reflection is important. Involvement and engagement in terrorism result in changes to those who join. Being able to withstand stress and being able to keep one's mouth shut in spite of the glory of membership and sense of mission are some of the abilities that leaders seek of recruits. However, personal accounts of former terrorists suggest that these qualities tend to be acquired and assimilated through involvement and engagement. While it may be possible to develop a set of guidelines to identify what kind of person is likely to be 'good material' for involvement, no recruit will be able to predict his or her own personal reactions and experiences from involvement in terrorist activity until they actually start. A good example is the case described in Chapter 7.

The common retort to criticisms of terrorist profiling is that the alternatives to micro-level individual profiles (i.e. macro-level models, often drawing on root cause notions for instance) are often so general and so broad as to be of little use, either in terms of prediction, or as a guide to operational applications. However, this seems unfair: perhaps the most obvious problem inherent in the profiling of terrorists is the abundance of unclear, inconsistent and unrealistic expectations that surround its practice. Profiling could not explain how and why people become involved in terrorism, no more than profiling could explain how and why people become involved in crime. While terrorism studies have witnessed exciting developments in recent times, the profiling of terrorists has become a pseudo-intellectual adventure reminiscent of the early sensationalising of offender profiling in the popular press before it gave way to more productive research in forensic and criminal psychology. Regrettably, terrorist profiling continues behind closed doors. It is sustained by audiences desperate for practical solutions and seduced by the allure of a quick fix. That quick fix is often promised by researchers adept at retreating, whenever necessary, behind the assumptions that occupy the blurred boundaries between disciplines.

There are some broader issues. That psychological perspectives on terrorism are synonymous with speculation on the existence of a terrorist personality is a regrettable testament to how little psychology as a *discipline* has had to say about terrorism.[13] Many claims about the psychology of the terrorist would not hold up to even casual scrutiny within contemporary psychological science. While terrorist profiling may need a further push before it gives way to more productive approaches, we should be mindful of the allure offered by some current practices. One of these is the practice of 'psychological autopsies'. While of value in specific forensic contexts, its use in analyses of terrorist behaviour has been premature and naïve at best, and if current efforts are anything to go by, the psychological autopsy will soon fill the gap left behind by terrorist profiling.

Concepts such as abnormality, and those like it, are insufficient to explain much about terrorism.[14] The truth is while abnormality distinguishes the abhorrent activity that is a major part of terrorism, it does not help explain it or further our understanding of those who perpetrate it. Though mental illness may be a consequence of long-term involvement, terrorist leaders do not encourage initial involvement from individuals who appear to suffer mental illness. There are exceptions (as always) but these exceptions reveal a tactical decision to engage the mentally ill. In movements like the Provisional IRA in Northern Ireland, individuals with overly violent and sadistic tendencies were found on the fringes of the movement. These individuals meted out 'punishment' (usually via a violent interpersonal assault) for some infraction. Such was the notoriety of IRA punishment assaults, that an IRA member, a former bomber, reported: 'I could *never* do that sort of thing.'[15] The remark is striking. Though willing to engage in a bombing operation, the IRA member felt that he could not bring himself to beat someone up. We can understand the paradox when we compare the qualities associated with each activity. Delivering severe interpersonal violence to an individual suggests a different kind of activity from bombing. Except for cases of suicide bombing, the bomber does not have to remain at the location when the device explodes. This dynamic places a different psychological demand on the perpetrator. A related case became apparent in 2007, when Al Qaeda in Iraq used female psychiatric patients as unwitting suicide bombers.[16] Hospital staff members at Baghdad's Ibn Rusd psychiatric hospital passed on patient files to Al Qaeda members, and it emerged that one of the women suffered from schizophrenia and depression. A key difference here, however, is that the women were duped into carrying explosive devices that were remote-detonated, killing the women and scores of civilians around them.

To consider one final example, another characterisation of abnormality concerns those who leave their movement because of some dispute or personality clash. In late 2006, a former IRA terrorist related a story about a colleague and close friend who left the parent movement to form a splinter cell.[17] Reflecting on his friend's decision, the IRA member suggests:

> It's one of the things that I've never been able to get my head around, but I suspect it's a kind of *interior* rebellion, you know? And it's also the kind of guy that thinks, *I would rather be in charge of a tiny group*. [He] was the classic kind of guy that would have gone with a splinter group, right? Absolutely the classic and he would have went down the road of, killing people mainly because, well . . . he had a bit of ability, charisma, and had utter determination. I just really do wonder about the kind of guys that go off into splinter groups because, I think most of it is predicated upon inadequacy. They can't handle the bigger organisation. I think there is something in that mindset that I think does bring a certain kind of a person . . . that has a certain amount of ability . . . a kind of a . . . strange kind of commitment . . . the kind that says *I would rather have six people with me than have these [people] talking, all evening* . . . It is *self*-motivation.

A further lesson from these examples is that neither plausibility nor common-sense explanations substitute for analysis. Psychologist Hans Eysenck[18] warned of:

> . . . the almost universal belief that anyone is competent to discuss psychological problems, whether he or she has taken the trouble to study the subject or not and that while everybody's opinion is of equal value, that

of the professional psychologist must be excluded at all costs because he might spoil the fun by producing some facts which would completely upset the speculation.

Psychology students learn this early, particularly in appreciating the differences between common-sense and scientific explanations. But Eysenck's observation does not suggest that we should prioritise one kind of explanation over another or one discipline over another; instead, it is a recommendation that when we develop some basic assumptions and assertions about the terrorist, we value that which has traditionally escaped much of the research on terrorism – rigour and evidence.[19]

From profile to process

Though terrorism is much more than the sum of individual acts, we need some understanding of the individual terrorist and the ways in which other issues (e.g. fellow group members, the larger movement, the ideology, etc.) impinge upon him or her. A consequence of some false starts[20] is that there is a poor sense of what an *individual* perspective on terrorism might imply. This confusion was apparent in an exchange between Bruce Hoffman and Marc Sageman[21] in *Foreign Affairs*, in which an unfair and limited representation implicitly emerges in the debate between the authors. Hoffman questions Sageman's choice of 'an individual perspective, rather than taking an organizational or collective approach', which Sageman subsequently (and accurately) refutes, asserting that he has not done this. However, given this characterisation, it may appear that an assumption *does* exist that we can explain terrorism at the level of the individual. We cannot, but without an effort to integrate findings from such a perspective, the 'organizational or collective approach' highlighted by Hoffman will be limited.

It would be useful then to assert that an individual perspective on terrorism is one that would seek to encompass the following types of questions:

1   How do individuals become involved in terrorism?
2   What reasons do they give (to themselves and to others) for becoming involved?
3   Are there any *a priori* qualities or traits that might act as risk factors for involvement in terrorism?
4   Are there any *a priori* qualities or traits that might correlate with an attraction to specific roles or functions within the movement?
5   How does the individual acquire the qualities inherent in, and necessary for, sustained terrorist membership?
6   What is the meaning of involvement, to:

    a   someone who is thinking about becoming involved?
    b   someone who is involved on the periphery?

    c   someone who is involved in a sustained and focused way?
    d   someone who is thinking about leaving?
    e   someone who has left?

7   How does the individual make decisions as a member of the movement?
8   What are the ways in which a) ideological content and b) ideological processes impinge upon the individual behaviour of the terrorist?

If we want to understand the development of the terrorist, we should ask questions about how decisions emerge, what is the meaning of those decisions to the individual and what are the consequences for the individual. Yet, to properly answer such questions, we must pay attention not only to individual accounts of terrorists but also the broader context which gives meaning to everything he or she does and aspires to become – thus echoing Hoffman's concerns and following the recommendation made by Reich.[22] To reiterate, we cannot explain terrorism at the level of the individual, nor can we reduce the terrorist mindset to a collection of presumed inherent qualities (or set of traits) that people bring with them to a movement. Rather, the mindset should be considered a *product* of the terrorist group: expressed more formally, it is a reflection of repeated social and psychological interactions with an ideology (however diffuse or unstructured), the community of practice it engenders and the meaning that is derived by the individual terrorist from sustained involvement and engagement with the group and activity.

    This is not to say that the individual perspective as a category or level of analysis is a fallacy, but rather that in understanding the individual terrorist, we cannot remain *at* the level of the individual. The psychologist or psychiatrist interested in understanding the terrorist will inevitably drift into other areas to address the group, organisation, culture and community.[23] To speak of rejecting the individual perspective, as implied in the debate between Hoffman and Sageman, misses the point. The individual perspective is an attempt to understand the *individual in context* and is about recognising the way in which group processes impinge upon the individual and become apparent to that person.[24]

Process

The 7/7 Report issued by the House of Commons (referred to earlier) was the subject of intense attention upon its release. One journalist[25] remarked how the author of the report could 'hardly conceal his bewilderment as he relates how [Hasib] Hussain's mother found him in his pyjamas, eating a bowl of cereal, 24 hours before he blew himself to pieces on top of the No. 30 bus, killing 13 other people'. Amid the drama, the minutiae attract attention. Little provokes more fascination than the juxtaposition of banal everyday behaviour and dramatic events with global consequences. How these seemingly inconsistent behaviours can co-exist is a source of confusion, yet history is replete with such pairings. Wartime examples of this contrast abound. Georg Seitz, a former U-boat crew member described the last evening ashore in the French port of Brest before his mission on board U-604:

> We would be in the bars in town, making the most of our last time ashore. Of course we were young and our comradeship was very strong so we would drink and dance with the girls and get rowdy . . . Of course we had high spirits, but it was war and everybody did what they could to enjoy life. But nor were we gloomy and expecting the worst. Drinking and celebrating with our crew and comrades would keep us in high spirits, and then we would get back to the job that we had to do.[26]

As Macintyre[27] argues, while the House of Commons narrative did not explain very much, it brought us closer to understanding elements of the process involved. It is critical to acknowledge that a useful way of understanding terrorism is by seeing it as a *process*. In an earlier work with Max Taylor,[28] we described what that meant as we defined it. A process, we argued, refers to a sequence of events that are usually ordered and/or interdependent (but not in a linear, 'stage-like' way). We used process to imply:[29]

> . . . actions of some kind associated with other actions and reactions, often expressed in some sort of reciprocal relationship (in an immediate sense between the various actors involved, such as governments, terrorists, media, politicians, the public, and also perhaps in a more long-term sense in terms of sociological, psychological, and political forces).

Naturally, and as we argued in the original article, the nature of that reciprocity can be expressed in a variety of ways. But, even when we seek to identify any or all of the elements of that process, it does not necessarily imply that what we have arrived at is a deterministic account – in other words, it does not necessarily follow that each element of the process inevitably causes the next element to become apparent or set in motion. This is important, and we have to be mindful because of the ease with which a deterministic account easily follows from post-hoc analyses of events – with little effort, we could easily find ourselves tempted by 'profile-logic'. We will return to this critical issue in later chapters, but for the moment, let us consider the relevance of what a process approach implies for how we think about the terrorist.[30]

There are significant disadvantages to the pursuit of profiles at the expense of understanding process. In assuming the existence of a profile, in addition to the problems identified earlier, we invite a danger of missing several critical process-relevant features associated with the development of the terrorist.

- First, we neglect the *gradual nature* of how involvement is shaped and socialised. There is no available evidence to suggest that violent radicalisation is anything but a gradual process. If radicalisation into a terrorist movement appears quick, it is only because we do not have access to the individual's life history and the chain of events that characterised his or her recruitment, initial apprenticeship and subsequent escalation of involvement and engagement.

- Second, we miss a sense of the *supportive qualities* associated with that recruitment. In other words, we fail to appreciate the significance of pull factors, the lures that attract people to either becoming involved in terrorism in a broad sense (e.g. being part of a social movement in which involvement would appear to offer benefits of some sort); the 'push' factors might explain why an entire community is radicalised, but only by considering the additional 'pull' factors can we understand the decisions made by those few who engage in terrorism.

- Third, we risk neglecting *role migration* – the process of moving from one role to another. Involvement in terrorism does not result in occupying a role or function that remains static. The reality is that there is a dynamic process of moving from one kind of role into another and sometimes back again. Sometimes this involves moving from fringe activity such as public protest to unambiguous terrorist behaviour (i.e. shootings or bombings, or related activities such as storing or moving weapons or components).

- Fourth, we overlook the importance of role qualities as perceived by potential and actual recruits. In other words, we miss the ability to appreciate the specific lures that entertain the desire to become a sniper as opposed to, say, the specific lures that entertain the desire to become a suicide bomber. We also miss how these role qualities become apparent to the onlooker or potential recruit that may only have a vague perception about what being involved entails (e.g. through seeking out and viewing Internet material).

There are additional potentially neglected issues, but overall there is a risk of becoming blind to the process dynamics that shape and support the development of the terrorist. Because of all of this, we also obscure the basis from which a more practical counter-terrorism strategy can develop to prevent or control the extent of those who initially become involved in terrorism. There is resistance within the counter-terrorism community to suggestions that we move beyond profiling. In late 2006, at a presentation on terrorist psychology, a senior British counter-terrorism official exclaimed: 'Hang on a second. Profiles *are* useful. Of course they are. The reason . . . is that your average suicide bomber is not going to be the middle-aged, white, father of three kids.'[31] A logical question from this might be: *how do we know?* A logical answer is that we adhere to this assumption because so far, this kind of bomber has not yet emerged. The point of the response is not to feed unrealistic appraisals of non-existing threats, or to encourage the imagination of anything being possible. Rather, it is to serve as a reminder that the assumptions that feed into how we think about the terrorist grow from actuarial projections based on a small, and statistically insignificant, sample of individuals. This is especially important now given the diversity inherent in what Sageman[32] has termed the *Al Qaeda social movement* as distinct from the *Al Qaeda organisation*. As a result, the danger exists for over-generalisation across and within contexts.

Becoming a terrorist

One critical question remains: if a large number of people experience the same root causes that increase the likelihood of becoming involved in terrorism, why is it that so few become involved in terrorism? The most appropriate answer is that we do not really know. Worse still, it is probable that we will never know. We will probably never be able to predict with any certainty, given certain social, economic or political circumstances, which person, or 'kind' of person, is likely to become a terrorist (and conversely, who is not). However, there are ways in which we can progress. What we can do is work towards identifying predisposing *risk factors* for involvement in terrorism. If proven reliable and valid, these serve as a prelude to risk assessment for prediction of involvement and provide us with a basis for a strategy for limiting and controlling the levels of recruitment to terrorist movements.

Risk factors for involvement in terrorism include:

- The existence of some **temporary emotional state** that renders the individual to have a greater openness to the use of, or support for the use of, violence. This might arise from feelings of anger, alienation (often synonymous with feelings of being culturally uprooted, displaced and longing for a sense of community) and disenfranchisement. For example, this might be expressed through looking for guidance and leadership which alienated young Muslims do not get in mosques – in Britain there is a perception among many young radical Muslims that mosque leaders are too old, too conservative and too out of touch with their world and that young people have no choice but to turn elsewhere (e.g. radical preachers) for guidance and clarity.
- More **permanent relevant individual factors** that might contribute to an openness to or compatibility with particular qualities of or expressions of involvement for the individual (e.g. stress-seeking, ability to withstand negative stress) through particular roles; it may be that particular personalities are attracted to particular kinds of activities or roles.
- **Dissatisfaction with current activity**, whether it be political or social protest of some kind. The current activity may not necessarily be public, like going on marches or being active in the community, but the dissatisfaction results from the perception that conventional political activity just does not work or produce effective results. A related issue is that the violent radical views terrorism as *necessary*; in Mohammad Siddique

Khan's video message before blowing himself (and six others) up in London in 2005, he urged British Muslims to oppose the Government.[33] He used the language of war and viewed terrorism as a necessary, defensive and, above all, *urgent* activity against an offensive enemy perceived as hell-bent on humiliating and subjugating passive Muslim victims. For Khan and his colleagues, engaging in terrorism was constructed into an escape from victimhood.

- Related to this dissatisfaction, the ***desire to 'do something'*** – to engage in activity as opposed to talking about activity and the acknowledgement of ***personal agency*** in the timeliness associated with the need for action (i.e. that there is no time to wait around for someone else to take action).

- ***Identification with victims*** – this may be real in terms of personal victimisation (e.g. by the military or police, or some religious or ethnic discrimination) or it may be something less tangible. For UK Muslims who become involved in terrorist activity, this identification is with Palestinian victims of the Palestinian-Israeli conflict, victims in Iraq or the conflict in Kashmir. In Khan's video testimony, he placed responsibility for his behaviour on the US and UK for the: 'bombing, gassing, imprisonment and torture of *my* people' in Afghanistan, Iraq and elsewhere. Though Khan came from Yorkshire, in northern England, he identified with the suffering of Muslims worldwide.

- Crucially, the potential terrorist has to be of the ***belief that there is nothing inherently immoral in violence*** against the state or its symbols; this belief may be fine-tuned by a religious or ideological figure, but to a large extent this view is held to some degree by the time the person has decided to engage in terrorist activity.

- An ***expectation of reward to accompany increased involvement*** – all suicide bombers (including potential bombers) have at least one thing in common: they come to believe that they will achieve more in death than they ever could in life. This belief, and the expectations it engenders, is a powerful motivating factor not only as far as initial recruitment is concerned, but also in terms of sustaining that person's commitment to the movement once a member. In practical terms, involvement (in any terrorist activity) might result in heightened status, respect, authority, both within the immediate peer group, the broader radical movement and, of course, at least as imagined by the recruit, the broader 'represented' community. The point is that the recruit feels *important* in what they do – the clearest answer to why someone wants to become involved in a suicidal mission is that they seek martyrdom and its accompanying expectant rewards. This is well documented in Middle Eastern movements, but is increasingly apparent in western Europe where violent radical websites hail the 7 July London bombers as heroic martyrs.

- ***Kinship or other relevant social ties*** to those experiencing similar issues or, alternatively, already involved.

With more data, we could easily identify other similar factors.[34] These, or any other set of risk factors, could be made more specific with respect to particular movements, regions or times, but also could be made broader so as to inform a more general theory of risk of involvement in terrorism. However, the important conclusion is that individually, none of the risk factors identified above may necessarily be of any major significance. Only when they combine do they provide a powerful framework for an openness to socialisation into terrorism, or a *nurtured* predisposition for involvement. For the purposes of analysis, however, what these risk factors essentially do is highlight why, given a group of people exposed to the same conditions (even from the same family), one person may step further towards involvement in terrorism and the other(s) may not. Given this, the area of terrorist risk assessment is critically underdeveloped, yet may be of vital importance as a practical alternative to terrorist profiling.[35]

We should also bear in mind that these risk factors are potent at a specific juncture in the process – the phase of *initially becoming involved*. Once the potential recruit begins to move towards belonging to a group (before engaging in operations – whether violent or non-violent), the individual will be subject to a further set of issues that exert unique influence at this new phase. These factors include the power of the group, the content and process of ideology (or ideological control), the influence of a particular leader and feedback from experiences both inside and outside the movement.

Additionally, individuals will experience increased involvement in different ways. The pathways as experienced by individuals differ. The availability or accessibility of different routes will depend on a variety of factors (e.g. including what the organisation decides to make available), and the availability of particular roles or functions for any one individual will depend on a host of issues (e.g. skills, available time to devote to the movement, etc.). Overall, for any individual, there may be broader shared qualities to that process, but the process of violent radicalisation as experienced by the *individual* will reflect a dynamic, idiosyncratic experience of incremental assimilation and accommodation for each person.

Understanding involvement

This chapter began with the argument that if we are to move beyond sterile debates about profiling and unrealistic analyses of terrorist motivation, we need to systematically understand what involvement in terrorism entails. We then achieve two things: conceptual clarity about the processes involved and, on a practical basis, avenues for counter-terrorism initiatives that can draw on the kinds of concepts under development. Eventually this will lay the groundwork for the evidence to develop a strategy to disrupt the process so that we can manage and control violent radicalisation and actual recruitment.

To achieve this, we need to address a number of issues. First, we can characterise the reality of involvement in terrorism today by its *complexity*: involvement in terrorism implies and results in different things for different people. Even the smallest of terrorist networks comprise a variety of roles and functions into which recruits are assigned or encouraged to move toward. Adoption and retention of those roles is neither discrete, linear, nor static. There is often migration *between* roles: moving from illegal activity (e.g. engaging in violence against civilians) to 'grey area' activity (e.g. supporting the process of engagement in violent activity) to activity that may be perfectly legal (e.g. peaceful protest, visiting certain kinds of websites). In fact, when we look at individual terrorist movements and the activities of its members, many members engage in activities that are not actually illegal, *per se*. These cannot be meaningfully encompassed under the label 'terrorism', but might merit the label of *subversion*. Without them, however, actual terrorist operations might be limited or constrained and fail to be sustained over time and place.

Second, involvement in terrorism may also imply – and result in – different things for the *same* person over time, place and experience. As evidenced by the Al Qaeda activities uncovered via Operation Crevice[36] and related cases in the United Kingdom, the terrorist group may expect the potential suicide bomber to engage in various criminal activities to finance operations.

The confusion around what constitutes involvement in terrorism poses major challenges to the ways in which we might construct a risk assessment. An illustration of this confusion became apparent when on 24 July 2007, Awaab Iqbal, from Bradford in England, was found guilty of a terrorism offence. Iqbal put a digital image of his face and those of his friends on a poster of the faces of the 9/11 hijackers.[37] He was charged under Section 57 of the UK's Terrorism Act for 'having articles for terrorism'. On the one hand, this case illustrates the need to have an explicit definition of what constitutes terrorism. However, the definition debate should not get in the way of progress on other fronts. A paradox in having a narrow (possibly clearer and more consistent) definition of terrorism is that it may result in an equally narrow conceptualisation of terrorism that, in turn, may actually limit our analysis and obscure our understanding of the processes.

For the most part, violence is what we readily associate with terrorism. However, the reality of terrorist operations is that this public expression represents the tip of an iceberg of activity. Supporting the execution of a violent attack, directly aiding and abetting the event, those who house the terrorist or provide other kinds of support, those who raise funds, generate publicity, provide intelligence and so forth are crucial to any operation. The person we think of as the terrorist fulfils only one, albeit the most dramatic in terms of consequences, of multiple functions for the movement. To paraphrase Kalyvas'[38] argument about civil wars, ambiguity is endemic to terrorism, yet is unsatisfactorily appreciated in the context of involvement.

Studying disengagement

Jerrold Post recently stated that 'too many terrorism experts have never laid eyes upon a terrorist, much less spoken with one.'[39] Post is correct, but laying one's eyes upon a terrorist is not of much value unless the researcher has a realistic sense of what is possible to accomplish when interviewing terrorists. David Gadd explains: 'often ... researchers expect their respondents to answer their research questions for them, hoping to eschew the challenge of interpretation that narratives of life present them with.'[40] While the individuals approached for this book were interviewed in a formal sense, they were not engaged in a clinical sense, nor were they subjected to psychometric testing. We may not have found a terrorist profile or the ability to compare personal characteristics with organisational roles, but to do this would require the kind of assessment that would be challenging given the circumstances of such meetings. The case studies in the following chapters are snapshots at best, glimpses into how individuals have engaged in and experienced a complex process. Furthermore, the details of that process are selectively recalled by those who give what they want to give, describe what they want to describe, and in their own words.

Related to this, we might ask how we know if someone is telling the truth? One can verify descriptions of events through triangulation of sources, but we ought to realise that, as explained by Kennedy: 'It is not a question of knowing the facts of past events but of the meaning of the events and how they can be re-emplotted ... Historical narratives are not only models of past events and processes, but also metaphorical statements, not just a reproduction of past events but a complex of symbols' (cited by Gadd[41]). Seeking truth from interviews suggests that the researcher has already missed the point. Interviews represent only one method in the researcher's toolbox. Because most terrorist researchers do not conduct interviews with former terrorists does not imply that we should afford those who do some sort of special status. Interviews bring with them the same limitations one can expect to find with any method. However, the great benefit of accessing accounts is that we are afforded another way to move the field of terrorism studies forward. By listening carefully to what terrorists say about themselves, and others, we may tease out some of the social and psychological qualities of these accounts. We can identify common themes or patterns,[42] especially regarding the meaning of events and roles to the participants. However, there is no illusion as to the limitations of these accounts: it is impossible to be certain of their accuracy (interviewees themselves, in frank moments, will admit this), and to echo the warning of Reich,[43] we must be mindful of the dangers of overextending what we might think is the significance of anything that is said. We should consider such accounts *exploratory* case studies (not descriptive, nor explanatory), the primary objective of which is to lead to the development of working hypotheses and contribute to a broader research agenda.

To echo Hoffman's[44] experiences of how 'normal' he found the terrorists he interviewed (p7), what was striking was not so much how normal the interviewees for this project were, but how it is that seemingly inconsistent attitudes, experiences and behaviours can co-exist in a way that is uncomfortable for the onlooker. Most of those terrorists interviewed for the project had killed people and/or had organised operations that resulted in deaths or injury. During the initial stages of the interview process, they offered tea, lunch, dinner, drinks, showed (one or two exceptions aside) great patience with the questions posed to them time and time again, and showed even greater patience in some cases when I requested a return visit. Some facilitated access to others in their immediate social network. At times, some of those interviewed for this book were aggressive, but none was violent in any way (except for one who kicked his cat in frustration at the end of an interview).

It is understandable why we have difficulty letting go of the stereotyped images of 'the terrorist'. In June 2007, two attempted bombings in London and Glasgow were perpetrated by a group of doctors who worked in the UK's National Health Service. Many people were shocked and surprised that 'doctors could be terrorists'. This is more a reflection of how deeply embedded in us are the stereotypes surrounding who or what *kind* of person we consider to be likely to be recruited to terrorist movements. In his work on the IRA, Rogelio Alonso[45] explains that 'the undoubted problem of obtaining access to sources of information that help to shed light on the secret world of a terrorist organization may explain such shortcomings, but the result has been a distorted perception of this group' (p3). Because of the challenges of collecting data in this area, there is always a danger of presenting what amounts to a limited and narrow view of what in time emerges as a different picture. A problem with published work on terrorism is that, to paraphrase Abraham Miller, (some) academics that study terrorism have a tendency to rush to print as quickly as journalists.[46] In the last few years, attempts to write about specific events have produced 'analyses' that, when fuller facts emerged months after publication in some leading journals, revealed just how premature they were.

Mindful of Reich's sentiments, the accounts presented in this book should not be considered 'complete'. When this project began in 2006, what I intended to be a series of interviews to focus on disengagement expanded to address a wider set of issues surrounding involvement and engagement. It was clear that despite the interview schedule brought to meetings, each of these interviewees had a story to tell and in their own way. The reader will see in the case studies that there is no neatly structured narrative in the way offered by the House of Commons report into the Al Qaeda bombings in London. Each source of information carries with it its own limitations and the case studies range from lesser to more complete and rounded accounts. This became obvious to me following an exchange with one of the interviewees. Commenting on his own near-600 page autobiography, the man described writing the volume as a 'stupid exercise'. He felt that no book, however long or detailed, could adequately explain how he felt about what he had done as a terrorist. What he attempted was to make sense of what in hindsight was a series of interrelated decisions amid an engagement with a complex process. What emerged was a sense of the meaning of those decisions to him and how his interpretation of particular opportunities and events elicited particular decisions and courses of action.

The interviews in the present volume aspire to illustrate that complexity and to illuminate the nature of the decisions and turning points in an individual's involvement. In turn, the objective is for these interviews to lead us to develop more specific questions about the behaviour of the terrorist and the disengagement process. Perhaps the most valuable feature of the interviews is that they are accounts of what terrorists 'do', what involvement entails and how disengagement comes about. To echo Luisella de Cataldo Neuburger and Tiziana Valentini, the objectives of this enquiry are to help in describing very particular situations.[47] The semi-structured interview schedule employed in these interviews does not try to produce complete life stories, rather to instead access accounts of activity, and meaning attributed to that activity, against a background of disengagement.

One of the challenges that emerged from the interviews was identifying when a terrorist can no longer be considered a terrorist? On one level, this might be answered by identifying when someone is no longer engaged in explicit terrorist activity (e.g. shootings, bombings, etc.). However, involvement in terrorism goes beyond the activities that result in the most dramatic and public behaviours associated with terrorism. Because involvement in terrorism entails more than engaging in violence, this raises questions not only about what constitutes involvement, but what can truly be meant by describing someone as *disengaged*. Some of those interviewed are inactive in the sense that they are no longer involved in the commission of terrorist operations. But it is also the case that they have remained active in a different kind of role. That role may not involve committing violence, but certainly involves behaviour of importance to the aims of the terrorist group. While it would be misleading, therefore, to say they remain involved in terrorism, several are committed to *subversion* of one kind or another. An important consequence of this, and one that has significant implications for policy, is that just because someone has disengaged from a particular role in a terrorist movement, it does not necessarily follow that they are *de-radicalised*. Some of the case studies in this book illustrate just how complex and seemingly incongruous accounts can be about what it means to be disengaged and not de-radicalised. We will see in later chapters that the term de-radicalisation is deeply problematic and carries with it equally troubling expectations.

Returning to concerns raised in the opening pages, one question that people will have is how I was able to gain access to interviewees. The simple answer to this is that this is not really as difficult as one imagines. With considerable patience, extensive preparation and willingness to travel, it is possible to arrange interviews with former terrorists. Requests for interviews can be made through a variety of formal and informal channels. Cultural and social norms demand respect and protocol be followed in all settings and during all dealings with people. Of course, interviewing in fieldwork settings can sometimes be dangerous and there is always a need to carefully evaluate risks and follow relevant procedures. No academic engaged in fieldwork should be unaware of those instances in which those traditionally associated with meetings with terrorists – journalists – have been put in very real danger and have in increasing numbers been kidnapped and murdered. However, it is easy to overstate the presumed dangers associated with meeting terrorists. Sometimes, there is an aura of excitement and danger not far removed from a Robert Ludlum novel that permeates accounts by researchers about their work in the field. While researchers may have different and unique experiences, gaining access to combatants tends to be straightforward. While never discounting the real possibility of danger, mostly arising from avoidable misunderstandings and deviations from agreed procedures, it is easy to distort the risks.

Finally, and an issue we cannot escape, is that we must admit how easy it can be to hide behind a neutral position in studying terrorism. Some academics would say that the fact that an academic uses the word terrorism already indicates that any claims to objectivity are invalid. Others would suggest that it is not the position or role of the academic to condemn or judge. But should we not condemn terrorism outright, let alone actually seek out meetings with those who engage in it? The former Chief Constable of the Royal Ulster Constabulary in Northern Ireland, Sir Ronnie Flanagan, once said to a journalist that he could not bring himself to understand the terrorist because understanding came too close to excusing terrorist behaviour.[48] His concerns are merited, but while understanding terrorism may not be the responsibility of the police officer, it is a responsibility of the academic. Ariel Merari suggested that the role of the academic terrorism researcher was to 'make terrorism known'. And this is precisely the objective with this book: to make known, and in their own words, how and why people join terrorist movements, what happens once they are involved in terrorism and ultimately how and why they disengage.

Conclusions

This chapter addressed some of the challenges to understanding how and why people become involved in terrorism and briefly addressed some of the problematic assumptions that continue to feed stereotypes of who becomes a terrorist and why. Given the major features of terrorism, as well as the fact that relatively few engage in it, a concern of terrorism studies has been the development of a profile. Though profiling has taken multiple shapes and forms, attempts to profile the terrorist have typically funnelled the complexity of the terrorism process into a narrower, static concept. This chapter illustrates the dangers of pursuing this line of argument. We explored the idea of seeing involvement in terrorism as a *process*, and made a case for considering what involvement ultimately means. Given this, the chapter outlined what we ultimately miss when we continue to assume the existence of a terrorist profile. Perhaps one of the biggest problems is that the continued effort to identify a profile simply encourages a 'one size fits all' approach to how we can manage and respond to terrorism. A worrying problem is the continuing assumption that there *should* be some kind of terrorist profile, rather than our acceptance of the fact that this may be one of the most significant conceptual errors in the entire study of terrorism. Given the heterogeneity (e.g. of those who become involved, of roles, functions and even pathways into involvement), no profile as currently imagined could ever capture that complexity. In other words, there simply is no terrorist profile to be found.

In the next chapter, we extend our examination of involvement with a focus on *disengagement*. The next chapter sets the scene for the interviews by providing an overview of our current knowledge on how terrorism ends, for both the movements and the individuals that comprise them.

2 How, when and why terrorism ends

Introduction

In the previous chapter, we considered some of the issues surrounding how and why people become involved in terrorism. In this chapter, we examine the process of disengagement. This will be explored from an organisational and an individual perspective.

While knowledge of each of the three phases of involvement in terrorism (becoming, remaining and disengaging) is underdeveloped, disengagement remains the least understood and has seen the least research.[1] This should appear surprising.[2] Not only are there significant implications for counter-terrorism in understanding how and why terrorism ends,[3] but there is a more pressing reason as to why we might expect there to be more research. The history of political violence by non-state actors is not only one of terrorist movements emerging and developing, but also declining and fading away. In fact, Rapoport suggests that the average life expectancy of a terrorist group is only about one year.[4] Despite some initial and promising research,[5] the literature on how terrorism ends is sparse.

While Chapter 1 provided a more general reflection on individual issues, this chapter presents a more substantive overview of the existing literature on how terrorism ends and outlines a series of issues for consideration on understanding individual disengagement.

Organisational decline

Much of the work on how terrorism ends has largely emerged through case studies on the decline of individual groups. Notable examples include Horchem's case study of the Red Army Faction,[6] Jamieson's work on the fall of the Red Brigades[7] (see also Weinberg and Eubank's[8] research on the same movement), Alonso's comparison of experiences in Northern Ireland and in the Basque country,[9] Gerges' study of the decline of radical Islam both in Egypt and Algeria,[10] Kassimeris' work on the fall of the 17 November movement in Greece,[11] and the decline of the Uruguyan Tupamoros as documented by Lopez-Alves.[12]

In her work on how Al Qaeda might be brought to an end, Audrey Cronin[13] explains that there is, on the whole, 'little agreement amongst experts as to how terrorist campaigns die' (p23). In making her case, she identifies five myths about the end of terrorism (pp23–8):

1) that terrorism is endless
2) that terrorism is situation-dependent and can only be understood in the narrow and specific context of a particular group and cause
3) that terrorism's demise is simple and straightforward, because with enough force and oppression any campaign can be killed
4) that dealing with the causes of terrorism will always lead to its end
5) that the best way to end terrorism is for states to engage in policies designed to win the sympathy of the populations from which terrorist groups emerge.

Cronin explains that while each contains a grain of truth, they essentially represent fallacies. These myths, she suggests, betray the complexity of the issues they seek to address. In particular, perhaps one of the most pervasive of these myths is the notion that terrorism does not, or cannot, end. The strength of this myth on the one hand might serve as a reminder of just how politicised threat assessments of terrorist movements have become.[14] Also, the persistence of this myth is as much a reflection of how analyses of terrorism have ignored the factors that lead to the ending of terrorist movements.

Martha Crenshaw has argued that terrorist movements tend to fall into decline for three broad sets of reasons:[15]

- defeat by their enemies
- defeat by a rival group, or
- defeat from within, with a fall into decline due to internal factors.

In a similar vein, Dipak Gupta[16] presents his three reasons for what he terms the 'endgame' of terrorism:

- absolute victory for the movement
- the transformation of the movement into a largely criminal movement, and
- a military or political defeat.

Before we consider examples to illustrate arguments from these and other authors, we need to highlight some issues. Both Crenshaw and Gupta emphasise that although the reasons for the end of terrorist movements may represent clear-cut factors in themselves, the reality (as also conveyed in Cronin's analysis[17]) is likely to reflect a combination of factors that explains this process.[18] Additionally, specific cases highlight other complicating factors. For instance, the demise of one movement may give direct rise to another. The defeat of the leaders of the 1916 rebellion in Ireland proved the inspiration for four generations of militant Irish Republicanism and continues to inspire marginalised splinter groups even to this day. Therefore, to simply equate the 'end of terrorism' with the decline of a movement may be difficult.

A common theme across Crenshaw, Cronin and Gupta's work is that any attempt to explain how or why terrorism ends can only be understood with reference to a broad array of factors – internal, external and interactive. For example, Cronin reminds us that in some cases (and echoing Crenshaw) the reasons for a group's decline actually 'may have little to do with the measures taken against it' (p11). Conversely, as Gupta explains, what is widely viewed as the success of the Algerian FLN is in no small part owed to the divisive and polarising policies of the French.

Perhaps no better laboratory in which we can examine a variety of movements undergoing significant organisational change is Northern Ireland. Given the progress of the peace process from 1994 to the present day, the experiences of several of the Irish movements illustrate a variety of issues on organisational decline and disengagement.

A good example of a terrorist movement becoming consumed by organised criminal activity is the Ulster Defence Association (UDA). The fact that the UDA became so steeped in crime is probably one of the main reasons that Northern Ireland's once most powerful terrorist movement has escaped serious analysis by the terrorism research community. In the 1970s, the UDA commanded formidable influence across Ulster. Its once 40,000-strong membership brought Northern Ireland to a standstill with a general strike. The strike was organised via the Ulster Workers' Council, which at the time was more or less directed by several senior UDA members. The UDA's principal goal was to bring about reform in Ulster, most prominently through the abolition of the Northern Irish Executive and greater political representation at Westminster. Yet, following the assassination by the Provisional IRA (PIRA) of arguably the UDA's most effective leader and strategist, John McMichael, the UDA was in terminal decline. So steeped in racketeering, prostitution, extortion and drug smuggling, the UDA's image as community defenders (against the IRA) was widely caricatured.[19] While the UDA leadership learned many lessons from the IRA's experiences, it failed to realise that a dedicated finance department went a long way in avoiding the problem of 'sticky fingers' and widespread profiteering. The UDA's preoccupation with money-raising ultimately distanced the movement from the community it claimed to represent. The UDA subsequently turned inward and, in the words of a former UDA commander interviewed in Chapter 7, 'imploded'.

Other examples from the region illustrate what can happen when terrorist movements enter into a peace process that inadvertently threatens the continued existence of the movement. The Independent Monitoring Commission (IMC) was established to observe the paramilitary ceasefires in Northern Ireland. At the time of its first report (issued in 2004), the Commission deemed the PIRA to be 'highly active in paramilitary shootings short of murder'[20]. In fact, and supported with statistical analysis from the Commission, while the numbers of murders and attacks on members of the security services declined, the level of 'other paramilitary violence' showed a sharp increase.[21] The reasons for this, according to the Commission, arise from 'growing illegal activities by paramilitary groups . . . their imposition of control over individuals or whole communities, and their involvement in organised crime'.[22] In some cases, the leadership will mask their involvement in such activities due to the potential political repercussions associated with being identified as the perpetrators. The PIRA leadership recognised this when on 20 February 2004, four men (described later by the IMC as an 'IRA gang') entered Kelly's Cellars bar in Bank Street, Belfast. The men used pepper spray to incapacitate Robert Tohill, a dissident Irish Republican. They then severely beat him, dragged him from the bar and bundled him into an awaiting vehicle. Witnesses described the perpetrators as dressed in 'white forensic suits, balaclavas, and surgical gloves'.[23]

Ironically, as the peace process developed, reports from the IMC painted a worsening picture for a time. The Third Report of the IMC,[24] issued in late 2004, cited findings from the Northern Ireland Organised Crime Task Force demonstrating that of the '230 organised criminal gangs believed to be operating in Northern Ireland . . . about 60% or some 140 have paramilitary links and that, of the top 25 criminal gangs involved in international activities operating in early 2004, 17, some two-thirds, had paramilitary associations' (p27).

Other changes occurred during this time that illustrate the ways in which terrorist movements decline as a result of defeat not by the security forces, but from within or by rival groups. One of the defining characteristics of terrorism in Ireland is the propensity for groups to split and factionalise. This frequently sets the scene for severe internecine feuding. In the late 1980s, the Irish National Liberation Army (an offshoot of the Provisional IRA) was attacked by former rank and file INLA members who had defected to form their own movement, the IPLO – Irish People's Liberation Organisation. The Provisional IRA eventually attacked and defeated the IPLO.

Ross and Gurr[25] identify other factors contributing to the decline of terrorist movements. The authorities may *pre-empt* the movement and inhibit its ability to operate. Related to this, the security services may find ways to *deter* the movement from engaging in terrorist activity. Members may experience *burnout*, resulting in a decrease in commitment to the movement. And finally, the movement may suffer from a lack of political support – a consequence of *backlash*.

Oots[26] makes an interesting observation that the factors giving rise to the *formation* of terrorist groups are sometimes related to the reasons they fall into decline. For example, while having an entrepreneurial figure at the helm of a terrorist group may be a factor in its development, the absence of that leader would logically damage the group's ability to survive. The imprisonment of Michael McKevitt in 1999 for directing terrorism reduced the operational effectiveness and organising capacity of the Real IRA (an IRA splinter group) to launch high-level attacks. Cronin explains that so pronounced was this effect, that eventually: 'from prison, McKevitt declared that further armed resistance was futile, and that the Real IRA was "at an end" ' (p29). In a similar vein, Crenshaw describes how the downfall of the Black Panther movement in the 1970s was largely due to the leadership being incarcerated, killed or exiled. An unanticipated consequence of this incapacitation, however, is that it may lead to factionalism and splintering that may or may not result in the overall decline of terrorism.[27]

A second organisational problem considered by Oots is recruitment. Put simply, a movement must replace members as they die, are imprisoned or leave. This issue echoes Hirschman's[28] sentiments about the challenges faced by members of organisations more generally. A reason for the disintegration of a terrorist movement, Oots suggests, might be because of a failure to engage in opportunities that might consequently result in the weakening of the movement. Oots specifically argues that the failure to form alliances with bigger, stronger groups can ultimately leave a movement exposed and vulnerable. Osama Bin Laden recognised this when in early 2000 he hosted a 'lavish banquet' in Kandahar.[29] The gathering was a virtual 'conference of Jihadists from around the Arab world', whom Bin Laden had assembled to attempt to win over in his efforts to form a global coalition in the furtherance of the Al Qaeda grand vision.

Another example of the importance of coalitions comes from Ireland, when several dissident Republican groups called a meeting in August 2006 in an attempt to forge an alliance.[30] The Real IRA, Continuity IRA, INLA and several disaffected Provisional IRA members were scheduled to meet to discuss common strategies for opposing Sinn Fein and capitalising on the increasing disaffection within the mainstream Republican movement. The timing of the meeting was to coincide with rumours of a split in the South Derry Brigade of the IRA, in which almost 40 members quit the Republican movement.[31] Eventually, however, the meeting's organisers called off the conference 'after the [IRA] moved in' and threatened violence against the dissidents.

Until the development of these moves aimed at formulating a common strategy, the Irish dissident movement had been, as Dowling[32] describes, 'ridden in faction-fighting' and until then did not pose a serious security threat to the peace process. One of the organisers of the meeting, Paddy Murray (a former IRA bomb-maker), said that the aim of the gathering was to: 'get as many people as possible genuinely thinking of an alternative to the Provos ... People are looking for an alternative that is both political and military.'[33]

Similarly, as Gupta[34] illustrates with the case of the Abu Sayyaf movement in the Philippines and its predecessors, ideologically allying oneself to another group, such as the prevailing global movement, can ensure survival when at risk. Likewise the Islamic Movement of Uzbekistan (IMU), by allying themselves with Mullah Omar and the Afghan Taleban, vastly improved their survivability.[35]

There are other ways in which splintering occurs. Sometimes it is the result of a deliberate, strategic decision taken by leaders. An example of this is when a movement has a *better* chance of achieving its objectives by creating another movement, focused on the task at hand and willing to pursue those objectives with the tactics the parent group has disavowed.[36] On the other hand, and as illustrated in more than one of the chapters to follow, individual factors can also frequently drive splitting, with forceful personalities playing a major role in the development of splinter cells and groups.

A failure to harness and sustain outside support, a failure to compete for constituents and a failure to safeguard against internal divisions are other areas highlighted by Oots. When the Egyptian Al-Gama'a al-Islamiyya (GAI) killed 62 people in Luxor, the Egyptian public was outraged. Victims of the attack included: 'young children, honeymooners and a man beheaded in front of his daughter' (p46). After the Luxor massacre, Lawrence Wright alleged that 'attacks by Islamists in Egypt abruptly stopped' (cited by Cronin). Elsewhere, the failure to compete for constituents was an issue not lost on the Popular Front for Liberation of Palestine. In her research on the Popular Front for the Liberation of Palestine (PFLP) and other movements, Bloom[37] found that terrorist groups tend to use suicide bombing given the presence of three conditions: when conventional terrorist or military tactics (e.g. bombings) fail, when there is some level of support in the community for use of the tactic and when the terrorist movement in question enters into some form of 'competition' with other terrorist groups to harness that popular support. She describes the case in early 2002 when the previously secular PFLP adopted the language of *Jihad* and turned to suicidal terror tactics when it looked like it was about to lose significant support in local elections. According to Bloom, following the movement's adoption of the tactic (previously denounced by PFLP leader George Habash), popular support for the PFLP increased.

Oots identifies an irony of terrorist organisations in that the greater their membership, the greater the difficulties they will face in maintaining organisational cohesion.[38] The point is a simple one, but important to appreciate. After the events of Bloody Sunday in 1972, the Provisional IRA enjoyed a massive surge in support. However, the IRA's subsequent inability to effectively police just who was being recruited meant that it was soon infiltrated by British security forces. It was not until late 1977 that Seamus Twomey, a leading IRA figure, developed what was to become the IRA's cell-based structure of active service units, ensuring a tighter and ultimately more cohesive movement.

On the other hand, a terrorist movement might do more than just survive and actually achieve its goals. Gupta argues that the most successful non-state violent groups have been those aimed at expelling foreign occupiers from their lands: 'The Taleban gained victories against the Soviet Military,

Hizbullah in Lebanon were successful against the Israelis, just like the Algerian FLN won against the French, the Mau Mau in Kenya, the EOKA in Cyprus, and the Jewish groups in Palestine were able to drive out the British forces' (p190). Other exceptions to Rapoport's '1-year lifespan' rule include the November 17th movement in Greece, Breton revolutionary movements in the north of France, the Armenian Secret Army for the Liberation of Armenia (ASALA) and Irish and Basque separatist terrorist movements. These movements have lasted decades and continue to survive in one form or another.

Though the impact of terrorism is undeniable, its overall effectiveness remains debatable and truly successful cases are few.[39] Terrorist groups rarely achieve their aims unless it is at the expense of major tactical change and the compromising of core ideological principles. In some campaigns, particularly ethno-nationalist ones, terrorism hardly ever ends completely; the most successful of movements are apparently successful only in a limited sense.[40] Temporary truces and ceasefires rarely ease lasting tensions that eventually bubble back up to the surface. A major concern of observers in Northern Ireland throughout the peace process has been that although the IRA was not involved in attacking the security services, the movement 'has been undertaking training . . . It maintains a capability on intelligence, both on political events and on potential targets, and on weaponry. This provides ample evidence of an organisation maintaining its capacity to undertake acts of violence or to participate in a terrorist campaign if that seemed necessary to it.'[41] The Liberation Tigers of Tamil Eelam (LTTE) in Sri Lanka are no different.

Related to this, Regis Debray argued that revolutionary movements face problems of 'drift'.[42] For example, in times of ceasefire or peace processes, the leadership of terrorist movements may have difficulty maintaining a day-to-day sense of focus and direction. Individual members may drift into peripheral activities, with the risk of allowing those activities to take centre stage (e.g. organised crime). The leadership may respond by allowing the movement to function in other, more acceptable ways. Ironically, this can be expressed in ways that show how the movement attempts to exercise even more control in times of ceasefires. In August 2007, the radical Shia cleric, Moqtada al Sadr, called on his Mahdi Army in Iraq to cease military activity for a period of six months.[43] Al Sadr's reason for this was to 'reorganise' and 'rehabilitate' the Army or, put another way, to reassert control and discipline over already fragmenting ranks.

Al Sadr's actions echoed events in Northern Ireland. During the IRA's ceasefires in 1972, and again in 1994 (ironically, under much of the same leadership), there was a noticeable increase in the amount of peripheral activity by IRA members.[44] Some cases are more discrete though no less significant in organisational and psychological terms. On 4 September 2007, the Belfast City Council passed a declaration condemning a Sinn Fein march through the city a month earlier. That march featured masked men wearing army jackets and brandishing replica Kalashnikov rifles. Though technically defunct and no longer engaging in terrorist activity, the function of the IRA's march was to serve as a sign to the community that the movement could show military strength when needed.[45] Such displays serve a powerful psychological function to the movement itself that it retains a position of strength, unity and purpose during periods of rapid change and uncertainty.

It might be premature to think of terrorist movements as 'ending' *per se*. What often happens is that movements that previously used terrorism go through some change that will result in lesser (e.g. often more discriminating) use of violence while at the same time engaging in parallel democratic political processes. Sometimes that change can happen so incrementally that it is only when a terrorist movement has formally disbanded that one can trace back the catalyst for their disengagement to many years previously. One could argue that the dissolution of the IRA throughout 2006–08 was set in motion by the decision in the mid-1980s to engage in the 'Tactical Use of the Armed Struggle'. That is not to say that at the time the movement would never again use terrorism, but that their gradual transformation was largely a one-way process towards decreasing their dependence on terrorist tactics to influence the social and political process.

Something we know little about is the process whereby virtually defunct movements revitalise and re-emerge. Cusack and Taylor[46] describe how the Ulster Defence Association came back from a state of terminal decline in the late 1980s to become a resurgent and newly equipped movement. An interview with a former UDA commander in Chapter 7 provides some context to this. Despite a host of internal conflicts, widespread internal corruption and lax security (illustrated by British Agent Brian Nelson's infiltration of the UDA), the movement resurrected to become more powerful than before. Another example of this is the extraordinary developmental pattern of the Kurdistan Workers' Party (PKK), which transformed itself on numerous occasions since the 1970s, each time re-emerging with a new identity, new tactics and a revitalised mission. Additionally, at the time of writing (late 2008) it is clear that while routed from Iraq, Al Qaeda is undergoing a significant resurgence in Pakistan and Afghanistan and is reasserting dominance in regions where its influence was viewed as all but academic.

Individual decline

The preceding examples demonstrate the complexity of the issues that emerge when we consider how terrorism ends. This literature is focused at the level of organisations and networks. There is little within that research about how and why individual terrorists disengage and to what extent, if any, this can be considered a truly individual process. In terms of those who end up leaving terrorism behind, much of the existing literature comes from the commentary on terrorist informers.[47] Equally relevant research on disengagement issues comes from work on right-wing extremist and skinhead gangs.[48] In addition, there is a broader empirical and theoretical basis to individual issues in the criminological literature on *desistance*.[49] Though theoretically rich, however, it is unclear the extent to which the assumptions in this literature can be considered valid in the context of political violence. We return to this in detail in Chapter 9.

Overall, however, the lack of attention to individual disengagement from terrorism is confusing, perhaps especially given the obvious availability of, and accessibility to, disengaged individuals. In Northern Ireland, with the advancement of the peace process, there has never been a better time to gain access to individuals who once engaged in violent terrorist activity. Just as there appears to be a constant stream of individuals flowing into terrorist movements, there is a less visible but equally steady stream of individuals who, for one reason or another, leave.[50]

Bergen and Cruickshank[51] list some of the individuals who left Al Qaeda and its affiliates. Individuals who once shrouded every detail of their lives in secrecy are often willing to engage researchers on the thorniest questions related to their former terrorist lives.[52] Yet researchers continue to ignore the valuable opportunities afforded by this accessibility. A major reason for this remains the short-sightedness about the 'relevance' of terrorist campaigns, or individuals, when they disengage. From a research standpoint the terrorist is never more relevant than when he or she is disengaged. It is at that point that they are far more likely to realistically (and safely) engage with researchers about past activity.

In addition, weblogs and other Internet sites increasingly contain contributions by former terrorists determined to speak out against their former comrades and leaders and, in some cases, to share their own opinions about what should be done to prevent future involvement by others. There are even think-tanks helmed by former members of radical and extremist movements. Key figures in such initiatives are often eager to forge a role in countering extremism, armed with the legitimacy of having 'been involved'.[53] Others are less apologetic. As detailed by Christopher Harmon,[54] and the subject of much controversy during the 2008 United States Presidential election, former weatherman Bill Ayers was appointed to Distinguished Professor of Education at the University of Illinois and 'renounces little' about his previous life.

Furthermore, dozens of former terrorists around the world have written autobiographies. In addition to communiqués, statements by movements[55] and contributions on Internet discussions, we have valuable data sources from which we may develop hypotheses. Notwithstanding that, there are obvious limitations to the data gleaned from such sources. While dozens of autobiographies of former terrorists exist, there are also increasing examples of accounts by those whose involvement and engagement amounts, upon closer inspection, to little more than peripheral activity. This does not mean we should discount them, but we ought to realise their limitations and the possibility that some, to paraphrase Reich,[56] may have little sense of the confines of their explanations.

In the fast-changing climate of policy-relevant discussion and debate about terrorism, there is a newfound credibility in being an 'ex-terrorist'. In some cases, however, this has led to bitter recriminations and acrimony. Sometimes this is the result of unrealistic expectations about what 'ex-terrorists' are assumed to be like. Walid Shoebat, a self-proclaimed former Palestinian terrorist, was invited in early 2008 to speak to an audience of US Air Force cadets in Colorado. Shoebat was invited with two other former terrorists, Kamal Saleem and Zak Anani, to help cadets understand the 'Islamic fundamentalist mind set'. What followed, according to multiple news reports, was an outcry that Shoebat did nothing more than stir up anti-Muslim sentiment in an attempt to confer self-legitimacy.[57]

However, and though we should be mindful of their limitations, that we have not subjected the content of terrorist autobiographies to even the most basic of structured analysis now represents a gap in our efforts. Over 20 years ago, Bonnie Cordes[58] argued that we should pay more attention to what terrorists say about themselves and others. In doing so, she presented a framework for understanding terrorist perceptions through an examination of both their external (i.e. propaganda) and internal (i.e. 'auto'-propaganda) communications. Yet, analyses of terrorism have shown little evidence of the ability or willingness to build on our knowledge of these issues.

While there is research on how and why terrorist organisations might decline and fall, there is little on the implications of this for the *individual* terrorist. In thinking about disengagement from terrorism, we need to answer the following questions:

- What does disengagement mean for the individual (e.g. does it mean leaving the movement behind completely or simply moving into a different kind of role, such as non-violent)?
- Why do people leave (e.g. is it a voluntary or an involuntary process, what are the principal driving factors in this)?
- What happens to people who leave terrorism (e.g. where do they go, what do they do, and how do they change)?
- How does the leadership of the movement view issues to do with disengagement (e.g. are there procedures or policies in place to deal with those who want to, or have to, leave)?
- How do we know that someone has actually disengaged (e.g. what kind of assessment can be done to ascertain the risk of someone 're-engaging')?

These questions represent only a beginning. There is no clear sense to date of what disengagement even implies. The idea of disengaging, on the one hand, might suggest critical cognitive and social changes in leaving behind the shared social norms, values, attitudes, relationships and social networks forged while a member of a terrorist group.[59] This expectation is likely in the case of a terrorist who has had a complete split from the movement.

On the other hand, disengagement might occur in a more nuanced manner, expressed though a more discrete role-specific process. For example, a terrorist may disengage from a *specific* role or function, but remain engaged with the broader movement through some other activity. While a terrorist may have disengaged, they may not have left. As explained in the previous chapter, all terrorist networks have multiple roles and functions to be fulfilled. In some cases, an individual may be expected to simultaneously occupy more than one of those. For some, therefore, there may well be a continued adherence to the same values and attitudes and the individual ex-terrorist may still engage in other support behaviour, despite not being involved in any actual terrorist operations. A broader involvement in and commitment to *subversion* may supersede a narrower and more focused engagement in *terrorism*.

These issues are of immense significance from a counter-terrorism perspective. They not only relate to an exploration of how we can assess dangerousness or risk (e.g. of re-engagement – a return to terrorism), but also raise uncomfortable questions about whether or not subversion may be a more realistic and manageable (and desirable) outcome than terrorism. We return to this issue in the interview with Omar Bakri Mohammed in Chapter 8.

There is some relevant literature on these issues. Garfinkel[60] outlined factors involved in the psychological transformation from involvement in violence to non-violent activity. She conducted a series of telephone interviews with former members of militant groups (in Nigeria, Israel, Kashmir, Lebanon and elsewhere) all of whom are 'now working for peaceful change' (p3). Garfinkel describes this transformation as taking place against a backdrop of vulnerability, catalysed by stress, crisis and trauma. She describes how some interviewees, particularly religious extremists, underwent – 'a reorientation in outlook and direction'. A key factor in the transformation, Garfinkel notes, was the role played by personal relationships: 'change often hinges on a relationship with a mentor or friend who supports and affirms peaceful behavior' (p1).

In a remarkable study, Ebaugh[61] examined 185 accounts of people who underwent significant role change. Her sample comprised ex-convicts, ex-alcoholics, ex-doctors, ex-nuns and others who experienced voluntary 'role exit processes'. Recurring themes among these diverse cases included:

- a sense of disillusionment with the individual's current persona or identity
- an attempt to identify and locate an alternative, more satisfactory role
- the existence of particular triggering factors that facilitate final decisions to leave the role; to finally
- the creation of a new identity as an 'ex-'.

As a precursor to theoretical and conceptual development of these issues, we can develop some principles that are consistent with the processes described here.

In earlier work,[62] I developed a simple categorisation system asserting hypothetical parameters within which we explore how and why individuals disengage from terrorism. Broadly speaking, the factors affecting individual disengagement from terrorism might be *psychological* (e.g. disillusionment) or *physical* (e.g. role change).[63] Additionally, while physical change brings with it subsequent psychological change, the latter can serve as a catalyst for the former (e.g. seeking out involvement in a less 'stressful' role). Also, expressions of both psychological and physical disengagement might be experienced as either *voluntary* (e.g. a personal decision the individual has made to leave) or *involuntary* (e.g. an individual is forced to leave in the face of some external issue). And, to further complicate matters, it might be difficult to treat as distinct *issues promoting disengagement* from *factors that sustain involvement*: a person might remain involved in a terrorist movement because disengagement avenues are not perceived to be available or open to them.

Psychological disengagement

Factors contributing to *psychological* disengagement can include:

- disillusionment arising from incongruence between the initial ideals and fantasies that shaped a person's initial involvement and their subsequent experiences with the reality of what is entailed by involvement – i.e. the mismatch between the fantasy and the reality[64]
- disillusionment arising from internal disagreement over tactical issues
- disillusionment arising from internal strategic, political or ideological differences
- becoming 'burned out'
- changing and conflicting personal priorities (e.g. getting married, having children, growing older).

The seeds of disappointment and disillusionment take many forms and might emerge very early in the person's involvement. Patrizio Peci, the Italian Red Brigades member, reported that his disillusionment occurred after his very first meeting with his new superior.[65] As Peci ate, his superior took off his shoes and socks and began picking at his dirty toenails:

> Fiore, who wolfed down his food, finished before I did. I kept on eating. He settled down to watch television. I kept on eating. He put his feet, those enormous feet, on the table and then, suddenly he took off his shoes, without even undoing the laces. There was a horrible stench. But the worst was yet to come. He took off his socks as well; he grabbed the bread knife, one of those long, serrated knives and began to pry off the filth from between his toes with the point of the knife. Zap! And off came the filth from between two toes. He was very adept. Zap! Zap! Zap! Zap! What kind of manners are these? I said nothing and I tried to minimize

things in my mind. 'They are just little things, nothing', I thought, but I was worried. 'If everybody behaves like this, how will I be able to live among them? (p11)

This is an extremely important aspect of psychological disengagement. A common realisation for new recruits is the crushing discrepancy between the fantasies that influenced their initial mobilisation and involvement, with the subsequent reality of involvement. Shattering the romantic dream is a theme consistently found in accounts across several different movements. Disillusionment frequently stems from the behaviour of peers that the individual previously respected. Eamon Collins, the IRA Intelligence Officer murdered as a result of testifying against a former IRA leader, once recalled a pivotal event in his experiences:

> On the news that night I was delighted to witness the impact that the bomb had made on the town. A local Catholic politician was interviewed. He said that the bomb had torn the heart out of Warrenpoint. I was pleased to listen to him confirming my analysis. Then the hotel owner came on. He claimed that the IRA team had rifled the hotel's till and stuffed their pockets with money before leaving. I thought he was talking nonsense: I could not believe that the team would have done something like that in the middle of an operation. When I next saw Mickey I told him what the hotel owner had said. Mickey looked a little embarrassed. He said: 'It's true. Hardbap robbed the tills.' . . . I felt that Hardbap's behaviour had taken the shine off the operation and had made the IRA look like common criminals . . . My romantic image of the IRA soldier was receiving its first hard knock. (p103)[66]

Terrorist groups rely heavily on maintaining a positive image and a successful challenge to this can have severe repercussions. In 1987, British investigative journalist Roger Cook conducted an undercover expose of the racketeering activities of the UDA in Northern Ireland. Cook's co-investigators set up a meeting between one of their team (who posed as a businessman) and a local UDA Brigadier, Eddie Sayers. Sayers represented one of the UDA's many 'front' security companies. The meeting was covertly filmed and Sayers was shown attempting to extort money from the 'businessman'. When the documentary aired in 1988, its outcome was dramatic. It was a sustained source of extreme embarrassment to the UDA leadership and to Sayers in particular who was shown having difficulty with simple arithmetic during his calculation of the extortion demand. As described in Cusack and Taylor's[67] case study of the development of the UDA in the years that followed, the Cook Report proved to be a powerful catalyst (among other factors) that led to massive internal upheaval within the UDA, particularly between those within the UDA who had made concerted efforts to 'clean up' the movement and those heavily engaged in criminality. The internecine feuding that followed led to such bitter recriminations that assassinations followed, but perhaps more damaging to the long-term sustenance of the movement, the UDA's reputation within the communities it claimed to represent never fully recovered.

Omar Nasiri, a former Al Qaeda member, recalls how he realised just how much Al Qaeda relied on preserving a particular image to sustain credibility. He recalls a meeting with the London-based cleric Abu Hamza al-Masri:

> Abu Hamza looked at me with his one good eye as we were introduced. 'Masha'Allah, brother,' he said. 'Can you meet me in the office after prayers?' 'Of course,' I told him. When prayers were finished I stood outside the office on the first floor of the Finsbury Park Mosque in north London . . . Hamza asked me which of the camps in Afghanistan I had been in, and I told him . . . 'I met someone you know,' I said in a conspiratorial voice. Hamza raised his brow just slightly. 'I trained with Assad Allah,' I told him. 'He told me about the nitroglycerine, and how you lost your hands.' Hamza looked away. 'Brother,' he whispered, not meeting my gaze, 'please don't share that story with anyone.' As I was to learn later, Hamza claimed he had lost his hands defusing a landmine on the front lines in Afghanistan. I knew the real story.[68]

In Colombia, increasing numbers of FARC terrorists sought a way out of the movement in 2008 and have begun testifying as to the treatment they received while involved: 'They teach you this Marxist philosophy and then treat you like a slave'.[69] 'Lina', a former combatant with FARC, describes how her father struggled to raise his five children once her mother deserted the family: 'I didn't want to be a problem for him. FARC promised me an education and a wage, so I went to live with them'.[70] Upon arrival, it was clear to Lina that not only were such promises never kept, but that any attempt to leave would result in execution. Lina described the particular challenges faced by female members of the movement in her interview with O'Keefe; she revealed that: 'contraceptive injections are administered forcibly and pregnancies are dealt with by means of abortions with whatever basic medical equipment is [available].' Furthermore, a Human Rights Watch report revealed that many of FARC's female 'members' were children as young as 12.[71] In addition to raising issues of personal agency, there are clear implications of these realities for the development of psychological operations to disrupt and undermine the existing commitment of members, as well as for initiatives aimed at preempting the flow of recruits to the movement in the first place.

A major psychological factor lies in the disillusionment that some members have with a group's tactical decisions. Mohammed Nasir Bin Abbas' decision to leave the Indonesian movement Jemaah Islamiyyah was in large part due to the movement's bombing on the island of Bali in October 2002. Jemaah Islamiyyah placed two bombs outside Paddy's Bar and the Sari Club, two nightspots popular with tourists. Over 200 people were killed in the blasts.[72]

Another high-profile defection was that of a former senior figure in the Egyptian Islamic Jihad movement, Sayyid Imam al-Sharif, known also as Dr Fadl. Al-Sharif was a major figure in Al Qaeda. He is considered to have been the mentor of Ayman al-Zawahiri, Al Qaeda's second in command, and to have been a one-time major ideological organising force for the movement. Al-Sharif's disillusionment with Al Qaeda was so pronounced that he went so far as to write a detailed book (*The Rationalization of Jihad*) setting out the case against Al Qaeda's doctrine, tactics and overall strategy. So influential was Al-Sharif's book that a large majority of al-Zawahiri's close followers in Egyptian prison promised to 'end their armed struggle',[73] and al-Zawahiri himself released a tape criticising his former mentor and denouncing him as an enemy.

Another example of disillusionment comes from the case of Al Qaeda members described in the 9/11 Commission Report. The report details how L'Houssaine Kherchtou defected from Al Qaeda and proceeded to testify against the movement in a US court.[74] Kherchtou's decision to break ties with Al Qaeda was, in his own words, because of Bin Laden's unwillingness or inability to provide Kherchtou with funds for Kherchtou's wife to have a Caesarean section following a difficult pregnancy. Furthermore, Bergen and Cruickshank described the case of Sheikh Salman Fahd al-Oudah, a Saudi religious scholar and one-time proponent of Osama Bin Laden. Al-Oudah engaged in a very public disassociation from Al Qaeda's tactics. In 2007, al-Oudah went on a prominent Middle Eastern television network to ask: 'My brother Osama, how much blood has been spilt? How many innocent people, children, elderly, and women have been killed . . . in the name of Al Qaeda? Will you be happy to meet God Almighty carrying the burden of these hundreds of thousands or millions [of victims] on your back?'[75]

It is not uncommon for change in personal priorities to catalyse a psychological crisis for the individual. One former IRA member reported that it was not until he spent some time away from the group that he wondered about where his life was going and what would be left for him to do once the struggle ended.[76] The individual engaged in terrorism may long for a social and psychological state (real or imaginary) that might have been attainable prior to membership. The effects of prolonged involvement in an underground movement can have devastating social, psychological and physical consequences for the individual's mental well-being. The strong desire to begin a family is a common theme in accounts of both men and women in FARC who have sought an exit from the movement.[77] O'Keefe describes how romance in FARC is frowned upon, and that commanders typically separated couples: 'I wanted to die. I felt like part of my soul had gone,' reported one member who became disillusioned with life in the movement.[78]

Kuldip Singh, a former member of the Khalistan Liberation Force, surrendered to the police in 2000 for crimes committed in 1991.[79] Police reports stated that Singh's confession was spurred by his strong desire to start a new life following his trial.

Physical disengagement

A different set of factors relates to issues we could characterise as *physical* in nature. To preface this, we should acknowledge why, when we discuss the factors that relate to walking away from terrorism, that *disengagement* is a more appropriate term than *leaving*. Disengagement does not necessarily imply that the individual leaves terrorism – the person may disengage by simply moving (or by being moved) from one role into another: terrorists may technically stop being terrorists in that they are not engaged in the commission of violent acts but may continue to engage in subversive activity. This supportive role, which may not involve engaging in illegal activities, may be no less significant for the movement's objectives. Occupying a different role or function within the broader movement is, in one sense, a kind of disengagement. During terrorist ceasefires, disengagement becomes apparent in terms of role change in that one-time 'front-line' members will be put to work on different kinds of activities by their leadership. This organisational reallocation serves a number of purposes (as detailed in earlier work[80]) but also reflects a leadership effort to keep focus and direction for followers and thereby avoid organisational drift.[81]

In many ways, the reasons for physical disengagement are easier to identify than those considered (primarily) psychological. Relevant disengagement behaviours and their antecedents might be thought of as *physical* where there is a change in the role of an individual terrorist. Moving from direct action to involvement in an ancillary function (e.g. storing weapons, moving weapons, assembling IEDs) is a common occurrence in terrorist networks but also the individual may move back into a violent role again. This may be due to internal concerns (e.g. organisational reshuffling) or external ones (e.g. avoiding surveillance or suspicion of security services), but moving from one role to another does not necessarily occur in a linear fashion.

Physical disengagement may be expressed as, and owing to:

1 voluntary exit from the movement
2 involuntary exit from the movement
3 involuntary movement into another role
4 voluntary movement into another role
5 involuntary exit from the movement altogether
6 experiences stemming from psychological disengagement acting as a catalyst for physical disengagement across factors 1–5 above.

Arrest, imprisonment and, obviously, death represent the most dramatic kinds of physical disengagement. There are cases where a terrorist may voluntarily exit from the movement. One example of this is in surrendering to authorities. In May 2008, the FARC senior commander Nelly Avila Moreno (better known as 'Karina') surrendered to the Colombian police.[82] More common are instances when someone is physically removed from the movement against their will or they involuntarily exit in some other way. In December 2007, Taleban leader Omar Mullah dismissed Mansoor Dadullah, a leading military commander in Helmand and Kandahar provinces.[83] Dadullah allegedly 'disobeyed orders' (though it was unclear how) and the Taleban issued a statement stating: 'Mansoor Dadullah does not obey the rules of the Islamic emirate and violates it. Therefore it was decided not to appoint any post in the emirate to him.'

There are well-known cases of how imprisonment signalled the end of not only an individual terrorist's career, but also dealt a mortal blow to the movement. This clearly is a reflection of the nature of the role from which the individual disengages. The arrest in 1992 of Abimael Guzman, the founder and leader of Peruvian Sendero Luminoso (Shining Path); the arrest in 1998 of Kurdistan Workers Party (PKK) leader Abdullah Ocalan in Kenya, and the arrest of Real IRA leader Michael McKevitt. Audrey Cronin (pp28–32) lists a host of these and other examples. Though in each case the movements technically survived, their decapitation dealt severe blows to the movement and in each case severely limited their ability to organise, plan and execute operations.

The role of prison in the disengagement process, however, can be complex. For some, prison represents an escape from the movement. In one of the interviews to follow in Chapter 3, a former right-wing extremist bomber reported how prison offered him the physical and psychological space to disengage on his own terms. However, for many Republican and Loyalist prisoners in Northern Ireland, imprisonment by no means marked the end of involvement. This is illustrated through the interview in Chapter 4.

Though the IRA would often tell would-be recruits that the only life awaiting potential members was spending a long time in prison, or ending up dead, the movement saw to it that imprisonment carried with it opportunities for continued involvement and engagement. Complete with localised command structures, movement-specific prison wings and with key prisoners' rights gained in the wake of the hunger strikes of 1981, there are many instances of imprisoned IRA terrorists who became significant political figures via ongoing political radicalisation and training within the prison system: involuntary disengagement, through arrest and imprisonment, was often the catalyst for the development of a substitute role. Similar dynamics can be observed in prisons both in Israel and in South Africa.

There are also examples of a direct continuation in the *same* role. In August 2007, Colombian paramilitary leader Carlos Mario Jimenez became the first terrorist prisoner to lose benefits promised to him for 'demobilising'.[84] Colombian officials determined that despite being locked in a prison cell that Jimenez continued to direct a criminal enterprise and smuggle drugs from prison.

Sometimes, an active member of a terrorist network may be asked to step into another role. This might result from staff shortages, a temporary ceasefire or from a leadership decision to place that person under internal surveillance for a host of reasons.[85] A terrorist suspect may attract unwanted attention from the security services and the leadership may decide to move that person into another role or function. Additionally, a member may be forced to move into another role as a result of disobeying orders or by sanctioning activity that was not approved by the overall leadership. The former Director of Operations for the IRA's Southern Command was shot in the ankle and removed from his position as a result of his decision to sanction an operation that caused significant community backlash against the IRA.[86] There are many cases where the member may be ostracised, but it is also common to have outright execution. Members who are found to have engaged in improper use of arms or money can expect death as the most severe form of dismissal from the movement.

Elsewhere, we see even more dramatic role shifts particularly when the former terrorist may be relevant for efforts at conflict resolution. In early September 2007, senior politicians from Northern Ireland, including former IRA leader Martin McGuinness, participated in four days of talks held in Finland.[87] The talks included 30 members of the warring Sunni and Shia Arab factions in a series of discussions aimed at identifying lessons for Iraq from experiences in Northern Ireland.

At a more localised level, many examples abound and are probably more significant in terms of their potential roles in counter-radicalisation activity. Robert Swann, from Larne, County Antrim, was sentenced to 10 years in prison for his one-time involvement in the Loyalist Ulster Volunteer Force. Described in April 2007 as a 'leading light' in his community,[88] the Antrim Gateway Centre nominated Swann for an award for his cross-community work. Swann was heavily involved in music and other social activity at a local club and was described as 'an inspiration for many young people'. One of the observers of Swann's experiences explains: 'You could hear a pin drop when Robert talked about himself, and the choices he had made and why . . . He made no secret of the fact that he was sucked into a life he later regretted . . . .'

One major area for exploration is how the leadership manages, facilitates, prevents or otherwise hinders voluntary role exit. The Combating Terrorism Center at West Point revealed through its second report on Al Qaeda's foreign fighters in Iraq[89] that Al Qaeda in Iraq (AQI) designed and used 'Separation Contracts' (for those leaving Iraq permanently) as well as 'Temporary Leave Contracts' (for those leaving Iraq temporarily). The contracts were to be read and signed by members. The contracts explicitly stated that the individual was 'not to divulge any factual information about his activities in Iraq', and that 'his personal rights are forfeited if he leaves Iraq without permission'. Though unusual to see such a formal procedure for handling issues of disengagement, such documents offer a glimpse into how some movements recognise that membership and involvement is fleeting. Interestingly, they also hint that disengagement may be equally fleeting.

Terrorist leaders may take more extreme steps to prevent disengagement and risk security breaches, perhaps through subsequent interrogation of arrested members. To protect the security of the movement, some movements convince their members that death is preferable to capture. Recruits of the Liberation Tigers of Tamil Eelam, otherwise known as the Tamil Tigers, sport cyanide capsules contained in a necklace bestowed upon each *Tiger* following recruitment. Tigers are instructed to bite down on the capsule once capture is imminent.

An additional issue here that relates to changes in personal priorities is how in some cases, though the terrorist may have long disengaged, cut ties with the movement completely or developed a new life, they may face prosecution well into the future for crimes committed while involved with a movement. In 2002, some 27 years after the Symbionese Liberation Army robbed a bank in California, DNA evidence brought charges against five former members of the movement for the murder of Myrna Opsahl, a customer at the bank.[90] In 2000, a court tried Hans Joachin Klein, a former colleague-in-arms of Carlos the Jackal, 25 years after his role in the infamous Carlos-led attack on the Organization of Petroleum-Exporting Countries (OPEC) oil ministers' meeting in 1974. Prior to his arrest, Klein spent a lifetime on the run from the authorities. And in the same year, the founding member of the Japanese Red Army terror group, Fusako Shigenobu, was arrested in western Japan after more than 25 years underground. While protection from the enemy may not be enough to keep the members part of the group at the initial phase(s), there may be little to protect them from relentless efforts to bring them to justice regardless of how 'disengaged' they aspire to be.

Reflecting on each of these cases, a clear contrast can be made with examples from Northern Ireland, whereby through the Good Friday peace agreement and the development of the Early Release Scheme, sentences were substantially reduced for those found guilty of terrorist offences.

An interesting example of the tensions that arise from the contrast with the demands of life inside and outside the movement comes from the findings of the 9/11 Commission Report. Mohammed Atta, the alleged ringleader of the 9/11 hijackers, expressly forbade all 18 other members of his team to contact their respective families to bid them goodbye prior to the 9/11 operation. Tension arose between Atta and Ziad Jarrah, who piloted United flight 93, which crashed in rural Pennsylvania. Flouting Attah's directives, Jarrah 'maintained much closer contact with his family and continued his intimate relationship with Senguen' [his partner of several years, whom he married in Germany in 1999] (p163). Jarrah's reluctance to sever ties with Senguen saw him send hundreds of email and phone call messages even while inside the United States and preparing for the operation (p225).[91] Because of persistent conflict and doubt, Jarrah required regular encouragement from his colleagues both in the US and Europe to 'see the plan through' (p246). In the hours before the actual flight, Jarrah even made one final phone call to his fiancée from his hotel room (p532).

Naturally, it may be a psychological issue that lies at the heart of migration between one role and another. If someone becomes burned out, the leadership may decide that they are more beneficial to the movement in another role. Additionally, feedback from engaging in a particular kind of activity may lead to the personal realisation that the individual would be better off in another role. As illustrated in Chapter 6, the reality of what it feels like to personally murder someone cannot be known about or planned for until it happens. The terrorist's experiences, both during and after the event, and the particular context in which that feedback is experienced and worked through, may heavily influence the likelihood of the terrorist's ability to continue in that particular role or function.

Finally, it is also the case that an individual may remain involved in the group for little other than the fact that *not* being a part of the movement may have negative consequences. As recalled by Dipak Gupta on his own formative experiences in India: 'Belonging to a group not only accorded me with psychological comfort, it also provided me with physical security. Calcutta at that time was bubbling with energy and it was dangerous for a young man not to belong to a group. The name Naxalite was itself a deterrent to others from assault' (pxvi). Attempting to avoid reprisal from enemies or rivals may be enough, both to catalyse initial involvement or sustain existing involvement, regardless of the level of psychological commitment to the movement.[92]

Conclusion

Though the disengagement factors asserted here remain exploratory, we have some useful starting points. Many of the issues briefly discussed in this chapter are returned to in Chapter 9. In the meantime, what follows are the case study interviews with select members of a disengaged sample. While the case study chapters have been chosen and organised subjectively, they are presented to the reader with a sense of increasing complexity. Some of the shorter, simpler accounts appear before the more complex and challenging accounts. That complexity reflects both the circumstances of the person's disengagement, but also closely reflects the nature of the person's involvement and their reflections on, and insight into, those experiences. As we will see, the ease with which disengagement can be conceptualised may well be a function of the nature of involvement and type of role or roles held. The case studies are now presented, before we return at the end of the book to reflect on their significance and re-engage with some of the critical features of the discussion presented in this chapter.

3   'Prison was a good thing'

Introduction

On 13 June 1985, a young member of the Norwegian right-wing extremist group, the *Nasjonalt Folkeparti* (National People's Party) detonated a bomb outside an Oslo Mosque. *Nasjonalt Folkeparti* was the successor organisation of *Norsk Front*. *Norsk Front* came to an end in the early 1980s after it was revealed that one of its members had engaged in a bombing operation in 1979. *Norsk Front*'s successors in *Nasjonalt Folkeparti*, however, claimed responsibility for neither the mosque bombing in 1985 nor any other criminal activity. Though *Nasjonalt Folkeparti* is not a national socialist party *per se*, many of its members were clearly Nazis. The mosque in question was built in 1980 and was the European home of the *Ahmadiya* sect, a branch of Sunni Muslims. The mosque was mostly frequented by Pakistani Muslims. In this short chapter, we are introduced to 'Lars' (not his real name), a former member of *Nasjonalt Folkeparti* imprisoned for his role in the bombing.

Meeting 'Lars'

Lars is in his early 40s and works as a civil administrator. He left home when he was 16, moving out of his parents' house on the western Norwegian coast. Lars responded quickly and positively to a request for an interview: 'I am willing to speak about my own experiences. My only concerns are the safety and well-being for my children, but it seems like you are handling that well.' When I clarified to Lars that I am an academic researcher, he responded: 'You are writing that you do not work for the police or intelligence services in any way shape or form. It would be no problem if you did. I would be happy to help the police or intelligence if I could be any help.' Lars was a very cooperative interviewee, though he appeared nervous and uncomfortable at the beginning of the interview. Though he acknowledges remembering events 'very clearly', he would give very brief answers to questions and would wait for a reaction before proceeding. He needed a lot of encouragement to elaborate on specific issues.

Speaking about the background and context to his involvement in

Nasjonalt Folkeparti, Lars explained that the most important element in this was his move away from home. He describes how the move served a number of purposes. He recalled in detail wanting to find independence by getting away from his parents as well as finding a new purpose in life and decided that the best way to achieve these goals was to move to the city. The move to Oslo was primarily characterised by Lars joining a new school, but he described this as a difficult and challenging time: 'When I came to Oslo, I found it difficult to fit in. I had no friends and felt alone.' Lars' initial involvement in the *Nasjonalt Folkeparti* he puts down to complete chance. 'So I was out walking one day and saw a sticker. It was a sticker on a car window. I looked at it and there was an address to something called the National People's Party. I decided to contact them.'

Lars' decision to make contact with the party was not completely devoid of context. In addition to wanting to make friends and grow a social network in Oslo, he describes having at the very least a vague sense of what the *Nasjonalt Folkeparti* was about and that the party was characterised by themes of paramilitarism: 'Well I was always interested in war and history as a kid. As a youngster I would read a lot about the war. I had some idea about the National People's Party when I decided to contact them. I did have some idea, but not much. I was not very political at all.' One of the first issues Lars himself raised was how he felt events were the result of chance. Reiterating how 'not very political' he was, he acknowledges about politics in general: 'I don't think that was very important for me' and suggests his susceptibility to getting involved with some group was 'very much so a coincidence whether you are involved in the left or in the right. This is especially like this when you are very young. You are always trying out very different things.'

One issue in particular however that may have flagged the *Nasjonalt Folkeparti* to Lars was the perception that 'they were involved in military things' because 'I always had an interest in military things.' Lars explains how this interest developed:

> One of the reasons for this is that my father always wanted to do a military career himself, but he failed at the school and so he could not have such a career. He wasn't good enough. But he always talked about it at home. He glorified the military, and he would talk a lot about it. The military life was some kind of ideal . . . for him. He talked a lot about it and I was always interested in hearing about it. I think that ah . . . made me think that the military was something . . . exciting. And I knew that those groups [the National People's Party] had some kind of military clothes, shooting, guns. So, I decided that I would write to them. I wrote them a letter.

Becoming involved

Lars' initial involvement in the party was characterised by gradual progression. It took several weeks before the politics of the movement became apparent to him, but his initial involvement was very firmly non-political and took a non-ideological social character. Upon seeing the car bumper sticker, he recorded the contact details of the movement before writing to them and requesting information. The leaders of the movement responded to his letter and invited him to a social gathering – a barbeque – at the house of one of the leaders. The meeting was very informal and there was no talk about politics. It was, for all intents and purposes, a social function:

> So I decided to write them a letter. And they contacted me back. It did not take a long time for them to contact me. And what happened then was that I was invited to a barbecue, a social event that they organised. And, well, that was the start of it. There was a lot of people at these social events and I remember that there was very little politics at the beginning . . . It was just very social and everyone was having a good time. There was very little . . . very little politics. And they were very . . . I think now, that they were very careful about talking about politics, about the extreme things. But it was really just like an ordinary barbecue with youths of my own age. It was not even really a 'meeting'. It was just very informal, not a meeting, and it was also the home of the leader of the party. I remember at the time he was about 40 years, and the young people he invited to his home were about 15–20 years old. We just met, barbecued, and drank beer. And we had a very good time. But there was no politics . . . I don't remember any at that stage. We just met socially, at weekends. There were very few formal meetings. When I think about it now, there was very little formal *anything*.

Lars reiterated just how receptive he was to the social nature of the group and how this was the most important factor underlying his initial involvement:

> Again, when I moved to Oslo from the north-western coast, I moved to go to school because there were no colleges there, so I *wanted* to go to Oslo. And I did, I went to a college, but a problem was that it was in the rich part of the city. So I didn't fit in very well. I was isolated, so I was going around, looking for other things. So when I started going to these social events and the barbecues, I found an environment I did like in that they somewhat took care of me. I made friends and I liked it.

But while keen to place his own actions into a broader personal context, Lars acknowledged that his experiences were not necessarily typical and that not everyone became involved in the party in the same way as he:

> I spoke to other people who had been in the movement and they all said that in one school I know, they made someone bully another pupil, and then they went to the pupil and offered him protection, and then he became part of the movement. It was a set-up.

Being involved

Once Lars became a regular attendee at the *Nasjonalt Folkeparti*'s social gatherings, his apprenticeship in the party took form. The level of his involvement changed and his commitment to the movement began to escalate. The escalation in commitment was marked with an increasing engagement in illegal activity, and at the same time, his development with the group was still characterised through a slow, gradual process of progression:

> It's very, very gradual. It does not happen quickly. Remember this is a very *social* group still. It starts with small things like am . . . shops for ah . . . shops owned by Pakistanis and Indians. We would know where they would own shops and we would see them. We would know who they were and we would watch them leave at night. We would attack them by doing only small things at the start. We started by gluing . . . putting glue in the locks of the doors in their shops. I know it's not a good thing to do but it's not a very *big* thing to do. And then, it's a bit . . . it's gradually . . . well, next time it's to smash something through the windows of the shop. Next time it's different. Gradually you do more and more. And it's always different.

Lars places this escalation clearly within an explicit group context and describes how his commitment to the group was harnessed through engagement in violent activity. His acts of vandalism were committed 'in a small group, usually four or five', and were primarily opportunistic. In the context of his involvement, however, Lars was now engaging in regular activities with the group and his loyalty was sustained by repeated acts of vandalism.

But while Lars' initial involvement in *Nasjonalt Folkeparti* was primarily characterised by environmentally proximate opportunities for involvement in low-level criminal activity, he went from this to assisting in the preparation and movement of explosives. This would culminate in his role in the bombing of the Sunni Mosque. Though the attack was initially thought to have signalled the beginning of a campaign against Muslims in Norway, the details of the event, and Lars' participation in it, reveal a different explanation:

> The bomb was not actually as planned as it may seem. We were in a location on the western coast. It was the summer, and we were all there in a kind of summer . . . in some kind of summer camp. It was down by the sea and there was a boathouse nearby. And I remember there was some work being done on the house. The house was not finished. For some reason, and it might be to do with work that was being done on the coast; there was some dynamite lying around. It was not secure or locked up, and right away we recognised that it was dynamite. So . . . some of us picked up some of the dynamite and brought it home. But there was no plan about how to use it at the time. Or what we would do to use it. But

after some time we did use it. We did use it once or twice, and did things like laying it outside the stores of foreigners.

Soon, however, other plans materialised for use of the explosives, and the Party developed a plan to target Norwegian Jews directly with a bomb. It appears that the initial target of the Party was not the mosque, but in fact a synagogue:

> I remember it very well, the leader of the party, drove me past a synagogue and he told me 'someone should do something there'. But he didn't tell me actually . . . I mean directly. It was very implicit. He didn't say *do it*, he just took me there and said *someone should do it*. But I took that as a clear signal. And also obviously because of something else that happened quickly. To fire dynamite you need ah . . . the fuse . . . and on the same drive, ah, later, he told me that he was going to get me some fuses. A few days later, I got the fuse. I didn't get the fuse from him, but from another person in the movement.

Lars' repeated demonstrations of his loyalty and commitment to the group meant that to the leadership he was a prime candidate for being tasked with the delivery of the bomb. He was instructed to place the bomb on the steps of the front entrance of the synagogue and then leave. His reaction, however, betrayed a lack of preparedness. A lack of explicit instructions resulted in confusion that had major repercussions for the execution of the operation:

> One evening I went from home, with the dynamite. Actually I was not sure where to go, what to do . . . so I was . . . ah . . . I remember I was thinking about the synagogue, but there was a problem. When I was outside I realised that there was no public transport in that direction. There was the tram, but the tram went in another direction. So I got on it, and when I was on it, I saw that it went just past a mosque. And that's when I got off, and I placed the dynamite outside, on the stairway . . . I didn't know about synagogues, or mosques, but I remember thinking and remembering that it should probably be like a Norwegian church. And so I remember thinking that there would be no people in a church in the evening. So I was sure that there were no people.

The bomb exploded with several people inside the mosque. No one was killed but those inside suffered several serious injuries. Shortly afterwards, Lars was apprehended by the police and quickly convicted of the bombing. Unusually, however, he was not convicted for attempted murder, but for, in his words:

> I was convicted for ah . . . I'm not sure how to say it . . . bad fire damage. It was a property crime, not human crime, because the court believed me. It was not an attempt to harm people. I know that [*Nasjonalt Folkeparti*]

harmed people in other places. But when I was there, we never did things *directly* to harm people. It was against properties all the time. There was no fighting either. We were always doing things against property.

Disengaging

At all times, and though he viewed such acts as 'wrong', Lars viewed the gluing of the locks and the acts of leaving explosives outside shop fronts as crimes against property and relegated their significance to 'nuisance' acts. He stressed throughout the interview that the attempt to bomb the synagogue (eventually a mosque) was also motivated by wanting to 'do things against property'. Whatever views had been shaped as a result of his socialisation into *Nasjonalt Folkeparti*, however, his commitment to the movement decreased substantially shortly after his conviction.

Upon conviction, imprisonment marked Lars' disengagement from the movement, both physically and psychologically:

> Well, I think for me, prison was a good thing because I was moved away from the movement. Prison was the best thing that happened to me then. I didn't meet people in the movement and was not around them any more. They did come to visit me sometimes, but I did make some new friends in the prison from at least two other different countries. Normal people. One was from Sierra Leone. Ah . . . but it was when I was in prison that my world completely changed. I discovered that everything I had done, and everything that I was thinking about before, was completely wrong. In prison, meeting these people, I realised how very wrong I was. [The man from Sierra Leone] and other people I had talked to in prison were nice people. It was a different world.

Lars' exposure to and engagement with people from different nationalities helped increase the contrast between him and those in *Nasjonalt Folkeparti* from whom he would increasingly distance himself. Soon, however, the deepening contemplation he would undergo would create another distancing between Lars and the other inmates at the prison:

> I also think I am not a typical criminal because in the prison, all the other prisoners said to me *you are not one of us*. They were kind to me, but it was very clear to me . . . *you are not one of us* they would say. There were a few reasons for this. A big reason was because I had never used drugs. And also they didn't believe I would be back. 90% of the people in the prison were coming back to prison because of new crimes, so they meant that I was not one of them because they knew I would not be back.

In prison, Lars found himself reflecting on how he had initially become involved, and how he viewed himself as 'vulnerable' to involvement with the movement:

> I had time to think about what I did in prison. Gradually, I began to think that one factor was related to my childhood. When I was growing up, my mother was very, very religious. She was a Mormon, and when growing up, I learned the difference between right and wrong. I think that when I moved to Oslo, I was still young. I gradually slipped . . . And after a time, I just got out of the church. I didn't go to the church. And I remember thinking that I was used to thinking about right or wrong only because of the Bible and other books that I read. When I didn't have the church any more I had no guidance about right and wrong, and there was nobody to say to me 'this is what's right, and this is what's wrong'. I really didn't feel at any stage that it was very wrong to do all the things that I did. I didn't have those guidelines, and I didn't feel there was anything wrong with it.

A recurring theme in Lars' explanatory style was a sense of him having minimal personal agency in the group activities in which he found himself engaging. Being in prison, however, appears to have changed this for him, and brought with it the realisation for Lars to atone for his crimes that he would personally 'need to do good things':

> Prison changed everything. When I went to prison, it was there when I really started to study. The first year I was there, I began to study philosophy. For a whole half year, I just read and read. I read all about the different philosophers. I learned about just very simple ideas. For example, I learned for the first time in prison that it is possible to look at the world in many, many different ways. There doesn't have to be a right or a wrong answer. There's a lot of different ways. But the other big factor I think was that I just met other people from other cultures. They were very different, but I understood that they were just like me.

Lars came to the realisation that he was finished with *Nasjonalt Folkeparti* and also that he would have to take tangible steps towards convincing others in prison and outside of the distance he sought between himself and the party: 'There was no doubt about that. When I was inside prison, I did call one of the largest newspapers in Norway. I told them that I was through with the movement.' In fact, Lars was quick to welcome visits from the media: 'They made a few visits to me while I was in prison. I told them that I had done a lot of wrong things that I regret, but [the journalists] would keep visiting me for a while to ask me about it.'

Again, in contrast to a sense of Lars' emphasis on external factors driving his initial involvement with the group, Lars stressed that his decision to speak out about his involvement and his change of mind was the result of his own decision: 'The prison authorities did not play a role in me changing my mind. I realised this *myself*. I decided I should call a journalist. And what happened was that I told them I wanted to speak because [the bombing] was still something they were writing about so my name was known. When I called out to them, they came at once.'

The significance of doing this was not lost on Lars and he acknowledges realising that publicly burning his bridges would likely be met with a negative reaction from his former comrades:

> Once the newspaper wrote about that, the fact that I had called them, and that I wanted to tell my story, there was no way back. I had told the rest of Norway that I was finished with *Nasjonalt Folkeparti*. And then, that's when I started to get a few letters with threats from former colleagues. The letters were very careful. The threats were not direct, but they were implicit threats. They would write to me, and tell me that I was a traitor, and say other things like that.

Upon meeting with and engaging the journalists, Lars' disengagement from the party was swift, clear-cut and was to become even more public. Upon his release from prison, he continued to reinforce the message that he was putting distance between himself and his former movement. Lars stressed that he was so committed to this increasingly public atonement that he began to seek out employment opportunities that would offer him a platform for spreading his message:

> Well I started education as a pre-school teacher. I never worked with [children] before, and when I think about . . . I think that what motivated me more than anything else in taking on even more education after prison was that . . . I think I did it mostly because I wanted to show the rest of the world that I was not dangerous. And I thought that the least dangerous thing I can do is to show that I can work with children. So I finished my education, and started to work in a child-care office, attached to kindergartens.

This did not prove successful and very soon Lars began to explore working in a different kind of setting:

> When I spent time working in an office, I realised that I was good at it. And soon then I started to realise that I wanted to learn more about public administration. So I actually started all over again. I went back into university and took a master's degree in public administration, and that's what I'm working with now. But all the time, wherever I worked, I felt it was important to speak to children. In the first 5 to 10 years after I went out from prison, I travelled all over the country. I spoke to youths, mostly, aged from 15–17 years, in schools.

In fact, Lars became a regular speaker about his experiences in the *Nasjonalt Folkeparti* movement. So eager to alter the image he had been identified with, and to reinforce his new persona, Lars began to grasp every opportunity to accept speaking engagements where he was offered the prospect of warning children of the dangers of becoming involved in extremism and youth gangs: 'I felt really good about doing this. I think it did it a lot of good at the beginning.'

He stresses how his engagement in this activity, as well as the adherence to this new counter-identity, was time-limited:

> I gradually did it less and less. It's not easy to explain why. I don't know. After some time, I felt it was starting to get too much in the past and I couldn't really speak too much about it any more. When I started to get a little older, it became more distant. It's just that as I grow older, it doesn't mean so much to me anymore. Also of course there is an obvious thing that I just don't look like a Neo-Nazi any more.

Though less regularly, Lars continued to speak with different audiences, including academics as well as more journalists. He described his readjustment to his life in mainstream society as being largely without major difficulties:

> I didn't have problems readjusting to life outside prison. I did get a tip from a journalist a few years later, that they [*Nasjonalt Folkeparti*] were planning to do something against me, but it never happened. I think my education helped me in getting accepted into society, and also that I travelled and spoke to children and young people about the dangers of getting involved in a movement. They believed me when I said I was finished with it. So really I didn't have any problems.

Interim conclusions

Lars' account, though brief and telegraphic in expression, highlights a series of issues. For Lars, there was clearly a significance associated with his pre-involvement fantasies about involvement in particular activities (positive perceptions of involvement in militarism of some sort). The role of chance in a pre-radicalisation phase (e.g. in seeing the car sticker) was significant to Lars and was an issue he returned to stressing more than once. Lars' behaviour prior to joining the group seems to be characterised by, at least in part by some, the identification of *involvement-seeking behaviours* (e.g. seeking out contact with *Nasjonalt Folkeparti*). The informal, largely social nature of the process that shaped his initial involvement (e.g. Lars' constant assertions that the initial meetings, over several weeks, involved no political discussions) is also a theme that is repeated while he is clearly engaged in the movement's activities.

There is an equally gradual progression from legal to illegal activity through the movement. The group plays a role in reinforcing that initial involvement, sustaining involvement and engagement in violent activity. Lars' activities inside the movement were always engaged in through the company of others and engagement in illegal activity in that group context served to reinforce his loyalty and commitment to the movement.

Equally gradual is Lars' upward escalation of activity from non-violent to violent and this is accompanied by a minimisation of consequences of activities on victims (e.g. his repeated view that property crimes and intimidation of the immigrant shop owners was 'wrong', but not serious or 'violent').

While the role of chance was an issue that appeared in the phase of his initial involvement, it recurred much later on in influencing the timing and nature of the escalation (e.g. finding the dynamite and deciding it ought to be used) and its parallel role in influencing the seeking out of an opportunity to use the material.

Lars' time in prison raises a host of issues. Clearly, prison played a significant social and psychological role in providing the setting and context for significant personal change (e.g. the significance of physical distancing from other members of *Nasjonalt Folkeparti* as a result of imprisonment and the role this played in Lars' subsequent psychological disengagement).

Lars' disengagement appeared to develop in parallel with the seeking out of an explicit new identity as an 'ex-member' (e.g. the educational role played by Lars for several years in warning children about the dangers of becoming involved) and the enthusiasm with which Lars embraced this new identity was significant. In time the adherence to that explicit new identity lessened in intensity and that gradual disengagement and distancing from that newly acquired identity shifted into a more settled phase of reintegration (e.g. Lars' move into the job he now holds and the accompanying perception that he can no longer meaningfully fulfil his post-prison role given the increasing time and psychological distancing from his prior life).

Though we are presented in this chapter with a brief, seemingly linear and relatively straightforward account of movement into, out of and beyond an extremist movement, Lars' case reveals some rich and complex themes with important implications for counter-radicalisation, and counter-terrorism more broadly. Significantly, there is also a hint here at the role of explanatory and attribution styles in attempting to understand insight and remorse and perhaps illustrate how we might conceptualise and assess 'de-radicalisation'. We will return to this issue in detail in Chapter 9. The cases to follow build upon these so that we may integrate the collective themes and interpret their significance for counter-terrorism initiatives.

In the chapter to follow, we also examine a case of a former terrorist for whom imprisonment played a pivotal, though less dramatic and subtler, role in facilitating his disengagement from direct involvement in the movement. There are some immediate and obvious similarities to the case of Lars (indeed, across several issues), but we see how, in the case to follow, imprisonment and the post-imprisonment phase posed a more complex and challenging environment for the individual in question.

4 'I volunteered'

Introduction

The Ulster Volunteer Force (UVF) was a Loyalist terrorist movement in Northern Ireland. Though tracing its historical inspiration to its predecessor movement of 1912, the UVF as we currently know it was established in 1966. Until the recent peace process, the UVF waged a campaign of violence across Northern Ireland. The operational domain of the UVF extended primarily to east Antrim, Belfast (the Protestant Shankill Road area in particular – home to most of the Loyalist paramilitaries) and areas of County Armagh. The primary goal of the UVF was to uphold the union of Northern Ireland with Great Britain (i.e. the United Kingdom).

The UVF engaged in a long 'tit-for-tat' campaign with the Irish Republican Army (IRA) and frequently targeted Roman Catholic civilians the UVF assumed to be supportive of the IRA.[1] The UVF was responsible for a series of high-profile attacks and murders beginning in the 1970s and continuing throughout the most recent phase of the conflict. Among these were the 1971 bombing of McGurk's Bar, one of the very first atrocities of the Troubles. Fifteen Catholics were killed, with a further 20 people injured. The UVF was also responsible for bombings in Dublin and Monaghan in 1974, which killed 33 civilians. Persistent allegations of collusion between the UVF and rogue elements of the security services in Northern Ireland stemmed from this and other incidents, and have been the subject of ongoing investigations in Northern Ireland.

With several hundred members at the movement's height in the 1970s and 1980s, the UVF is believed by many to have killed more civilians than any other Loyalist paramilitary organisation. They have also been implicated in substantial drug-related seizures, despite a public stance against drugs. Together with sister movements Ulster Resistance and the Ulster Defence Association (UDA), the UVF imported large numbers of arms from South Africa. But perhaps most notorious of all UVF activities were those that emerged from a particular cell of the movement better known as the 'Shankill Butchers'. Led by Lenny Murphy, this UVF active service unit was responsible for over 30 killings. These civilian murders were characterised by abductions that were accompanied by horrific, often elaborate, torture.[2] The Shankill Butchers were eventually apprehended and the Provisional IRA assassinated Murphy.[3]

Throughout the 1980s, the UVF expanded their target range to include not only Catholic civilians but also Irish Republican terrorists and related political figures. During that decade, the UVF suffered major setbacks with the arrests of key members. A series of internecine feuds occurred in relation to the UVF ceasefire in 1994 and these gave rise to the formation of the Loyalist Volunteer Force (LVF). Led by Billy Wright, in the years following the 1994 ceasefire, continuous clashes took place between the UVF and LVF, and at times between both UVF factions and the larger Loyalist movement, the UDA. Wright himself was murdered by Irish Republicans while in prison.

In contrast to the IRA, the UVF had mixed success in its transition into the mainstream democratic process. Its political representatives, along with key figures in the UVF, formed the Progressive Unionist Party (PUP) in the early 1990s. The PUP participated in multi-party talks that led to the Good Friday Agreement in 1998 and even won two seats in the Northern Ireland Assembly later that year. Despite these gains, however, the PUP failed to develop a long-lasting political presence in Northern Ireland. In the face of increasing irrelevance against a backdrop of stability across the region, in 2007 the UVF officially renounced violence in a statement that reiterated its commitment to decommissioning weapons and completely ending its involvement in terrorism.

Meeting 'Alan'

'Alan' (not his real name) is a former member of the Ulster Volunteer Force (UVF). He served a lengthy prison sentence for a variety of terrorist offences. He was interviewed in a house on the Shankill Road, Belfast. Alan was a cooperative interviewee. It was clear that he had significant experience in giving interviews, and he was relaxed and confident in the answers that he gave throughout.

The process that characterises Alan's initial involvement in the UVF is in many ways quite similar to that which characterises the way in which many others became involved in activism in Northern Ireland during the early phases of the Troubles. The backdrop of civil strife in the late 1960s saw Protestant and Catholic communities divided along ethnic, religious and eventually geographic lines. Becoming involved in paramilitary activity on either side was not unusual and in some cases it was even a rite of passage.

Becoming involved

In reflecting upon his initial involvement in the UVF, Alan points to having a strong awareness of the instability spreading across Northern Ireland in the late 1960s:

I grew up in Northern Ireland, during the 60s, and the civil rights campaign began in the late 60s. I had no real particular interest in politics or anything like that. Because as far as I was concerned, all my friends, and eh, people that I had grown up around, be they Catholics or otherwise, well, we all didn't have a lot. So the only thing surprising me about it was wondering what the Catholics were complaining about, because we were equally as poor if you like, we were all working class.

On more than one occasion, Alan stressed that 'politically' he 'had no interest, and I just ignored it.' What he felt influenced his growing awareness of unfolding social and political events was 'just a bit of curiosity . . . I was wondering what [Catholics] were complaining about.' The proximity to violence, however, meant that Alan became increasingly aware of the seriousness of the situation:

With resistance from extreme militants of Unionism eventually the civil rights campaign degenerated into violence and subsequently an IRA campaign began then. I was aware of it [extreme Unionism] but determined to keep myself aloof from it because I didn't hold any extreme political views or religious ones for that matter. The reason for this is because some people were motivated by . . . sectarianism.

Alan recalls being disgusted at the sectarian nature of the Troubles, while at the same time he says he remained separated from playing any role in the conflict. Though 'concerned', like everybody else, he describes being largely uninterested in being involved in any way as he got on with his life:

[The violence] went on for a number of years, obviously I became concerned, but I was . . . I got myself a fairly good career, I was working for the Post Office, working on telephones then. This later became British Telecom. I was really pleased with the progress I was making in my career. And I had a steady relationship with a girl that I subsequently married.

However, Alan eventually did become involved in the UVF. Against an ongoing awareness of the situational backdrop, and the escalating civil strife engulfing Northern Ireland, Alan describes the issues surrounding his personal decision to become involved, and places significant emphasis on personal responsibility, despite an acute awareness of community influences:

It was purely a *personal* thing with me that motivated me to become involved. People that I had come up through school with . . . had chosen careers in the security forces, and a couple of them were killed. We weren't close friends, but when you go 11 years through your school life with somebody, there is some kind of relationship there, you know. And that had a profound effect on me, particularly combined with the fact that the IRA campaign at that time was pretty . . . well, you were heading up towards the worst years of violence in terms of deaths and casualties and it just seemed that no matter what material possessions you were accumulating or what way your life was going, it just seemed all meaningless. The country seemed to be just collapsing into anarchy.

Despite what Alan describes as a depressing situation, with a seemingly inevitable downward direction, he did not view his involvement with the UVF as equally inevitable. In fact, he describes having considered a variety of options with which he would be able to express some kind of participation:

I thought for quite a while about joining the part-time security forces. A lot of people did this . . . in reaction to . . . the . . . because of the existing security forces seemed pretty inept in being able to contain the IRA violence. They [the IRA] were just to me . . . it seemed that they were able to kill with impunity. So I thought for a while about either joining what was then the UDR [Ulster Defence Regiment – a regiment of the British Army that was formed to assist the police with special security duties] or some form of reserve police force.

Though the UDR would have offered a legitimate outlet for participation, in the end, Alan's decision to seek out involvement in the Ulster Volunteer Force he presents in logical and strategic terms:

I decided with the nature of the work that I was doing, which had me going into quite staunchly Republican areas such as South Armagh, that the only thing I would be doing would be giving them another easy legitimate target. So I didn't think it would be a very good idea to do that. So then the next option which I thought for quite a while about was to fight the IRA on the same type of terms, mainly illegally through the Ulster Volunteer Force, which was eh . . . the most active of the Loyalist organisations in my particular area, where I grew up. So that was really it; that was how I joined the UVF.

Following his decision to join, Alan's ability to become involved with the movement was heavily influenced by the close availability of local opportunities:

Well you know, with growing up in an area, you fairly well know who the players were. And some of the guys that I had grown up with had taken that course quite a number of years before I eventually joined, so it was . . . I probably socialised with some of them, and so it was just a matter of them, ah, making them aware that you were interested in becoming involved with them.

Upon deciding to seek out involvement, however, the actual process of becoming involved was very gradual. Alan describes how the UVF's recruiters responded to him:

> Their selection in later years of the conflict became less discriminatory. But at the time . . . like, you know they didn't just *allow* me to become involved straight away. It was quite a number of months after I first expressed my interest.

Alan recalls not reacting positively to this, and felt personally rebuked: 'You know . . . it sort of irked me at the time [I thought] *why did they not think I was sort of good enough type of thing*, you know?' He explains how he later accepted that there were organisational concerns underpinning this process:

> They just didn't accept people at time purely just because they wanted extra numbers. And they probably had a closer look at me to see what was motivating me, and . . . you know, they were probably guarding against all sorts of things, like infiltration and what not . . . And they eventually came back to me, and said was I still interested?

Alan described how the months between his initial involvement-seeking and the initial response from the movement was sufficient to sow the seeds of doubt in his mind: 'My interest probably had waned in that period, you know, but well, I approached *them*. I approached them in the first place so I can't very well hold back now!'

Being involved

By the time Alan was approached by the UVF for active duty, he was holding down a full-time job. This did not deter him from agreeing to join and adopt what he called 'the double life'. Consequently, in addition to the challenges of making the transition into illegal activity, juggling the demands of routine daily life on top of UVF duty was not without its own difficulties:

> Because all my upbringing and all that was very law-abiding, that type of stuff, respect for law and order, and am . . . you did have to cross a rubicon to become involved in illegal activity, and . . . for instance I wouldn't have dreamed of driving my car without tax or insurance, things like that, all the mundane things that people do, the rules that we adhere to. My life on that side was perfect. But you know sometimes I wonder about it now, the other side of my life when I was killing, or trying to kill people, you know, so . . . It was difficult, but then again I would always have viewed myself as very much a 'part-time' activist.

Despite being a fully-fledged though part-time member of the UVF, Alan's double life did not entail the movement governing his every thought or action. He describes the reality of his involvement:

> You know, it wasn't like I was doing something every day. You would have had that [full-time involvement] in certain places. I lived in [Mk] which, probably outside of Belfast, would have been the most acutely affected area in terms of violence, you know. We were on the hinterland of South Armagh [a major IRA stronghold at the time]. And it was probably the last Unionist stronghold east of the Bann, or west of the Bann. But it wasn't a full-time sort of occupation with me. You did fit it in, you worked around it. That's a bit flippant, but that's how it was.

Alan describes the challenge of reconciling the pre-existing perceptions about his involvement with the reality of his time in the UVF: 'I knew about the UVF before I joined, you know? I had a clear sense of what joining the UVF meant . . . but being honest now, even when I did commit acts of violence, I was never ever *entirely* comfortable with it.' He described the efforts required to cope with the demands of involvement and engagement in illegal activity: 'You know, it took a lot of . . . am . . . with the events that go on, you are able to *justify* what you are doing, you know . . . if you understand what I'm saying. Like if I had to kill somebody for self-gain or gratification, I just couldn't do it.'

With a little elaboration, Alan explained how he worked through the discomfort with violence by stressing the nature of his role as a UVF gunman. He emphasised the autonomy given him by the movement, a point reinforced by his emphasis on 'volunteering' and on which he drew a sharp contrast with the IRA:

> I was never *told* to do anything in particular. What we had was a unit, and we would have identified a Republican target, and it was up to ourselves to take them out, or take him out, whoever it was. But the, the point I'm making there . . . I take personal responsibility for anything I was ever involved in. You know, if you're talking to Republicans for instance, you very seldom get personal responsibility, it's always *the movement* that does it, but you know as far as I . . . I don't blame . . . No, *blame* is the wrong word, but I don't hold anyone else responsible for the actions that I took. As far as I'm concerned, the name of the movement was the Ulster *Volunteer* Force, and I volunteered, and anything I subsequently did I take responsibility for it.

Alan spent seven years as an active terrorist before being apprehended by the security services. Throughout that time, and despite his part-time engagement with the UVF, the stress and pressures of involvement remained vivid on a daily basis. He describes the reality:

Well, obviously there's a certain amount of fear and apprehension that you're going to be killed yourself or apprehended en route, you know, to the operation, or coming away from it. You know, there's all that fear and apprehension that you're gonna be caught. That pressure was there right up until the day of my arrest. I was arrested several times before I was eventually ... before they had evidence to convict me. But you know, it's ... most people there ... you know, it's probably different in the *political* arena, but [it's not like] criminals that tend to get arrested for minor things until something major happens, [in my case] the very first time in my life that the police came to my door was to question me about murder, so it was just a ... it's a quantum leap if you like.

Alan was arrested by the police and was charged with murder. During interrogation, he made a full confession.

In one very obvious manner, prison marked Alan's disengagement from terrorist activity. Reflecting upon the significance of his arrest and his time in prison, Alan suggests that the seeds of psychological disengagement were beginning to show by the time of his arrest:

It's a strange situation, because [prior to arrest] I had come to my own conclusion that violence wasn't achieving anything. And at that particular time, I felt the IRA campaign was coming to an end. They weren't able to do what they were doing. I just came to the conclusion that some day ... we ... were going to have to talk and come to some form of accommodation here. And that we were going to have to question the morality of it ... if there was any morality about inflicting violence on people. It was really just a cycle then.

Significantly, Alan suggests that he had already begun to feel a strong sense of personal disillusionment with the overall purpose of engaging in violence and recognises this as a vulnerability he claims to have been aware of at the time:

You know I probably wouldn't have been involved in any more active service in the UVF even if I hadn't been apprehended. I look back on it now, and that's probably what weakened my resolve under interrogation about what I had been involved in. Because by that time I didn't have the same mindset or the same eh, motivation to keep me going.

Given that Alan was clearly working through doubts about the tactical effectiveness in reaching the UVF's objectives through violence, it might appear surprising then that prison did not mark either the end of Alan's involvement, nor his commitment to the movement: 'I went to prison, and then of course, my theory [of the futility of the cycle of violence and the

IRA's campaign coming to an end] was thrown out the window by, mainly by the actions of Margaret Thatcher.'

Margaret Thatcher, the former British Prime Minister, responded publicly to the IRA hunger strikes with the now infamous 'let them starve' remark that, in addition to her overall handling of the hunger strikes, was viewed as a major catalyst for renewed domestic and international support for the IRA. The Thatcher response is held up a classic example of the failure to counter terrorist propaganda.

For Alan, the Thatcher response and the reinvigoration of the IRA served to dampen his disillusionment and personal doubts about the UVF mission and his part in it. Instead, he argues that it actually reinforced his loyalty and commitment to the group. Despite harbouring doubts, Alan asserts that it immediately served as a backdrop to his continued adherence to UVF ideals within the prison, and among fellow UVF members:

> Because with her handling of the hunger strikes, it gave the IRA a whole new impetus and the campaign took off again, whereas I felt in the late 70s it was dying a death, you know, and that they [the IRA] would eventually come to that conclusion. But then as I say, she gave it a whole new impetus. I . . . and maybe people particularly from my own community had a perverse sense of admiration for the hunger strikers because they wanted exactly the same things as what I would have wanted, in terms of the political objectives. You've all those things, but . . . the other point about it I would make . . . was that when I was probably drawn away from the UVF, and I certainly wouldn't have become active again, but when you're in prison you're right back amongst them again. So by circumstances you do become involved with them again, not from a desire to have you engage in violence. But you're in a wing of the prison where all the UVF people have a command structure.

Though psychologically disenchanted with his involvement in the UVF, and struggling with issues of loyalty with his commitment still waning, Alan describes the obstacles to continued disengagement within the prison system. Being in prison meant that he was faced with having to struggle through a different kind of involvement:

> In prison . . . being involved, it just meant you know, you have a command structure . . . you adhere to the UVF code of discipline in the environment that you're in. But there's not a lot in relation to what they require of you. But mainly, in prison, I just immersed myself in education. There's *commitment* [and] much like the IRA, you know, we would have resisted attempts by the prison authorities to impose their regime upon us. And we all worked together as a unified body to achieve whatever conditions that we felt we required in the prison.

Disengaging

Alan served 13 years of his life sentence. He received an early release and explains the context to the decision behind this:

> I was released in 1993. The normal mechanism at that time was after 10 years of a life sentence you become . . . you go before a life sentence review commission, and then they recommend that you do another bit, and you come before them in another three years, and they may or may not let you out. And you do the same thing all over again in another couple of years. But I finished up being let out after 13 years.

I asked Alan to describe the risk assessment that was conducted on him and his response provides some insight into the decision-making process:

> In the end, and this is probably the nature of what you were involved with, the reality is the conflict here threw up a lot of people that probably were psychopathic by nature when you see the nature of some of the killings people were involved in, you know. And I suppose obviously there were times like that when they [the life sentence review commission] would try to see if you were naturally like that.

Alan drew a sharp contrast between his motivation and that of 'the criminal' and explains why there was a clear sense of why he would not have been seen as a recidivist:

> What I always knew is, to me, criminals can't help themselves. You know, there are people that are just straight criminal by nature that are just like that. I always was in complete control of what I wanted to do and what I didn't want to do. When I came out of prison I knew I would never be involved in violence again anyway. I think they [the panel] had a pragmatic approach to it, although they would never probably publicly declare that. They knew that things were different in nature, and for people who lived in an abnormal society, well you get normal people that were doing a lot of abnormal things.

Alan's reintegration into his community was not without challenges, but he describes his experiences with relevance only to key differences between his experiences and those of others in prison for similar offences:

> Maybe untypically in a lot of cases, I was married before [prison]. Most people who go into prison for a long time, their relationships break up, you know, but my marriage survived imprisonment. I was fortunate enough I had two young children when I went in. Both of them were under the age of two, so when I came out they were teenagers. I had a

good environment to come back out into. My wife and I had still had a good relationship, and we still have to this day. We'll be 33 years married this year, so we've survived quite a lot, and you know it made things a lot easier for me in that respect. A lot of prisoners, they go into prison, they're maybe those who went in quite young, they're living with their parents. [When released], their parents would have been deceased perhaps, or coming out to relationships, if they were married, or had girlfriends, if, if those relationships had ended, and so they're coming out, and had no structure to fit into you know, they obviously would have had a tougher time than what I did.

Alan became re-involved with the UVF, but in a different way. He ran a community support scheme to help former prisoners reintegrate into their communities: 'I always wanted to contribute some way to convincing many former comrades in the UVF that we should think about going on the ceasefire and getting involved in the process that would see ... eh ... non-violent methods of resolving what conflict remained you know.'

Once again, and a theme repeated throughout the interview, he stressed this was a personal choice and not something that had emerged from looking at efforts within other movements:

No, no it was internally with myself. The thing about is that some [people] take longer than others, but eventually the penny drops with most people, you know there is this question *how long are we gonna keep killing one another?* At the end of the day, in all conflicts, the various participants will eventually talk, so why not do it sooner rather than later?

Alan's experiences in prison and exposure to the experiences of other Loyalist prisoners at the time were influential to his commitment to his post-imprisonment role, but he reluctantly acknowledges that his new role was also shaped in part by his own difficulties of long-term reintegration into the community:

It certainly wasn't my intention to come out of prison and become full-time involved in what I'm involved in now. That was never my inten-tion. I was reasonably well educated when I went in. I enhanced that education during prison and finished up by getting a first class honours degree [in mathematics] naively thinking that that would help me back into some kind of meaningful employment. Theoretically it should have given me at least an opportunity to get at least decent employment, when I had been very well academically qualified, plus I had 10 years' experi-ence previously, although it was probably out of date when I came out, as a telephone engineer. But with all the barriers that exist preventing former prisoners from getting into employment, it was tough. You know once they heard I was in prison that was the end of the story, so you were condemned to menial jobs, like you know, I messed about buildings sites and what not for a couple of years. But when the ceasefires kicked in, there became opportunities for full-time employment in the community sector, and I've been employed here since.

The initiative that Alan began was established to provide support for former politically motivated prisoners from a Loyalist background. In the time since the Good Friday Agreement, many more prisoners were released from prison as part of the Early Release Scheme and other goodwill gestures facilitated by the Irish and British Governments. The reintegration dimension of Alan's work diminished and he now characterises his efforts as part of peace-building work in his local community. He has remained closely involved in facilitating consultative processes between Loyalist paramilitaries and others.

Even though the reasons and probably the nature of conflict throughout the world are different, there are common threads running through every conflict. We were in Colombia, and I was totally amazed about how what we were saying and what they were saying struck a chord with one another. Commonalities like, exactly the same things happened here that happened in Colombia, although you multiply them by a thousand or a million times, that was the nature of it you know? Degeneration of polit-ical ideologies into criminality, drugs, that type of thing, it's all there like. South Africa is the same; I've been there several times. Where we have problems now, you have an increase in criminality, people use skills they acquire during the conflict they put them to use for their own ends.

Interim conclusions

Alan's account reveals some interesting and complex issues. An overarching theme that emerged in his descriptions is the nature of the relationship between personal, individual issues and the larger social and political context. He describes having made a personal decision to become involved, but places this decision explicitly within a broader, ongoing social movement. His recurring emphasis on being a 'volunteer' was coupled with a contrast between his own role and that of his enemy opposites in the IRA. There is also a sense of urgency and timeliness surrounding his decision to become involved. His account of this phase displayed an acute awareness of the fact that many others around him were also becoming involved.

In one way there are interesting similarities between Lars' account and that presented here. Both involve (at least initially) involuntary physical disengagement through imprisonment. Prison for both men, however, saw a period of reflection that ultimately set the scene for psychological disengage-ment from the movement. What characterised Alan's disengagement, however, was ultimately more physical than psychological in the long run. His views about the utility and effectiveness of the tactical use of violence underwent significant change, yet his dedication to working towards political change has remained steadfast. The dampening of his loyalty to the movement only emerges in terms of a difference about tactical effectiveness, not about purpose or the legitimacy of those methods. Alan acknowledges how his disillusionment with the effectiveness of violence was so apparent to him by the time of his arrest that this played a role in how quickly he confessed to his crimes. At the same time, his involvement with, and commitment to, the UVF has clearly outlasted his changed views about the effectiveness of the UVF's 'military campaign'.

Though he recalls being 'aware' of the growing social and political crisis engulfing Northern Ireland, Alan's involvement is typified by a lack of any pre-existing political motivation at the outset of his involvement. Despite this lack of any apparent political motivation, however, there was a clear sense in which there was a timeliness and urgency to act in some way.

Alan acknowledges that despite the seeming inevitability of the spiralling conflict, that involvement in a paramilitary movement was not necessarily an inevitable step. Alan's pre-involvement activity saw him consider a number of options and an engagement with the rationale associated with choosing each of these options – i.e. how to become involved, with whom, not wanting to become an easy target and so on.

A significant factor identified by Alan was identifying with the victimisation of others in his community (his school friends he mentions in particular, in the context of a broader victimised community). Despite an awareness of powerful situational factors, there is an explicit embracing of personal agency (e.g. the reiteration of having 'volunteered'). This is a reliable reflection of UVF ideology and of Loyalism more generally. He repeats on several occasions the fact that he 'chose' to do what he did and that he 'always felt in control of what I did'. Alan's ability to express this to the prison panel, he argues, played a key role in the decision to grant him early release from his sentence.

As with the account in the previous chapter, we see evidence for a *gradual* sense of involvement and engagement. Throughout Alan's account, there is an issue of timing and its consequences for shaping the involvement process that appears, however implicit, relevant. Alan describes the seeds of doubt having crept in once some time had passed between his declaration of 'wanting to be involved' and the movement's reciprocation of that approach many weeks later. At this point, Alan's decision to go through with his earlier decision appears to have been heavily influenced by what he feels was an obligation to act on the prior commitment to the movement and of following through on the promise he made. There is a clear sense, therefore, in which issues of personal agency (which he stresses) and responsibility to a collective force appear contradictory and difficult to reconcile at particular points in Alan's account.

One very clear issue that emerges in Alan's account of being involved in the

UVF is a very clear sense of the psychological demands as a result of involvement. For example, despite being a part-time member, Alan describes dealing with a constant preoccupation with concerns and anxieties (e.g. of being caught or killed). He recalls having to work hard psychologically to 'cross a rubicon' into illegal activity, and a particular challenge was in having to work at reconciling the stark juxtaposition and contrast between mundane, everyday behaviours and engaging in terrorist violence ('even when I did commit acts of violence, I was never ever *entirely* comfortable with it').

There appears to be at least two distinct ways in which this is facilitated: a) Alan's ability to reference external events as a means of working through psychological demands of justifying personal actions (e.g. 'with the events that go on, you are able to *justify* what you are doing') and b) emphasis on the fact that despite the identification of specific points in the process where he felt involvement to be a one-way street, the recurring reminder and restating that he 'volunteered' for the UVF (in contrast to the IRA members he points to on more than one occasion).

The factors that relate to Alan's increased involvement and his reflections on that involvement are important to identify. There is clearly an acknowledgement of the growing disillusionment with the effectiveness of the tactical use of violence, yet this is expressed without necessarily being associated with a sense of guilt or remorse on a personal level. External circumstances appear to have played a role in possibly blocking disengagement routes. There is a clear sense in which Alan's 're-engagement' with the UVF, though different in character, was heavily influenced by the revitalisation of the IRA following the hunger strikes, and was sustained by Alan's continued exposure to the UVF command structure while in prison. This is despite what he acknowledges was a deepening disillusionment with the effectiveness of the UVF's 'military tactics'.

Alan's account also illustrates an important point that was made in Chapter 2. Disengagement from terrorist activity may arise from a tactical reassessment on a personal level (in this case, his increasing sense that violence was not producing what was expected), but does not necessarily have to be accompanied with a re-evaluation of the *legitimacy* of that tactic. It would be premature to say that Alan views his involvement in the UVF as having been illegitimate or wrong, but his perceptions about the continued effectiveness of a reliance on violence alone proved a powerful catalyst for reassessing the nature of his involvement.

This we will see is a recurring theme across a variety of different accounts. In the following chapter, however, we encounter a graphic account of how first exposure to particular tactics can lead to a dramatic reversal of commitment and loyalty to the movement.

5 'There is no conscious decision'

Introduction

The events of 11 September 2001 instantly and forever burned the name *Al Qaeda* into the public's consciousness. Reference to Al Qaeda is now immediately associated with its worldwide modus operandi – well-planned, highly coordinated, synchronised terrorist bombings guaranteed to kill dozens and seriously maim hundreds more. Al Qaeda continues to shock and surprise, attacking a variety of hard and soft targets worldwide in pursuit of its short- and long-term objectives. Still, and despite a seemingly unending flow of research reports and detailed analysis of this global Sunni Islamist movement, there are substantial gaps in our knowledge and understanding of Al Qaeda. The movement continues to defy easy definition or categorisation. In truth, the movement comprises elements both of a centralised command and control structure, and at the same time reveals qualities characteristic of a regionally decentralised franchise, managed locally by entrepreneurs whose principal task is to attract and groom ever more recruits to the movement. In fact, in the years following 9/11, Al Qaeda has become much more than a terrorist network. It is also, in the words of Sageman,[1] a global *social movement*. In the years that followed 9/11, the War on Terror may well have disrupted the potential for large-scale attacks by Al Qaeda. But it is certain that it has not eliminated them completely. Coordinated attacks, albeit on a smaller scale than 9/11, will continue to frustrate counter-terrorism efforts and will contribute to the longevity of the threat posed by Al Qaeda and its offshoots.

Meeting 'Omar'

One of the principal ways in which counter-terrorist initiatives have yet to develop in disrupting Al Qaeda operations is in paying closer attention to increasing numbers of defectors from the movement. As revealed in Chapter 2, there are increasingly well-known examples of those who have turned away from Al Qaeda, and probably many lesser-known cases waiting to be unearthed. This chapter presents the case of an individual who walked away from Al Qaeda.

In early 2008, I met with and interviewed 'Omar'. Omar runs a community outreach service, engaging local Muslim youths from his office in London. Omar was recruited by Al Qaeda in early 2002. Before he could develop into a fully-fledged *Mujahid*, however, and based on his experiences on the Pakistan–Afghanistan border, the reality of what his looming involvement in the 'cause' would bring him was sufficient to shock him back to seeking a permanent exit from Al Qaeda. In a sense, Omar disengaged before he could become fully committed. He has since devoted himself to preventing young Muslims from being similarly targeted by Al Qaeda for grooming and recruitment.

Interviewing Omar proved a challenge. The interview took place in his London office and he expressed a preference to be interviewed 'out front', near the entrance to the building. The setting was noisy and the atmosphere busy. There were regular interruptions, and the interview was stopped halfway through for about 30 minutes when two police officers came to speak with Omar. The impression conveyed, however, was that Omar is a highly influential figure in his community and that his views about the local community carry weight both among the police community and local Muslims that Omar declares he is 'duty-bound to serve'. He spoke frankly about his experiences of being recruited to Al Qaeda and of how his experiences in Pakistan shocked him back into 'reality'.

Becoming involved

Omar's initial involvement with Al Qaeda coincided with the early days of the post-9/11 invasion of Afghanistan. Now in his early 40s, he attributes his personal readiness to 'get involved' in the struggle to what he describes as a growing awareness of the human cost of the invasion, as well as a sense of urgency for humanitarian response:

> It was . . . I think [involvement] was basically all borne out of being unselfish. I had always been supportive of people, who, you know, have been less fortunate in life. Especially when you see, you know, young children, old women, old people involved in conflict. And you see them displaced. Some of them injured, you know, people losing their families. I think it was the images, the *messages* that were coming out after the invasion into Afghanistan, that, ah . . . struck a chord with my emotions.

Omar stressed that this identification with those suffering from the effects of conflict should not be viewed as a 'Muslim issue' because, he argues, that identification was not just apparent 'with Muslims or Pakistani people. It was a whole range of people that used to work with me as well. Some English people, you know, some British people.' But, he explains 'the whole thing was about *wanting* to get involved, *wanting* to help the civilians, the victims that were caught up in the conflict, initially, that was what it was all about for me.'

Identifying with the victimisation of fellow Muslims provided Omar with a strong sense of wanting to 'do something' to help. His brother, Omar explains, felt the very same way.

The opportunity for Omar and his brother to become involved in helping victims became apparent to both of them in London upon meeting some individuals that were 'connected'. When asked what 'connected' implied, Omar turned to explain the role of two individuals, one of whom was an Al Qaeda recruiter who came to London in search of sympathetic Muslims:

> Well, I was ah, how shall I say . . . let's just say I was introduced to a couple of people, ah, who had direct links to Afghanistan, and then they came to us to sort of . . . gather funds for them. So you know, we were more than happy to support them. We were always sort of comfortable. We were in business, we were pretty much comfortable, so we wanted to get involved, and wanted to get involved in charity work, donating to charity.

Omar saw this as nothing unusual 'given the circumstances at the time'. However, at the time of this initial approach for help with fundraising, Omar had only a limited sense of who those specific individuals in London were, and apparently at the time there was no immediate association made with Al Qaeda or the Taleban:

> At that time you know, it was all about people who were representing the innocent civilians . . . but then shortly down the line, I'd say, maybe a couple of weeks into it, that was when I realised . . . ah, that was when they told me that ah . . . one of them was from Taleban, and one of them just introduced himself as an Arab brother, em, from Syria. And wanted to know, em . . . you know, wanted to get a sense of some of the kinds of thoughts I had about getting involved.

The Arab brother from Syria identified himself as 'Abu Sufiyan', a man Omar describes as 'not his real name', but that he was 'representing Al Qaeda'. This man 'spoke Arabic eloquently', and encouraged Omar to 'get more involved' by engaging in fundraising efforts for what Omar believed to be humanitarian aid for civilians caught up in the conflict in Afghanistan. To Omar, this again seemed normal, as did, apparently, the Abu Sufiyan character's approach to him: 'After the initial meetings, it was all just kind of informal. You would just carry on donating money. Donating as much money as possible. Bits of money here and there.' Soon, however, Omar's awareness of his own willingness to become involved in the effort in a more direct way soon became apparent and relevant to him:

> Ah . . . it came a point, where, you know, after seeing the kinds of images, the damage that was done, some of the images coming from Western

media . . . [hearing] about the way in which an American fighter pilot struck his bomb on a village because he didn't want to go back to his base empty, you know, with his weapons intact. Em . . . that's what . . . that really struck a chord . . . it *really* touched on an emotional thing. Once you're in that frame of mind . . . when something like that is touching the person that's most human, most unselfish, to some extent self-sacrificing . . . it's like . . . let me give you the example of, say, outside, if there's three people outside beating up on one young person. Some people would just jump in, and stop that fight. 'Cos it's wrong. It's not fair. *These* are the type of people that are most easy to be recruited . . . they are really easy to be recruited, and I was the person who would have jumped in to stop that fight rather than the person who walks by.

Omar's self-awareness of an altruistic streak was a recurring theme, and he spoke about the process of his increasing involvement as not stemming from a conscious decision, *or* reflecting a deliberate choice, *or* reflecting that Al Qaeda were deliberately attempting to recruit him:

No, it's not like that. There is *no* conscious decision. I wasn't specifically targeted. I think it was ah . . . they were travelling around, to my understanding, they were travelling around [London] trying to get support for the cause. And when they've realised how forthcoming support was from key individuals . . . It's like if you go into a hundred people, there's going to be five or six of them that are gonna relate to them.

Omar identifies 'the willingness to *do something*' that he felt distinguished him from the 'others who chose to just express support'. He explained that the Al Qaeda fundraiser-recruiter, Abu Sufiyan, 'really didn't have to do much, as far as I was concerned' in encouraging Omar's involvement:

Now out of that five or six [people] there might be one or two who have *strong* feelings, *strong* emotions, and want to do something, you know, like I said. That scenario when you jump in, and you don't consider your own safety, but you want to, you know, you want try to *stop* something that's unfair from happening . . . in all situations, and it wasn't particularly because I was a Muslim. This was in 2002, the summer of 2002. And then so . . . one thing led to another.

I asked Omar if, given his apparent enthusiasm for being willing to jump in, he had any prior perceptions about what 'jumping in' would entail in reality: 'Well yeah, it was the idea of helping the Mujahidin, who were fighting this Goliath, you know.' At this point, Omar explained that helping equated to donating money. He describes his pre-existing views of the Mujahidin as positive, expressing an admiration for them: 'How humble they are, how practising they are, how humble, and sort of simple they are. They were fighting with mere stones, compared to missiles.'

These two factors – Omar recognising and acknowledging that he felt compelled to not just express passive support but 'the desire to do something', combined with very positive attitudes towards the Mujahidin themselves combined to provide a powerful incentive for Omar to explore a more active role: 'It is *very* easy to draw a person in. And that's how I got drawn in, quite literally.' Omar was clearly radicalised. His views on justice and fairness were not new to him, nor were his views about the 'duty of all Muslims' to 'help those less fortunate than us'. But in light of the opportunity open to him, his views were acquiring a new significance and he was set on a path to violent radicalisation. Additionally, Omar's views were being reinforced by his friends and peers in his local group: 'Yeah, it wasn't just me. A few other people that were with me also, who were supporting the finance with contributions. So it's quite easy for people like that.'

Being involved

In late 2002, Omar prepared his last will and testament and arranged to fly to Pakistan. By this stage, the Al Qaeda fundraiser-recruiter was no longer present, but Omar had taken the decision to 'help': 'I flew on my own to Pakistan. This was in December. I wanted to ... I wanted to go, but obviously then, when it was put to the rest of the guys that ah ... contributed to the cause as well, I was selected.' Omar repeats that he was 'selected', but reiterates his own role in expressing the personal desire for he himself to go:

It was more [about] taking money and actually witnessing it with my own eyes, you know because it's like, if I'm taking money from you, I wanna make sure that I'm not gonna be, you know, taking it for the sake of taking money and not paying it back. Because I promised people that this money would be correctly given to the poor people. It wasn't for anything else, because a lot of people question that [belief] that it's not there for the elderly and so forth. They assumed that by giving it to me that it's for the victims, and I said 'yes'. So I took some money with me as well.

Omar reiterated his reasons for personally wanting to go to Pakistan as arising from both doubt and suspicion about how his money would be used, coupled with a firm intent to see first hand the consequences of conflict: 'We had some doubts, we had some doubts. That was one of the reasons why, you know, me in particular ... *I* wanted to go. I wanted to make sure that the money was being spent where it was supposed to be spent.'

Exploring this issue further, and after being asked about why he prepared a last will and testament, Omar eventually acknowledges he was already prepared to 'go' in another way:

The guys that were working with us [those who facilitated Omar's transport across the border into Afghanistan] didn't really know what our intentions were. Yes. My intentions were that if I *did* go there, and if I did see what we had seen on the TV, and what we'd been told, was true, then by nature of our, our ah, charitable sort of mind, and wanting to try and help somebody, I would probably just get sucked in. And my brother knew that. And we said that I would end up probably staying and getting involved in the fight. Am . . . so I took the journey, and went there.

It was clear that Omar was actually prepared to engage in violent activity. His positive perceptions about the Mujahidin take on a new significance with the acknowledgement that he was willing to 'just get sucked in', and this willingness appears to have been reinforced by his brother. Omar attributes the probability of getting involved in violence on his 'charitable sort of mind'.

What Omar encountered shortly after his arrival, however, presented him with an unexpected reality that proved difficult to reconcile with the bases of his 'intentions'. The gap between his initial expectations and his subsequent experiences quickly changed his willingness to 'get sucked in' to violence. In explaining this, Omar prefaces his criticism of those he felt duped by with an acknowledgement of what he argues is the legitimacy of militant struggles elsewhere:

You know, I'm not taking anything away from the Mujahidin in Kashmir. You *know* what they are fighting for. They are *freedom* fighters. And the Pakistani struggle, the Chechen struggle, you can't take *anything* away from them. People who would fight in defence of . . . or fight occupation, this is one thing I do not want to take away from them. But what I *will* say is that what happened whilst I was there, in Afghanistan wasn't what I, or my companions, were buying into. Pakistanis were going across the border, and they were getting *slaughtered*. And it wasn't always by the West. Most of the time it was by the Afghanis. It became obvious very quickly. I mean right away. The initial journey into Afghanistan can't have been more than 20 minutes. I saw young people and old people, you know, severely injured, severely traumatised by what *they* saw and what *I* saw. I was quite adamant that, at that time, that wasn't justifiable in my eyes. That wasn't right. And I didn't agree to that. My aim was to *help* those people, those very people that were being drawn into the conflict, you know, poor people. The ones that didn't have a future, and had lost all hope in life. They lost their family, lost limbs. I was helping them. I think it was just our basic human nature that we got so passionate about it.

The distinction Omar makes between what he terms 'freedom fighters' and what he would come to view as 'terrorism' by Al Qaeda and the Taleban may appear inconsistent and self-serving, but it is a distinction of immense significance to Omar. He explained how he has no difficulty in reconciling what might on the surface appear to be a contradiction, and stresses that this can be understood, from his perspective, via differences in motivation and methods between the various movements (a point he returns to in detail below).

Disengaging

Omar travelled to Pakistan on a first-class air ticket and made his way to Peshawar. There, he was instructed to wait to receive a telephone call. He spent four days waiting before he was contacted with details of his transport into Afghanistan. When asked if there was a specific issue in particular that led him to 'turn around on the road', Omar points to what he describes as a 'chance encounter', an 'instantaneous event', with two people who appeared to be returning from battle against US forces in Afghanistan:

> I was up until that point, *sure* that I was going into a camp, to see you know, to see refugee camps, and you know, to see what was going on. But, it didn't even get to that point. It was an instantaneous event that happened, which totally … At that point, when it happened, my immediate thought was to get those two people out. It was to help [an] elderly guy and [a] young kid out of that environment, where they were in danger. Get them back into safety, back into Pakistan. Get the young kid back off to his parents, because his parents didn't even know that where he was, and he was a poor kid from a village. And so was the old man. You know, and I wanted to go and help my Muslim brothers and sisters, the Muslim struggle, so at that point my main aim was to get them out of harm's way and into safety. And plus, I was angry! I was really angry at the mere fact that … ah, well, why should *they* be allowed to get involved in this sort of thing?

Omar's account moved dramatically back and forth across a number of issues at this point, but a recurring theme in his recollection is one of outrage at what he saw as an unfair situation coupled with his growing realisation that at least some people were being exploited and coerced into fighting: 'They were lied to. They were being used as cannon fodder, just cannon fodder.' A sense of fairness and justice pervades much of what he reveals about his view of the world as well as why he says he eventually decided to pull back from further engaging in activity on which his views were rapidly changing upon reaching Afghanistan. I asked Omar to elaborate on his specific experiences at the border crossing:

> We went through the [location] gates, it was about 20, 25 minutes, and we were all in pick-ups. There were pick-ups coming the other way. And there was one pick-up in particular. Both drivers got talking, our vehicle

and the oncoming vehicle. And at that point, some of the young ones, some of the old people, got off. And there was this kid looking up at the rest of the guys, and he's talking, and he's bleeding. And I think . . . well, seeing that, it's a thing you can't really forget. He was *so* young, and the old man was sort of bewildered, his arm gone, sort of tied up in rags, and the kid's crying out and he's telling me that there's this butchery going on. He's saying *these are animals, these are butchers* . . . you know, and I started to wonder. I said *what's wrong?* Because I understood the kid was from Pakistan. And you know, he's telling me what happened. He's saying *this is what happened, I wanted to go along, to go along, to join the Jihad, I wanted to get training, and this convoy of vehicles, we were told to stop. But when the vehicle was told to stop, we were told to get off and run, but as we were running, we were just getting shot at.* And I said: *by the truck driver?* He says: *no, there was people in the bushes, people all around, they were shooting at us.* I said: *was it the Americans?* He said: *I don't know.* So he said all this, and this just . . . this young . . . *kid* who was obviously very traumatised. The old man just sat there, he didn't say anything. So then, he says, the kid, he then ran back to the pick-up, and he goes: *while I was trying to get on, they were driving off,* but the old man picked him up by the head and put him back on again. And he just said: *I want to go home.*

In one clear way, the account of the boy's experience echoes Omar's own grooming by the Al Qaeda fundraiser-recruiter back in London. Both were duped in part as a reflection of their own 'willingness to help' fellow Muslims in combination with wanting to 'join the Jihad'. Both were 'sucked in' to a conflict, the nature and reality of which neither could be expected to be prepared for.

The situation Omar found himself in on the Afghan border seems to have been surrounded in confusion. He explained that not only did he want to turn around and go back into Pakistan, but that he wanted to bring the child and old man back with him:

So I'm standing out on the highway, with *our* driver, who couldn't really understand what I was saying to him. And I couldn't understand what *he* was trying to say. And we were stood there arguing. The reason why I backed off was because they were armed up, they weren't shouting using their guns, but . . . they were armed. I don't think it was like deliberate, that they were sending us in to get killed, but it was just like ah . . . I don't think it was . . . It just didn't seem to make sense, what was going on.

After some time, Omar managed to bribe the driver to turn the truck around and drive back across the border:

So I was offering them money to take us back to [town]. At which point, I showed them a fifty-pound note, because I had a lot of money, to give to the people there. Well . . . we went back to [town] and I got the old man tidied up, and got him all cleaned up. I spoke to the little kid. He was from Punjab. And the old man was from the other side of Pakistan. So I sent him off there, and I went straight back to Islamabad. I went straight back there from Peshawar.

Omar's relief at not remaining in Afghanistan soon turned to anger. He recalls being furious with those who had approached him in London, and immediately contacted his brother to attempt to locate the Al Qaeda and Taleban members:

I phoned my brother, and I told him to find the guys who were here, the contacts that were here [in London]. I had had no further contact with them. I completely lost contact with them. They didn't contact [my brother] since I'd gone. The last contact I had was someone who called me, who told me to go to Peshawar to meet somebody. So at that point, I think it was four in the morning when I got in the plane, back to the UK. From leaving Afghanistan I was back within the UK within 36 hours. At that point I was so . . . *angry*, I was . . . I wanted to you know, I wanna help young people, young kids, innocent people. And by coming here [Afghanistan] I'm seeing young people, being sent into battle zones without any ammunition, any training. They're just sent out there and allowed to fend for themselves. *No way*. And the majority of Pakistani people going over the border are coming back seriously, seriously, seriously injured. Or dead. And it was Pakistanis that were coming back. It wasn't Arabs, it wasn't Afghanis, it was Pakistanis that were coming back. People from my parents' country. And I had a serious issue with that.

The recurring themes of a) a strong sense of unfairness and injustice about the plight of others and b) the perceived 'need to do something' were pervasive in almost every aspect of what was reported by Omar. His outrage at recognising that he was 'lied to' by Al Qaeda might initially seem at odds, however, with what appears upon closer inspection to his clear enthusiasm and willingness to 'get sucked in' to violent activity in Afghanistan. When asked about these issues, Omar reflected on the distinction he continues to make to this day between Al Qaeda and what he views as 'legitimate Jihadis':

You got a lot of Mujahidin that are coming in from Kashmir into Afghanistan, you've got a lot of Mujahidin that are coming in from Chechnya. But when they get there, and they see the *methods* of Al Qaeda, it's totally different. They don't wanna buy into that. They don't wanna buy into beheading journalists, or beheading innocent civilians. That's not part of the deal, that's not part of Islam. They want to fight an occupation. Full stop. Under the guidelines of Islam. When they see Al Qaeda manoeuvring in different ways, you find, well, it's a fact that a lot of them move to go back, back to the original place where they were fighting their original struggle, Chechnya, Kashmir, you know. I was speaking to a gentleman who was living in Afghanistan for a long, long time, who was an English gentleman. And he lived there for 25 years, helping the local natives in agriculture, and water irrigation. He was captured by the Afghan Mujahidin. And he was about to get killed. He said: *we were put down, we were blindfolded, we were tied. We were on our knees, and we just heard firing.* He said: *and my friend passed out. Because you know, he thought he was gonna get shot.* It was a Salafi Mujahidin who saved them. So there are the true people who are fighting an occupation, and nobody can take anything away from them. They are *the Mujahid*. But the methods that Al Qaeda, and the Taleban are using . . . it's *not* an ideology, it is a different agenda that they have.

Despite his experiences at the Afghanistan border, Omar's sense of 'duty to [his] fellow Muslim' has not wavered. In 2004, Omar and his brother opened a gymnasium and community centre, which since grew into a larger initiative, a Muslim community group set up to: 'engage radical young people, but to prevent them from getting involved in violence. Channel their energy into something positive'. I asked Omar if his experiences in Afghanistan were the catalyst for his decision to set up the initiative:

Well, to an *extent* it was part of that. But also locally . . . the kids that I saw. The ones that I saw getting involved in some gangs that were terrorising some old people. But then finally coming across a young person that's been abused by his uncle, finding someone that's getting involved in prostitution . . . and again, the Muslim community not doing enough. The imam, the leaders of the mosque not doing enough, in denial that you know, gang violence or prostitution or theft was going on. They're still in denial, but my main focus really went to the forefront of tackling extremism shortly after 7/7 [the Al Qaeda suicide bombings of 7 July 2005]. I was telling the local authorities how important it is for us to engage young people, because there are people out there looking to recruit our young people not just into violent extremism, but into all sorts of vices. So my main focus was to sort of get local people, local community involved in how important it is to understand our young people. And I've been saying that since 2003. Young people need to be understood and the only way you can understand them is if you engage them. And respect them.

An important theme that is clear from the above excerpt, and has been implicit in his reaction to how the Al Qaeda fundraiser-recruiter 'lied to' Omar, is his relationship with authority. Omar places more emphasis on 'community' than 'authority' and is distrustful and suspicious both of the positioning of authority figures as well as their effectiveness. This was reinforced by his experience prior to arriving in Pakistan, and was echoed dramatically in his encounters with the young child and old man on the Afghanistan border.

The reaction to Omar's initiative has been mixed, particularly in relation to his decision to engage with young extremists involved in movements sympathetic to violent Jihadism. In the following excerpts, we see how Omar places great emphasis on his new role as a community figure, and there is a clear sense of the importance of how he continues his mission to 'help others' by drawing directly from his own experiences:

> Our local community and our local imans, say, if they find out you're from Al Muhajiroun, they're like: *No, get out! Get away.* We're saying: *No, no, come in, let's talk, don't go away.* Our approach is that there's some understanding between what *you're* saying and what *we're* saying, let's try and you know, let's try and negotiate. Let's talk about what's going on. If you're gonna try and represent our faith, right, let's try and understand where you're coming from, where you're getting your quotations from. You know, in what context are you quoting this? 'Cos you know, you are *representing* a faith. But at the moment, we tell them: *the faith is being alienated. The faith is being demonised, because of certain quotations that you're coming out with.* So we need to draw them in. I never used to think in that way, first, but my brother used to always want to engage with them, to talk to them. And then through the engagement, that's when I realised, it's very important to keep them close, to talk to them, to challenge them. If they're saying: *well I don't agree,* let's find out why. So let's ask them: *why?* Let's say to them: *ok, let's agree on certain things, and disagree on certain things. But let's get one thing straight, the faith that you're claiming to represent . . . you're not doing it.*

Omar's suspicion and distrust is rooted in his experiences with individuals who have claimed to be 'representative of Muslims'. He attributes this to recognition of hypocrisy and the lack of meaningful leadership. A successful voice, he argues, is one that is able to acknowledge the significance of the issues driving radicalisation while at the same time offering an alternative to *violent* radicalisation:

> It's not the ideology that's at blame, you know? It's not the *faith* that . . . because people are blaming the faith. It's nothing to do with the faith. There are a lot of small little things that have contributed to this, especially those that relate to Western foreign policy, of which going into Iraq and Afghanistan . . . You know? And all this, these double standards. But it's also lack of, lack of strong community leadership. You know,

the added issues of sectarian and caste issues, lack of opportunities, you know, drugs. All these kinds of things. And added onto that is unemployment, disaffected young people. Put that all together and you've got a cocktail for disaster. With the help of the Metropolitan Police we've got the chance to deliver. Think about how *easy* it is to recruit young people. How you break them down slowly but steadily, the *tone*, the *voice* . . . it's very easy. We apply similar tactics, but for the reverse effect. It's actually identifying and understanding the mindset of a recruiter, or a terrorist. Because I've actually been there, done it, you know.

Interim conclusions

The case of Omar is interesting not only in terms of his own experiences of disengagement, but also given that Omar's new role in many respects represents a potentially valuable development in counter-radicalisation efforts. On the one hand, his personal experiences illustrate the dramatic disjuncture between the idealised and romanticised views about involvement and the subsequent, jarring reality of what involvement actually entails. Making this known represents an important task, and not unlike Lars' case from Chapter 3, this is something Omar has decided to engage in.

On the other hand, the fact that Omar is a good example of a radical Muslim who draws a distinction between what he views 'legitimate' and 'illegitimate' violent jihad poses immense challenges for Western policy-makers. The co-existence of seemingly contradictory and ambiguous views makes his role in counter-radicalisation a difficult prospect for many, and the significance of distinctions made by Omar may not be understood or appreciated in the development or promotion of counter-radicalisation initiatives. He is, accordingly, a paradox to Western governments. To reiterate a point made earlier, though such distinctions may appear inappropriate, even offensive to the onlooker, this does not detract from the significance of these differences for the believer. Omar views Al Qaeda with disgust and disdain and came to realise the way in which Al Qaeda has exploited 'genuine concerns, the need to help fellow Muslims' into 'a different agenda'.

Across a host of issues, Omar is someone whose behaviour and general worldview is heavily influenced by a strong sense of community justice, fairness and equality. A community figure to begin with (through his business interests), he is keenly sensitive to social problems and the plight of disenfranchised and victimised members of the broader Muslim community. For Omar, the fact that the reality of involvement proved such a contrast to his initial expectations proved to be the catalyst for his disengagement. The realisation that 'my people' were being 'used as cannon fodder' sustained Omar's outrage at '[having] been lied to'. Omar's experiences demonstrate that negative views about the impact of foreign policy, combined with the victimisation of fellow Muslims, is insufficient in explaining why he wanted to become involved in fighting against the US in Afghanistan. Idealistic and romanticised expectations about what lay ahead of him propelled his acceptance of 'being selected' to go to Afghanistan. Despite Omar's retreat from Al Qaeda, however, he remains steadfast in his views about the 'aggressiveness' of US foreign policy and 'the problems they create'.

On the one hand, Omar is someone who has been radicalised in a general sense for several years. He has no moral qualms about the 'freedom struggles' throughout the world. From Omar's perspective, the fact that the Al Qaeda figure did not have to 'do very much' to engage him is as much a reflection of the significance for him of civilian casualties in Afghanistan as it is a reflection of Omar's once idealistic views about 'the struggle'. It is clear that Omar and others like him increasingly make that distinction. Additionally, that Omar highlights 'beheadings' and 'the murder of journalists' is an indicator of how such dissent among many radical Muslims who support 'freedom fighters' is equally a consequence of escalating and increasingly indiscriminate violence by Al Qaeda.

Though there are many apparent tensions surrounding issues of what role someone such as Omar could play in counter-radicalisation, it is clear there is enormous potential to be explored. To echo the point made in Chapter 2 by Bergen and Cruickshank, the global Jihadist struggle is clearly more amorphous and heterogeneous than is normally understood. In this sense, criticism of Al Qaeda by those who also consider themselves 'radical' is not particularly new. What is different is the increasingly visible expression of that dissent.

For some, it may be tempting to dismiss Omar's efforts because of his expressed support for 'legitimate Jihad'. Omar's objectives as described by him are not to prevent radicalisation *per se*, but to promote alternatives to *violent* radicalisation. Omar describes a picture of radicalisation in London as in part a reflection of 'an overwhelming generation gap', which, in his view, 'leads to some serious problems'. Omar believes that radicalisation is 'inevitable', given 'Western foreign policies'. However, the role that Omar has created for himself does not aspire to 'de-radicalisation' in this sense, which has other connotations that, as we see in Chapter 9, may prove unrealistic. Politically sensitive issues of 'partnership' and 'integration' as part of efforts aimed at counter-radicalisation often reflect an unrealistic sense of what is likely to be achieved by promoting former terrorists and activists alike in de-radicalisation efforts.

The kind of nuance apparent in Omar's account offers an important glimpse into an array of cultural and political splits between what is overly simplified as a singular global Jihadist community. We return to this issue of differences about legitimacy and justification again in the case of Omar Bakri Mohammed in Chapter 8. For the 'Omar' of the current chapter, there is a major difference of opinion and belief about methods and tactics of Al Qaeda and the Taleban. For the Omar of Chapter 8, a difference also exists, but it is not so much a difference about methods and tactics, rather a difference about where (in terms of location) specifically those tactics find legitimacy. As we see in Chapter 9, the fact that such splitting exists holds major potential for counter-radicalisation initiatives as well as those aimed at undermining those already radicalised in one way or another.

6 'A step too far'

Introduction

One of the first lessons learned by students and scholars of political violence is that the Provisional Irish Republican Army is probably the one terrorist movement on which most has been written in the academic literature. Journal editors frequently bemoan the fact that the majority of submissions from terrorism researchers still focus on Northern Ireland. Despite this, it is not that difficult to appreciate why there is still so much to be said about Northern Ireland. Terrorism has long been a major problem for the region, and the Provisional IRA in particular has enjoyed significant longevity. The IRA has existed in one form or another since the early twentieth century, and its origins can be traced back further still depending on how willing one is to stretch the concept of Irish Republican militancy. Additionally, however, the IRA has undergone significant internal change since the early 1990s. With the advent of the Good Friday Agreement, the broader peace process, the IRA as a terrorist movement has come to an end. That end has brought with it a plethora of valuable opportunities for the research community. To echo a point made in Chapter 2, former IRA members are willing and able to speak about their experiences to academics and other researchers. Failing to grasp the opportunities afforded by this is equally a failure of the terrorism research community to recognise the valuable lessons to be gained from studying a 'defunct' movement such as the IRA for our understanding of other terrorist groups.

To compare the IRA to Al Qaeda might seem odd, and certainly former IRA members would balk at the comparison. However, to fail to explore the possibilities that there may be similarities in terms of the social and psychological processes inherent in both movements reflects a lack of imagination on the part of the research community as well as an overly narrow view of how a counter-radicalisation initiative might develop that would be informed by lessons from both movements. One of the lessons from the extraordinary case study to follow is that the similarities in the process of becoming involved, remaining involved and disengaging between one major IRA volunteer's experiences and those of contemporary Al Qaeda foreign fighters is striking. In fact, it may well be that once the researcher ignores the group 'identifier' (IRA, Al Qaeda, Red Army Faction, and so on) that the similarities in processes appear more obvious.

In this chapter we consider the case of 'Michael' (not his real name). A former IRA member, Michael rose through the ranks of the IRA to become a bomb-maker and improvised explosive device (IED) teacher to a senior operational commander. He led many IRA operations and is himself responsible for committing more than one murder. He did all of this by the age of 19. Michael's notoriety, however, stems from the fact that he later turned his back on the IRA and became the most damaging informer the movement has ever had.

Meeting 'Michael'

Michael comes from the Republic of Ireland and was born into a family background that supported Irish militancy in the early twentieth century phase of the IRA's development. Shortly after the most recent phase of the Northern Irish Troubles broke out in the late 1960s and early 1970s, Michael joined the IRA when he was 15. He showed such promise to IRA leaders that by the time he was 19 he was promoted to a commander role. He became infamous within Irish Republican circles. By the age of 20, however, he left burned out and disillusioned: 'A lot of people do forget that I did actually leave the IRA before I was 21, you know? I did get out fairly early'. He subsequently returned to re-engage with the IRA, however, and was later revealed as one of the highest-ranking informers to ever compromise the movement. His role as informer was revealed after he spent eight years in prison for IRA offences. He is one of the few remaining IRA informers alive today and lives outside Ireland.

Michael was interviewed extensively throughout 2007. Following an initial interview lasting three hours, he agreed to several subsequent return visits and was generous with his time. Michael was interviewed over three weekends, and the transcript of the interviews ran over 110,000 words. He is articulate, highly intelligent and has written and spoken extensively about his life in the IRA. Because so many IRA informers have been murdered, Michael's security was an issue I was aware of from the outset. We met initially in a public venue, the location for which was conveyed to me by a text message shortly before the first meeting took place. When asked if he is always on the alert for his safety, Michael's response was characteristically self-deprecatory: 'No, not constantly. I mean, I am of course aware of stuff. If you keep looking over your shoulder you bump into things and get an awful crick in your neck.' He subsequently acknowledged that he does not take risks with his safety:

> It is a really strange way to live your life. You're not complacent, you can't be, but at the same time you don't let it impinge on, well, the way

you do stuff. I said to someone earlier on today, I'm going to meet a guy now who does this terrorism stuff. Now, am I supposed to believe for a second that what you are going to do now when you leave is make a phone call to an IRA hit squad, and you know, storm up the stairs and shoot me dead? That's fantasyland. I'm not interested in that.

Michael admitted to wanting to put me at ease and expressed a frustration at what he said was the widespread assumption that he is 'supposed to be scared all the time'. I asked Michael if it is true that he cannot visit Ireland: 'No, I go back from time to time. I don't advertise it, but I get to go every now and then, but here is where home is now.'

Becoming involved

Michael has played a major role in speaking out about the IRA and his experiences in it. In particular, and as we shall see from the accounts of his own involvement in later sections, he has publicly highlighted the sectarian nature of IRA targeting. This has made him a hate-figure within the IRA and the target of several years of propaganda to discredit his role within the movement. In particular, he has highlighted this aspect of the IRA to 'get away from this idea that it's a romantic thing, to fools like me who think it's all about shooting soldiers'. When asked about how he became involved in the IRA, Michael's answer was about how he might *not* have joined in the first place:

> Maybe I mightn't have joined in the first place had I had more exposure to people from Northern Ireland. I could so easily have become like a crusader for peace, do you know what I mean? You are looking just at idealism. It's why I say that, you know, some of the guys that are joining Sinn Fein now in the Irish Republic just need to join the Green Party. I don't mean that because Sinn Fein has lost all its values, I just simply mean that when you're a kid, you want to change stuff. I'm not making excuses now, but for example, my brother who is 4 ½ years older would not have touched the IRA because he was 4 ½ years older – that's what I really think. It is so important to remember the *time*. So when I'm 15, he's 19. And he's working in Dublin, he is away from home and he sees this stuff happening and he's got a good job, and says *I don't really want to get involved.*

Michael acknowledges that for a considerable period of time he has reflected on how and why he became involved in the IRA and concluded: 'I think it was just honestly, time and place, to a large extent. Honest to God, I think time and place to a large extent.'

Given what Michael describes as the real possibility that he could have joined a different kind of 'activist' group, I asked him what particular appeals becoming involved in the IRA had, compared to other groups: 'What happened in Northern Ireland meant, especially after 1972, that the IRA went mainstream.' Michael referred to the widespread civil unrest in Northern Ireland when the Provisional IRA emerged as a fully-fledged paramilitary organisation shortly after the events of Bloody Sunday, when on 30 January 1972, 26 civil rights protestors were shot by members of the British Parachute Regiment, 14 of whom were killed: 'They just appealed to a whole lot of people, a huge lot of people that would never have been . . . militant. Because really, when you look back, Northern Republicans sort of really just wanted equality. They never wanted the whole united Ireland business originally.'

Michael did not grow up in Northern Ireland, but in the Republic of Ireland. Though geographically small, the age-old saying in Ireland that 'the North' is a different world rings true especially in the context of the conflict. Northern Ireland was the IRA's principal operating theatre and long attracted sympathetic Republicans like Michael who grew up far from the social and political unrest that saw the emergence of the civil rights movement and, subsequently, terrorist movements on both sides of the divide.

The 'mainstream appeal' of struggling for Nationalist equality in Northern Ireland was particularly relevant in drawing in 'romantic fools like me', Michael explains. Additionally, Michael suggested that because of that mainstream appeal, the movement also attracted, and represented an outlet for, 'nutters':

> This is a mad thing to say to you but [MR] once said to me he said *look, Michael, understand one thing, this person here was a complete nutter before the bomb. The bomb did not make him a nutter.* He is saying that one of these guys was always a head case before that. He also says, *so and so was always a pretty level-headed guy before the bomb* and surprise, surprise, he says to me, *he's still a pretty level-headed guy.* So what I'm trying to say is that too much allowance can be made for circumstances.

This recognition, Michael argues, was not lost on the IRA leadership:

> There have always been very astute people involved in recruiting to the IRA who see that there are level-headed people and there are strange kinds of people. Not 'strange', but violent kinds of people who we know they are violent *to begin with* and they'll want to join the IRA. There is a sense in which people were evaluated and put into certain roles if you like. 'Cos every large organisation is going to have that challenge – how do you fit people into things?

The IRA, Michael explains, was in many ways similar to any large organisation. As explained in Chapter 1, there are multiple roles and functions into which a variety of different people have to be put. Michael suggests that the

IRA was equally skilled at finding roles for [explicitly] 'violent kinds of people':

> I don't think it worked like that early on. I think you know, the early days of the Provisional IRA were kind of just 'all hands to the wheel' and then it began to sort itself out. Some people, you know [MS] for instance would have been regarded as a very, very efficient guy. Violent and efficient. How do you harness that? Well simply, [MS] is good at doing stuff. Then he establishes a record – goes to jail, comes out, gets married, has a child, begins to settle – is kind of feared around the area – lots of IRA guys who knew him from his time in jail as the guy that beat up prison officers and wouldn't give in etc. etc. and that builds it all. So he goes from being the extraordinarily violent man that no one could control, except me, to being the elder statesman.

[MS] became involved in the IRA around the same time as Michael, and is now a senior Sinn Fein politician.

The IRA had, in Michael's words, an ability to detect qualities in potential members that would render them suitable for involvement: 'I think that one of the overwhelming qualities . . . quality . . . I think what the IRA has always looked for is people who have "gone through the mill" as it developed. You know, has he killed anybody? Has he gone to jail? Has he got balls? Does he display some political awareness? You know, basically has he been around?'

I asked Michael to explain, in his words, the background to his own decision to become involved with the IRA:

> I think involvement in the Republican movement was quite easy – being in [the South] that part of it, at that particular time it was quite easy. I suppose the general environment. I suspect that part of the reason I wanted to go to Northern Ireland was that was where it was at – that's where it was happening – that's where the Republican struggle was happening. But maybe there was kind of something else as well in that, you grow up in a place in [TE] where everybody talked about it but nobody actually seemed to do anything, so perhaps there was a part of me that, you know, wanted to be *seriously* involved rather than just be somebody that was sitting in [TE] talking about it.

Michael acknowledges two critical issues – having exposure and access to a supportive community, and being acutely dissatisfied at the failure of community figures to 'be seriously involved' instead of 'talking about it'. Michael suggests that he 'reached a point' where he decided that simply talking about engaging in the struggle wasn't enough, but also acknowledges the challenge of recalling any precise decision:

> I think that, crikey it's hard to sort of think back and work it out, but I

think it was like . . . you had a Republican *tradition* . . . and I am not saying that our tradition was in any sense of the word a mainstream tradition, but it was certainly, it was kind of born – there was a kind of civil war tradition – it was a little bit peculiar to parts of [TE]. So it was still kind of anti-state and . . . But I remember a public meeting in [TE] and at that stage I suppose the guys at the public meeting would have been what later become the official IRA, but over the next day or two I remember meeting all these people; guys I went to school that all wanted to join the IRA and I suppose at some level I thought they were all full of wind and hot air. You know, they were all sitting down in [TE] talking about doing this and that. I suppose my nature would be to be committed if I was doing something – even now I would be rather intolerant of someone that if they said they were doing something, I would kind of like to see what they are *doing*.

This theme has carried through from earlier chapters – a sense of wanting to 'do something' and engage in activity that involves more than 'meeting' and 'talking'. Michael elaborated on this initial phase and was asked if he had a sense of what 'being involved' would imply. Michael recalls having a clear sense of what involvement in the movement entailed, primarily as influenced by his own family's involvement:

Yes, yes I think I did. I suppose that would have come from home and particularly from my father's side and my father's family side. They were the kind of things that you learned very, very young about . . . and again, it does go back and it does . . . it sounds like there is a huge gap, but if you think that . . . the Irish civil war essentially ends about 1923, but if you think in 1939 . . . there are 43 people interned from the greater [TE] area – that's an awful lot of people. And some of these people went on to become successful businesspeople in their own right but they never joined any other political party – they always existed as a sort of sect, but they were very much looked up to because while many become very successful in their own right they never sold out. So they are kind of almost like men of honour. When I came to be around 15 or 16 and I'm very much anti-nationalist, I was a socialist, I mean I formed a young socialist group in [TE] but then kinda the revolution is beginning to happen on your patch so all this old stuff is suddenly becoming tremendously relevant – now it is actually becoming *real*.

But, Michael emphasises, there was a clear realisation that while 'some of these guys talk a good story, they aren't actually going to do anything . . . so as a kid . . . I've all this actually in common with [MS] you know . . . It's like we are going to do something about it . . . and stand out. And how do you do it? Well you do it by going to Northern Ireland. So there are huge waves of romanticism.'

For Michael, his peer group was a major facilitating influence in his decisions and he realised that there were others in his immediate social network that felt the same way. The 'huge waves of romanticism' played a significant role not only in facilitating his movement into the IRA, but also in sustaining his involvement in times of doubt and guilt. Initially, Michael's move to become involved in the IRA was almost a rite of passage. He describes how receptive figures in the community were to the steps he took in seeking out involvement in the movement:

> I went to a local shopkeeper who was also the local insurance agent and said I wanted to join the IRA. It was as simple as that. I mean they knew where I was coming from, they knew the family background. He looked at me and said *ah ... thought you'd turn up*, right? Now again ... don't forget these are different days. The Provos had just been formed, and [everything] is in a state of chaos. And he said *first of all you need to join Sinn Fein*. So I said okay. So I go to a meeting at the Trade Union Hall.

Going to the meeting, however, did not bring with it the excitement that Michael expected: 'Not at all. I had some doubts. I remember sitting in the back of the room thinking – I am in the wrong room, I am in the wrong room, but I thought – yeah – they [the Provisional IRA] are a popular front. They want to get the Brits out ... and they probably have more capacity to mobilise more people in a nationalist struggle than the officials [the official IRA] would.' Michael reflected on his enthusiasm and acknowledges critical peer influences:

> It's very hard to explain. Don't forget I was 15/16, right? I'm a pretty out of control kid anyway, you know? I'm rebelling at home. I'm reading far too much. And everyone around me tells me I am the brightest boy in the place. Suddenly you move into a world where I'm 15 and at my first IRA meeting the guy oldest to me must have been 29, right? So I am kind of like the local bright shining star. I don't think they were [engaging] me in a kind of an incredibly manipulative way. I think I was kind of precocious, and at the same time I was about the only thing they had, do you know what I mean? I mean I was about the only thing they had that could get other kids involved. I was the only person with any roots around the place that was in touch with any kind of recruitment policy you might get involved in. So you know I talked with the guys at school and I'm getting other people involved.

Romantic tales and elaborate stories of 'street battles' and 'action' continued to influence Michael's gradually increasing involvement, as well as his ability to get 'other kids involved':

> It's so simple to kind of tell stories of romance. Particularly if two things

are going on and one is that you are being told that you have been *conquered* and second is that that you are second or third generation. And they're a lethal combination . . . it's just *lethal* . . . like nitro-glycerine. And so my getting involved was almost from a self-expectation. I'm listening to this bunch of farts at some level and they are not going to do anything, [and] I'm listening to all these stories. And I suppose I'm going because I want to prove myself, I'm going to want to prove that *they* are a bunch of old farts anyway, and when I come back again, you know . . . there's going to be yellow ribbons all around the table and they're going to think that I'm a hero – I suppose.

Being involved

For Michael the distinction between becoming involved and *being* involved in the IRA was made clear by his first IRA meeting. This involved meeting other IRA members in the barn of a local farmhouse. Michael's very first task involved cleaning weapons that were being stored in the barn:

> It was in a house just outside [TE], a farm house, and we had to pull all of this grain back and they were pretty big farmers so they did barley and stuff like that. It was in like a drying shed, where barley would be dried and stuff like that. So you pull all the barley back with these wooden shovels and there are these guns. So the guns have got to be cleaned and the guns are going to Northern Ireland. So that's my first meeting.

Michael again acknowledges that the age difference between him and other members of the IRA unit was noticeable, and that that played a significant role in him being 'adopted' and groomed by more senior IRA members:

> I think, if I say 27–29 was the next guy in my age group, and then I was kind of adopted in a sense by the guy who was astute enough to realise that I was bright and that I had, ah . . . he saw huge potential. So when I was about 16½, I was promoted to be the training office on the [TE] Command Staff. Wow! Boy was I f****** moving! It meant that I finished up actually training loads of people from Belfast and Northern Ireland in training camps in [TE]. They came down to [TE] and I trained them in [TE]. Training was the first major thing I got involved in. I was important to the IRA. And then I was making stuff.

Michael had been involved in the IRA for less than a year and was already 'promoted to the training office' and involved in making explosives. He progressed further just as quickly. He started to train IRA members from Northern Ireland who travelled to the South of the country partly to escape intense security pressures and surveillance to an area that afforded refuge from the glare of Northern Ireland. This rapid progression was not without incident, however, and Michael encountered his first major negative experience as part of his daily involvement:

> It was April. I had been to the training camp and I was, I had got a whole load of stuff and I'm mixing some [explosives], 'cos I wanted to do a training thing with six guys the next day and I'm mixing stuff in the shed and it catches on fire. It blows up the house, absolutely blows up the f****** house. So I ran off and I got to a farm house about a mile and a half outside [TE] and a guy went to a hotel with me and we phoned [KB] and he turned up and he said to me, look *you have got to hand yourself in.*

The explosion was dramatic and was heard for miles around. Michael panicked and ran. The contact he telephoned in the IRA advised him that he would have to face the consequences of the accident:

> What [my contact] is getting at is they [the IRA leadership] have a certain responsibility in the area. Something awful has happened so you've got a young guy, 17 years old, and the picture is slightly changed. A bomb has gone off in [TE], and now this is going to bring heat on us. We got training camps on and we were very seriously involved in a lot of stuff and he is thinking best way to defuse this is for me to go in and say *oh look I'm really sorry – I was just messing about with some old stuff.*

The objective, Michael explains, was to 'keep it at district court level, keep it that way' to deflect 'the heat'. However, the police took a 'slightly different view'. But because Michael was a minor, he was sent to a young offenders' institute.

Several weeks into his sentence, he appeared in front of a local judge, and outside the courtroom, Michael was approached by a fellow IRA member who said: 'Look, we think you should escape. We've got a bicycle placed outside the courtroom, right, and we got 80 of our people here so if you hop on the bike and escape . . .' Michael's decision not to do so proved a significant boost to his already popular standing within the local IRA. He recalls saying to his colleague: 'You know, I want to grow up a bit. I will be out of jail one way or the other in a few months so what do I need to do that for?'

Upon his release from prison, Michael's reputation as an IRA 'star' was at its highest. His loyalty to the movement was unquestioned. He did not inform on his colleagues and served his time without any attempt to escape. Upon his release, he returned to IRA activity and soon was involved 'virtually on a full-time basis'. Michael dropped out of school completely and was now 'involved in the training camps full-time'. Michael's standing within the camp specifically was strengthened by the fact that he was significantly younger than those IRA members he trained in explosives use: 'I am training people that are older than me – there is nobody younger than me. [BD – local IRA leader] comes to me and says *will you go full-time and run this training camp we have down in South [TE]*? I say yes, and it's that training camp that I begin to meet scores of young people from Northern Ireland. Dozens and dozens and dozens.' Michael's role involved 'basically weapons training, mortar training, and explosives training.'

I asked Michael if he had any sense of the consequences of his activities at the training camp: 'I had a very clear sense of that. I had no direct experience of it. It is kind of difficult. I suppose it's a bit, it's a bit like maybe computer games.' Upon saying this, Michael retracted this answer and was uncomfortable with the choice of phrase:

> That's a bad way of putting it. You know it's kinda like . . . you *know*, but you don't *actually* know. So they're telling me. These guys are telling me about gun battles and at that stage don't forget there is a very hard sectarian edge to the whole thing, you know? I think it is kind of like, you grow up on mythology and myths and you are going to be involved in a kind of a struggle that's about getting the Brits out of Ireland. Now does that actually entail . . . actually killing people? So if you are sitting in [TE] training these guys, and these guys are telling you about gun battles with the Brits, I suppose it is extremely difficult for them to actually bring you the bits of body parts so you can look at them and think this is what it's actually all about. It all sounds great stuff.

The 'great stuff' and romantic view of the struggle that Michael absorbed through his fellow IRA members would soon be shattered, and very dramatically.

One of the principal themes that emerged through the interviews with Michael was his relationship with violence. This is an issue he has struggled with throughout his involvement in the IRA and played a major role in his eventual decision not only to leave the IRA, but to become an informer. He recalls an early vivid experience that he argues set the scene for much of the difficulty he had later as an IRA member attempting to justify his own actions and those of his comrades:

> I was out of jail. We were sitting in [our] house and on the television screen there were people scraping up bits of bodies. There were several bomb explosions which were pretty horrible and my mum said to me *nothing good ever came out of killing people* right. I think it was her way of saying to me . . . I think I'm right in saying this, her kind of core belief in life was that you have got to make your own mistakes and learn from your own lessons.

Michael elaborated on this:

> When we were about 9 or 10, right, it was the summer holidays. There was an ice cream guy that used to deliver, they used to deliver like blocks

of ice cream to shops and stuff. And we were, a gang of us, we're 8–9–10 years of age, and we steal some of the ice cream out of the back of the truck and we go along the railway track. Now we couldn't eat it. These were *big* blocks of ice cream. I go home to find my mum sitting by the fire and looking at me and saying *do you know what you have done? Sit down.* She's horrified. She said *you have let me down. You stole that stuff didn't you?*

Michael was asked to explain why he thought this to be significant:

I think what I'm getting at is that there was something in my mum's voice about . . . there was something about . . . you know *nothing good comes out of killing people* and then she said *you know before it's over, no one will know who started it.* Now my mum was completely uneducated, right, and she just said, *nothing good comes out of killing people . . . before it's all over no one will know who started it.* And, I always, I always had a . . . I never liked violence . . . I just never liked it.

To explore further the relationship Michael having 'never liked violence' and his activities within the Provisional IRA, two incidents illustrate how he struggled to reconcile the consequences of his involvement in terrorism with the romantic ideals he brought with him from the south of Ireland. They also illustrate, as we see later, how Michael's acknowledged inability to escape the consequences of the ice cream theft as a child echoed his inability to avoid accepting personal responsibility in the aftermath of those he personally murdered as part of an IRA active service unit.

Following his experience of training Northern Irish members of the IRA, Michael graduated to engaging in terrorist operations in the IRA's principal operational theatre – Northern Ireland. It was there that his peripheral apprenticeship would end and he would quickly rise to a senior position within the IRA, but also from where he would turn against the IRA and become an informer.

Experiencing murder

When Michael was involved in running the IRA training camp, he recalls having 'no direct experience' of violence. That changed dramatically as he became personally involved in IRA operations. He recalls the background to one specific operation that involved receiving an order to murder a police officer:

There were several strands to it. [PN] was a notorious Special Branch Officer. The IRA held him responsible, wrongly as it turned out, for being involved in very brutal interrogations. To the local IRA, he was almost a legendary kind of Special Branch Officer and, there was a guy called

[SN]. Well [SN] became the OC [Officer Commanding] of the Belfast brigade during this period. So he is placed in charge, and he was very close to [DL]. [DL] was very close to [KN] and [PN – the police officer] was the person that jailed [KN] for a bombing in which an RUC officer was killed. So [KN] had a pathological hatred for [PN] going way back.

Michael explains that the IRA constructed a view of [PN] that effectively served to demonise him, a common tactic used by the IRA in advance of an assassination:

They were viewing [PN] in a bigger landscape. There was a bomb in Carrickmore, planted by the Loyalists, and local mythology has it that [PN] was laughing at all of this. The point I'm making was that [PN]'s murder was bigger than just the man himself. This [mythology] has been going around the houses for a year or two and suddenly it became top priority. Everybody knew he went to this particular bar. He parked his Volkswagen there.

Michael was tasked with killing the police officer and was instructed to enter the bar and shoot him. Recalling the event, Michael makes reference to his disengagement from the IRA: 'If you find yourself in the wrong place or you believe you're in the wrong place then you kind of have to do something about it. My touchstones are, I have a horror of people that behave badly to other people. That might sound completely preposterous but . . .' The murder of the police officer, and the reaction to it, both from other IRA members as well as members of the Republican community, proved upsetting to Michael: 'I suppose I have a sense of decency. Decency is the word I was trying to come up with. There is a profound ignorance and stupidity and coldness about the guy that knows it all, you know? And back then I knew everything. I knew exactly how to sort everything out, you know? And I was, and still can be, a very formidable organiser, you know. But . . .' Michael reported feeling guilty about what he did to the police officer and stressed that 'you don't get over the guilt. You don't. You can't.'

Michael recalls the specific event and traces his reaction to it in the aftermath of the shooting:

I murdered [PN]. He is sitting in [the] pub. He is reading the *Irish Independent*. That's the newspaper he is reading, right. I go in with the Belfast lad [T]. I am the guy that kills him. I am in charge of the operation. I want to kill [PN] as quickly as possible. I want to make sure that we get out of there and everything is okay. I had a conversation with an RUC officer who was a friend of [PN]'s, and he said to me *if you had come into that bar 15 minutes earlier, by pure chance, there were 4 RUC officers, off duty, sitting there, armed.* It was a place where RUC officers went into. So we have got to go through these dragon's teeth. Now, this will sound like I am glamorising it, I'm not. But I mean essentially, you can just imagine it, we are walking down, there is [the] pub, and we know that pub is used by RUC officers. I absolutely knew it and I have got, well I say a 17-year-old kid, he might have been 20 but in my view he was a kid, from Belfast, and I have a Belfast woman driving a car who I'm really not sure about.

The 'Belfast kid' and 'Belfast woman' are terms used by Michael to signify that these individuals were not part of his local unit. They were sent by the leadership figure [KN] in Belfast to ensure a 'Belfast role' in the murder and to establish a Belfast signature on the operation. The involvement of outside figures contributed to Michael's unease about the operation and contributed to him focusing on the effectiveness of the operation: 'These people I'm just not sure about so I want to do this thing as clinically and as quickly as possible. I want to kill this guy who is this "notorious Special Branch Officer", who has "tortured IRA prisoners", right? If you like, it is a complete military operation. It has gotta be done, I have to got to make sure the people I am responsible for, get out that door in one piece.'

Michael recalls what went through his mind in the moments before the shooting:

Do it. Do it. That's the target. Do it. Do it as best you can. And don't forget you are on the tops of your toes. 20 years of age. At 20, you are invincible, you know? What happens is that [T] was the name of the lad that was with me. I say to him *have a look*. We have been told [PN] will be sitting on the end of the bar. He goes to the end of the bar. I have seen a photograph and he's got a huge big neck, right. He's a big man. And I push the door open. [T] looks at me and says *yeah he's at the end of the bar*. I push the door open, walked in and start shooting. He stumbles towards the toilet and I shoot him twice. I'm not sure, em . . . I think he was hit seven times. Of the two weapons, he was hit seven times by the gun I used. All [T]'s shots missed.

After shooting the police officer, Michael and his back-up gunman ran out of the pub into the awaiting vehicle:

We get in the car, right, and the girl proceeds to drive the wrong way up a one-way street. I'm trying to tell both of them to calm down. I'm trying to get her to drive. And . . . you see, there is something, there is something that clicks into mode. There is something I suspect that takes over. I am the guy from [TE], right? I come up, I am responsible for the biggest Republican area in Northern Ireland, and we have now completed an operation and we have shot at that stage the most senior RUC person in Northern Ireland who had been shot. I've got two tulips with me who aren't up to much and I want them to get away. *I* want to get away.

Michael's actions during the murder and the escape from the scene reinforced his reputation as 'effective', and what he described earlier as him being a 'formidable organiser' and his standing within the IRA would grow further as a result. Immediately after the shooting, the unit left the area, crossed the border and retreated to an IRA safe-house in the Republic of Ireland. Michael switched on the radio and listened to 'the 1:30 news, the lunchtime news on Athlone radio'. He recalls vividly the reaction to the shooting by the two Belfast IRA members:

> It came up [on the radio]. They said that an RUC inspector had been shot dead. And it also said, his mother was a widow. The girl said *shit, I feel sorry for his mother.* And [T] said *I don't* and I remember thinking . . . that . . . *I'm going to have to pay for that one day.* There was a huge sense of guilt. So at some level . . . I thought it was, at some level . . . I can't actually say . . . the important thing to remember is this, that when it comes on, at the news at 1:30, Athlone, I am really sure about this, I thought *you're gonna have to pay for that one day.*

I asked Michael about why he felt guilty at the safe-house: 'I don't know. Don't ask me what happens in the person's head. I've no idea, I've absolutely no idea. I suspect that in spite of everything I was that young romantic guy from [TE], d'you know? That's what I suspect. I don't know.' If the seeds of doubt were in Michael's mind as a result of having committed murder, the reaction to the shooting by [T] and other IRA colleagues further reinforced his dissatisfaction with the event. Michael spoke about what happened in the days and weeks after the murder of the police officer. The overwhelming reaction, he explains, was: '*excellent* – it has been done, right?' Michael returned to his own IRA unit less than two weeks after the murder, and recalls:

> I turn up in [M – a town] and [KA] looks at me and says *that was a great operation.* Now he doesn't know I've done it. He doesn't know I've been involved in it, he genuinely doesn't have a clue. And [SN] comes walking in and says to me *f****** hell man, well done . . . how many did you put in him? I heard it was seven.* And then *An Phoblacht* [The Republican newspaper] is there the next day and the headline on the front page is a big photograph, with [PN], and it says *Torture Chief Shot Dead.* *Torture Chief Shot Dead* is the big headline. It was huge. So when I went back into [OG] after that, I am this guy from [TE] that can walk on water.

Publicly, Michael was revered. The murder of [PN] reinforced his reputation throughout the IRA, north and south. Internally, for Michael, however, his doubts about the meaning and purpose of his activities were already developing:

There was a kind of build-up coming from . . . remember I'd said about [PN], you know, *I'll have to answer for that some day* and I suppose in a general sense . . . maybe it is a bit specific in my case, maybe but . . . I bought into something that I hadn't seen the real edge of. So, it's like you go to a place from [TE] in the belief that it is a 'war' and when you are dealing with . . . something that hasn't been resolved, you get there you find out it's just a hell of a lot more complicated.

Michael's romantic image of the IRA, like the cases reported in Chapter 2, received its first major challenge. After the murder, and similar to the case of Omar in Chapter 5, the reality of engagement was at odds with his pre-existing views about what involvement and engagement would entail. The 'real edge' that Michael 'bought into' was not what he expected or wanted. The feedback he received in the form of support from his colleagues contributed further to the growing realisation that Michael was now struggling to justify his continued engagement in terrorist activity. While the seeds of Michael's psychological disengagement had been sown, a pivotal event was to shatter any remaining romance about the IRA and provided the catalyst for his disillusionment and eventual disengagement from the movement.

'The policewoman'

The person to whom Michael referred in the context of [PN]'s murder, [KA], was one of the most senior figures in the IRA of Northern Ireland. Michael became very close to [KA], viewing him as a mentor. Michael recalls: 'he is a hero . . . and for many sensible reasons if I can say so,' and how [KA] in turn viewed Michael as 'sort of the best thing in the world.' The deterioration in Michael's overall relationship with the IRA, however, was catalysed by the reaction of [KA] to the murder of a female police officer by the IRA. The background to this event was at a time when Michael, [KA] and other IRA members occupied a safe-house, hiding from the security forces. Michael explains the background to the events that followed:

The IRA had a ceasefire and the kind of build-up to it is that, you know, I finished up in these extraordinary circumstances where essentially when I think back on it I'm 19 and I'm in charge of the largest Republican area in Northern Ireland, right. And, [KA] who later went on to be the Chief of Staff for years has just got out of Portlaoise jail where he has been on hunger strike, and he is recuperating. Now the ceasefire begins to unravel, and [KA] begins to send me messages to carry out operations. At the same time I knew I'm getting very clear messages from people like [GS – a senior Sinn Fein leader] that 'the ceasefire must hold'. I come out of [OG]. I go to [M] and we are sitting in the flat. And I am making tea, and there had been an explosion. Now the IRA ceasefire at that period, it hasn't come to an end but it's been flaking out a bit . . . it never came to a definitive end, ok, the IRA never said *this ceasefire is over*, it just began to unravel. It turned out anyway, it was a policewoman that was killed and I'm making tea and [KA] was sitting back and he said 'we might get two for the price of one'. She was pregnant [long pause]. I thought f***. I thought, f***, f***, f***.

Michael recalls his reaction vividly. He says he was 'devastated' at the remark. For the first time, he says, this graphically illustrated to him just how sectarian [KA] and fellow IRA members were:

> I admired this guy. I had some doubts [that] I was going to talk to him [KA] about. I had some doubts in [OG] about whether we were fighting a sectarian war or we were fighting a war against Britain. Look, in retro- spect maybe some of the doubts could be answered, do you know what I mean? But I was caught in a very localised, kind of almost a defender situation. So I wanted to attack British army patrols and the guys wanted to shoot the local UDR [Ulster Defence Regiment] down the road. That doesn't make them any better or any worse than me, I'm not saying that, I'm just saying that was their focus, that was their war, and that's how they seen it. Me coming from [TE], I wanted to attack the British army, that's what I wanted to do and so I had doubts.

Michael recalls feeling 'caught' on more than one occasion. He recalls the sense of conflict between the 'real edge' of the IRA as a sectarian movement and his 'ties' and 'loyalty': 'I thought it was a fun place. At some level I thought [that]. And don't forget I still had a huge loyalty to, you know, just, people and place. I'd also developed a huge warmth for the people who had been putting us up, the houses we stayed in, and you know I realised that you know, you've got you know a married couple and he's got a job and they are putting up four guys with guns, and I had to kind of think about why a married couple living in a reasonably nice house put up 4, 6, 8 [people] sometimes.'

Powerful sources of local, informal support that had served to sustain Michael's involvement with the IRA conflicted with his experiences of the reality: 'I cried desperately. I remember lying on the mattress, just f****** crying. And then you have got to get up in the morning and in this place at the time there were probably 9 or 10, 11 guys from [OG]. I mean, guys that were really serious operators that killed a lot of people and I am the only guy from the South of Ireland and I am responsible for [them]. I'm their boss. Do you know what I mean? You can't show weakness.'

Michael 'didn't say anything' to [KA], but acknowledges that [KA] detected a change in Michael after that event: '[he] says to me a couple of weeks later, he said *listen, you're getting too close to [OG]. I want you to go take over this place in [GA].*' Michael's response was that he: 'hitchhiked down to [TE] and a week or two later I resigned from the IRA.'

Disengaging

Like every other aspect of Michael's involvement with the IRA, his experiences of disengagement were neither simple nor straightforward. To provide some context to this, Michael explained that 'leaving' was not an uncommon occurrence for IRA members and that, perhaps surprisingly, 'it happened all the time'. Michael explained that [KA] and the other IRA leadership were 'ok' with him resigning because: 'the IRA thought it was better to leave me to go away for a few months or a year or two.' Leaving the IRA, Michael explains, was as much a practical step as anything else, but was predicated on two assumptions: 1) that the individual member 'keeps his mouth shut' and 2) that there is a strong probability that the member will want to come back 'of his own accord':

> Yes, of course you can [leave]. Why would you want to hold onto someone who doesn't want to be there? You should keep your mouth shut, you know. Basically just keep your mouth shut. But what are you going to do? Put a gun to this person's head and say *you will take part in this operation tomorrow morning?* It would be just madness. So when a person says they want to leave the IRA it is quite acceptable. Always has been, always will be. I know there is this mythology about you can't leave but clever people in the organisation of which [KA] was one I suspect would have said, *you know something, I think Michael's had a f****** bellyful and he is like, just about 20, he will be back in a couple of years.*

The event in the flat, however, while a tipping point for Michael, did not represent anything resembling a singular event that catalysed his disengagement. He provides more context to that point and ultimately suggests the existence of a more complex and gradual process:

> I had already shot [PN] which everyone was over the moon about. I had sort of ran what's now described as the [SR] Brigade of the IRA. I knew [OG] like the back of my hand and I kept being in there when everyone else left and then I turn up in [TE] and then just said *look I'm resigning.* But I also, I said, *I need a break* essentially. What I wasn't quite aware of and I wouldn't have been because I was 'on the ground' was the huge power struggle that was going on [between the [OG] IRA and the IRA leadership in Belfast]. So, when I came back it was interpreted by people like [KA] and [GS] as being on *their* side.

Michael returned to the IRA a few years later, but it was clear that he was still struggling with a wavering commitment to the movement:

> So when I go back, and I met [KA], I'm in a meeting in a house in Limerick. I'm sitting in a chair in the back, and he was sitting in a chair

in front of me. I hadn't met [KA] since [seven years previously]. [KA] turned around and he looked at me *F***, that's a face I didn't think I'd see again. Can we go and have a chat?* We go outside and he says to me *will you take over? Do you want to take over stuff again?* Do you understand what I mean? He would have thought that I went away because I had a pretty rough time, but that, well, *he was actually one of the best of us and he's here again now.*

[KA] didn't address the event that took place in the flat, nor did Michael raise it in conversation:

> I would have loved to but if I had, it would have . . . not so much raised suspicions, because you see I am just not sure about how it will go down. You know the thing about black humour, right, the thing that keeps people going in these kinds of [circumstances]. I was never *sure* if [KA] just said that as kind of like, uh . . . yes. But the point is that, for me it really was a step too far. It just was a step too far. I thought it was awful unworthy of him. Even if he *was* doing it as pandering. This is going to sound completely bonkers but you don't actually say *I hope she was pregnant and we get two for the price of one.*

Throughout, Michael not only recognised the importance of his role in killing members of the security forces and training others in how do to this, but he offers a contrast with how he felt others reacted to those incidents. The relationship between Michael and [KA] was pivotal to Michael's realisations about the IRA, and despite being back as an operational member of the Provisional IRA, the 'hatred' that Michael encountered, he argues, was sufficient such that Michael was unable to reconcile his continued engagement with the attitudes providing a supportive context, yet from which he felt alienated and without an ability to make his voice heard.

Michael's changing views led him to eventually deciding to inform against the IRA: 'As I got to know [KA] later on, I did understand that it was hatred. And I mean, look at [MS]. Jesus Christ, he grew up only six miles away from me, we knew each other. How could MS say *I don't know what all the screaming is about. They were only all Orangies anyway?*'

'Orangies' is a derogatory term used to refer to Unionists in Northern Ireland and is a label used by Republicans more generally to refer to Protestants. The remark 'I don't know what all the screaming is about' refers to the outrage over the IRA bombing in 1978 of the La Mon restaurant and hotel near Belfast. The IRA planted an incendiary device outside the window of the restaurant. Twelve people were killed instantly, with dozens more suffering from horrific injuries. No IRA members were ever charged with the atrocity:

> In [MS]'s heart, this is what he truly believes. He planted loads of bombs over here, he got involved with [BN], and another guy from [TE], and

killing and torturing a UDR man on the border. At this stage [MS] does know what it's about. No question, he knows what it's about. We both know about dead bodies we both know about the horrors of stuff. And yet, he is talking to me and says this kind of stuff [*I don't know what all the screaming is about*], and to me and *that* was the point.

Michael repeated: 'You just don't say those things.' Though the idealism and romance associated with the IRA's campaign had initially played a major influence in the decisions Michael had made to become and remain involved, the 'attitude' and 'blatant ignorance' of the reality of the IRA's activities and those such as Michael's friend [MS], played a major role in turning him away from the IRA. Michael reflects on this discrepancy as experienced by him in a variety of settings:

Someone once said to me that I was too intelligent to buy into it all the time and frankly I think I was, but you know years later, I see it crop up again. I am sitting in [TE]. These people walk into this bar and some kind of conversation strikes up, and this girl says to me, *are you the one they call *****? I said *what do you mean*? She said to me, you know, [PN – referring to the police officer Michael had shot and killed]. And I said to her *can we go outside and have a conversation*? I said *don't ever say that to me again.*

As a result of his activities within the IRA, Michael had become a folk hero with his own nickname. He was even being recognised in public. With the example above, however, he was also beginning to see mirror examples of the idealism that had influenced his decision to become involved in the IRA. Michael realised that the murder of [PN] was already feeding another mythology that could just as easily be relevant and significant for other potential recruits hearing tales of 'gun battles'. Reflecting on his eventual decision to become an informer, Michael explains the need to:

Stop the idiots like me that are idealists. In a sense because you aren't going to be able to stop the people with genuine grievances. There is a difference between insurgents and people with real difficulties, and real issues to handle and then people that see themselves as being able to handle the problems of the world. There are people who want to fight for their land, right, and the people who want to internationalise it and do all those things. I was one of the guys who almost wanted to internationalise it. I am one of the radicals coming in from outside into Northern Ireland and the guys there are actually dealing with serious problems on the ground. And let's imagine that they are at some level a popular insurgency. But it's not them. *I* am the guy you need to deal with. The guys you need to deal with are the foreign fighters coming from outside trying to make it worse. So, at one level I am the most dangerous one.

The parallels between Michael's situation and contemporary movements such as Al Qaeda and its relationship with foreign fighters are striking. If the Northern Irish identifiers were removed from the above account from Michael, one could easily be reading about the Mujahidin in Afghanistan, or Al Qaeda in Iraq. Again he emphasises: 'I have a bigger agenda at some level. They just want to shoot the guy that lives down the street but I am actually saying *it's about a united Ireland. It's a bigger concept than that, you know? You're not just shooting the guy down the road, you're fighting for the freedom of Ireland.* You know, they just didn't understand.'

I asked Michael if this played a role in how quickly the IRA accepted him and how equally quickly he rose to prominence in the movement: 'The fact that I ended up running that area of [OG] as a kid [is] because they were in awe of the fact that a guy would come from [TE]. I remember once a guy called [BH], he looked at me and he said *f*** man.* He said *if I was you I would just be down in [TE] enjoying myself, but here you are up here with us.* But I wanted a United Ireland. They didn't know Westminster. They didn't think Westminster was our enemy. They just wanted to get a bit of space for themselves but *I* had an agenda.'

Interim conclusions

The case of Michael is as important and interesting as it is complex and challenging. What is presented in this chapter is approximately one-eighth of Michael's entire account, but what we have here is the context to his disillusionment and disengagement from the IRA.

In brief, Michael's case effectively illustrates the case of a foreign fighter, an imported terrorist as opposed to a local, home-grown militant. He grew up far from the conflict in which he became involved, but eventually became intricately engaged to the extent that he became a major figure in the movement. Though with no initial experience of the same kinds of driving forces relevant to IRA members from Northern Ireland, Michael was exposed to a supportive community at three distinct levels – his family, his peers and the broader environment in which local figures played key roles (e.g. the shopkeeper who gave him specific instructions about joining). It was these background influences that provided not only a context and setting for Michael to explore initial involvement, but also provided him with a lure of what involvement would entail. Michael emphasises throughout his account the ease with which 'stories of romance' can be told, and acknowledges the 'lethal combination' of this added to 'the family background' and 'support' in the community.

A major issue for Michael's phase of initial involvement was the sense of needing to 'do' something. He draws a sharp contrast with those in his community who talked 'a lot of hot air' and acknowledges the self-expectation that led him to seek a separation from these individuals. The fact that Michael was younger than everyone around him was an issue that both spurred him on to impress upon others the seriousness of his commitment and also led to his grooming by senior IRA leaders. Michael embraced this, and combined with his technical and organisational acumen, started on a path of rapid apprenticeship and accelerated promotion within the IRA. In addition to his age, he differentiated himself from his comrades by having 'an agenda'.

To reflect on these issues in a broader way, one of the most striking themes inherent in his account includes the clear difference between motivational issues and perspectives between 'local' and 'imported' members of the IRA. Michael is an example of the latter, a foreign fighter whose motivational sources were heavily influenced by romanticised fantasies about involvement. We can appreciate the significance of this characteristic in a number of ways and one key issue relevant to counter-terrorism here would be in making a distinction about where (and how) to focus attention in controlling the level of involvement. For example, the kind of action needed to counter the involvement of imported fighters like Michael would appear to be different from the kinds of initiatives needed to address local issues and stem the tide of local recruits. Whereas Michael was heavily influenced by one particular set of issues in a locality far removed from Northern Ireland, it would be difficult to see how, in contrast, this awareness of anywhere other than local place would be found in the case of Chapter 4 with 'Alan's' process of becoming involved.

The distinction between local and imported is in many ways a key issue for current policy failures in counter-terrorism. There needs to be a way of distinguishing between different kinds of terrorist from a preventative perspective. The decisional calculus for a local terrorist will have to be different from that of an imported terrorist, and this basic distinction would be expected to lead to different preventative initiatives. A major lesson learned by British forces in Northern Ireland was that the conflict was unwinnable in military terms and that a key element to effective control and management of the conflict was addressing local issues – developing effective contacts, understanding individual experiences, and so on. Addressing terrorists like Michael, however, requires a different kind of approach and a focus on different sets of issues.

Additionally, we can see from Michael's account an illustration of the external factors that give rise to a localised, specific terrorist operation. An example of this is in not only the influence of leadership personalities on events, but also in the reaction that emanates from that same leadership. Michael's examples illustrate that through the control that extended from Belfast for the assassination of the police officer – both in terms of the decision to kill him as well as the operational involvement with the introduction of the two individuals – but also in the reaction of and tone set by [KA] following the murder of the female police officer. Michael describes on several occasions the feeling of being 'caught' and that relates not only to the jarring differences in perspectives between him and the localised members of the IRA, but also in the degree of autonomy (or lack thereof) even while he is essentially put into a senior role.

Though Michael recalls the significance of particular childhood influences in affecting his susceptibility to involvement with the IRA, the influence of his mother in providing Michael a sense of conscience was an issue at the heart of some of the psychological challenges he faced while a member of the IRA. Despite the fact that Michael embraced IRA activity, coming to know 'all about dead bodies', and there is abundant evidence for this, it is clear that he grappled with the consequences of his actions when removed from the operational context itself. There is clear conflict in his gradually creeping awareness of the IRA being different to his expectations, yet Michael describes how despite this, 'you have got to get up in the morning', and show that 'I am their boss. You can't show weakness.' Even after the jarring incident in the safe-house after the female police officer was killed, Michael's reactions illustrate what Hirschman[1] describes as the conflict between 'voice' and 'exit' in leaving organisations of all kinds. 'Voice' in Michael's context (i.e. expressing his shock and disapproval at his colleague's reaction) would have come with a high cost such that for him, exiting (albeit temporarily) was at that particular moment a more attractive option.

The major factor in Michael's disengagement, both psychologically and physically, was the creeping disillusionment with the image of the IRA and its activities that had formed the bedrock of the fantasies that shaped his initial involvement in the first place. Perhaps most significantly on this issue, the events surrounding Michael's reaction to that of others (in relation to IRA murders) raise interesting issues about the role of informal learning in terrorist movements and about ideas that relate to what we explore in Chapter 9, particularly in terms of making the reality of terrorism known to potential recruits. This may lie at the heart of the development of the counter-terrorism initiative that acknowledges the significance of the kinds of differences in perspectives and motivations that run through Michael's account.

7   'They were once my people'

Introduction

The widely held image of the Loyalist terrorist is that of a vicious, nakedly sectarian paramilitary, having, as one commentator argued, all the 'political nous of a Rottweiler'. In Chapter 4 we were introduced to 'Alan', a former member of the Ulster Volunteer Force. In this chapter, we are introduced to a very different kind of Loyalist. 'Doug' is a former Commander of the Ulster Freedom Fighters (UFF), the military wing of the Ulster Defence Association (UDA). The UDA was the largest Loyalist paramilitary organisation in Northern Ireland, which, like the UVF, sought to uphold Northern Ireland's place within the United Kingdom and defend Loyalist communities from the IRA. It was formed in 1971 as an umbrella group spanning a number of local vigilante associations. One of the features that distinguished the UDA from the UVF is that the UDA in the 1970s advocated total independence for Northern Ireland. Also long since forgotten is the fact that the UDA once functioned as a legal organisation under the motto of 'law before violence'. But it was during this legal period that the UDA committed many terrorist acts under the cover name 'Ulster Freedom Fighters'. The Republican community, particularly members of the Irish Republican Army, represented the UDA/UFF's primary target. Just like the UVF, the term 'tit for tat' was frequently used to refer to UDA/UFF retaliation against the Irish Republican violence.

In 1992, the UDA was eventually proscribed as a terrorist movement both by the British and Irish governments. Because of the UDA's descent into criminal activity, collusion with the rogue members of the security services in Northern Ireland and other various sinister events, the movement has frequently been dismissed as never having had genuine political aspirations. Consequently, for years Loyalism, in all its forms, largely went unexamined, and this is why its significance continues to remain poorly understood. In fact, it seems unbelievable even now that the UDA was once a formidable power that could command extensive social and political influence. Yet it remains the case that in the early 1970s, the then 40,000-strong movement brought Northern Ireland to a virtual standstill by organising a general strike through the Ulster Workers' Council (led by several senior UDA members). The UDA's objective was to bring about several reformist measures in Ulster, notably the abolition of the Northern Ireland Executive and greater political representation at Westminster. But a decade later, and following the assassination in 1987 of arguably its most effective and strategic leader, John McMichael, the UDA was in decline.

By 1989, the movement was in complete disarray and the security services in Northern Ireland had finally succeeded in virtually paralysing the movement. Ironically, it was a major journalistic investigation (referred to in Chapter 2) into Loyalist racketeering that combined with other events to ultimately lead to the UDA's internal reshuffle. There was a change of leadership and the UDA underwent a revitalisation with young, fresh recruits who would each play their part in the UDA's attempts to rearm itself from local, national and international sources.

Doug commanded a notorious UFF 'Company' during the 1990s. Under his command, Loyalist terrorists surpassed even the Provisional IRA in assassinations, murders and casualties in the period leading up to 1994. One of the UFF's most notorious acts occurred in October 1993 in the Catholic village of Greysteel, Londonderry, where a UFF unit ambushed a group of people celebrating Halloween. This attack, in which the UFF killed eight people, was blamed as a response to the IRA's bombing of a fish and chip shop (believed by the IRA to house senior UDA figures, including Doug) on the Shankill Road. That bomb killed nine people – the UDA leadership was not present at the location.

Meeting 'Doug'

Doug is nothing less than an icon in Northern Ireland. Feared, hated and reviled in some quarters, idolised and revered in others, he remains to this day both an enigmatic and divisive figure. Several dozen Catholics were murdered by the unit that Doug commanded. Doug's command, and indeed the UDA overall, never successfully shook off the image of being blatantly sectarian. The discovery that rogue members of the security services fed intelligence to the UDA only demonised it as typical of Northern Ireland's 'dirty war'. Convinced by the then Secretary of State for Northern Ireland, Mo Mowlam, of the merits of supporting political representatives, Doug was released four years into a 16-year prison sentence which began in 1995. Ironically, the 1994 ceasefire also served as the catalyst for years of savage internecine feuding, which ripped apart the remains of the once formidable Loyalist groups. Despite positive early signs, the UDA's representatives failed to establish an effective political presence in the wake of the ceasefire. The UDA, in Doug's words, 'imploded'. With no IRA to fight, the movement turned inward, unclear of its purpose and place within a rapidly changing political scene in Northern Ireland.

Examining Doug's history of involvement in terrorism, it is remarkable that he is alive to describe his role in the UFF and how he came to disengage from the movement. Despite his rise to power in the UFF, Doug was 'sidelined' following a series of disputes with other senior personnel. He was released from a Northern Irish prison to be flown, together with this family, to a new life in Britain. At the time of the interviews for this book, Doug was relocated to northern Scotland where he remains with several of his 'loyal followers', who, like Doug (and in his own words) 'cannot yet safely return to Northern Ireland and enjoy the peace'.

Despite significant leaps forward in the peace process since those eventful days of the UDA's virtual disintegration, Northern Ireland's newfound stability offers Doug little security. Doug says he 'sleep[s] soundly at night', but acknowledges that he will forever have to look over his shoulder. A spray-painted wall in Belfast warns that he, and his long-time mentor, are 'dead men walking'.

Doug was a nervous interviewee but at the same time was clearly experienced in giving interviews. Throughout the interview a constant challenge was to maintain focus on the issues of involvement, engagement and disengagement while allowing Doug the space to speak about issues he felt were of enormous significance. Regularly, Doug spoke at length about his 'betrayal' and 'abandonment' by his former colleagues – 'traitors'. He has spoken publicly about his involuntary disengagement from the UFF and a challenge throughout the interviews was guarding against what might have been a series of prepared propaganda statements. Doug remains bitterly opposed to former comrades who now run the remnants of the UDA. He laments that the UDA is:

> . . . now a criminal organisation. We were once to the UDA what the SAS are to the British Army. They were the elite. I was a charismatic leader. Billy Wright was a charismatic leader. That helps the movement. Gerry Adams was a charismatic leader. Eamon Collins was a charismatic leader. These guys today [in the UDA] what are they? What young fellas are gonna go out and follow them?

Doug's anger at the UDA leadership was evident from the outset and he did not waste any time in expressing this:

> The organisation is still in turmoil. I mean these are the thugs that threatened to have me murdered. They were once my people. Where are they now? They're still in turmoil. They're criminals, they're just gangsters. All of a sudden in the middle of the peace process, they decided they wanted to be Loyalists! They wanted to do what they couldn't do when we were asking for help after the Shankill bombing, and incidents like that. Where was the UDA when it could have helped us doing what we were doing?

Becoming involved

Like the case of the UVF member described in Chapter 4, the context to Doug's initial involvement is set against a backdrop of social and political turmoil that engulfed Northern Ireland in the early 1970s. One of the paradoxes of Doug's leadership role in the UFF is that his experience of initially becoming involved was highly unusual. Unlike the case of Alan, who emphasised the fact that he 'volunteered', and the case of Michael, who travelled to Northern Ireland from afar, Doug was actually coerced into joining the UDA as a teenager. He acknowledges how unusual this was, but explains it as a product of the times:

> Well yeah I know it's a bit odd . . . but I think way back in the early 70s . . . I can't speak too much about it now, because I was a kid then, but when there was thousands and thousands in that movement, I think it was just more or less that people ah . . . it was a sink or swim situation. The country was in turmoil. There was ongoing street riots. There was civil disorder on the streets, and most men had to come out and join one organisation or the other. Either the UVF or the UDA.

In contrast to accounts of involvement like Alan's, there was no gradual process of exploring involvement in particular roles, nor room for the kind of reflection worked through by Alan in the time between his initial approach to his leadership and the time it took the leadership to return to him with a decision. Doug's case was very different: 'It wasn't a case of going to a recruiting office and going through a training course to join an organisation of your choice, it was just like: *Get in here, stick your hand up, you're now a member of the UDA. There's a coat, there's a hat, there's a big baton.*'

At this point, Doug returned for the first of many criticisms of the motivational character of the UDA leadership:

> But remember, and they're not the kind of guys that go to church on a Sunday and pray. They're evil people. They're criminals. Their roots are in criminality. The majority of the UDA, and I'm speaking as a dedicated member of the UDA myself one time, their roots are born in criminality. And through this criminality, lots of them joined the UDA as a flag and protection for their criminality. And you just have to look at . . . even now as we speak, the UDA is in turmoil because of criminality, because of the current, the majority of the current leadership are nothing but criminals, thugs, gangsters. In my time, I put my hand up [raises hand], anything I fought for, I never went to jail for criminality.

So pronounced is Doug's hatred of his former colleagues that practically every issue about which he spoke was tied to his feelings towards those who 'isolated' and 'rejected' him. An important issue for Doug is the context in which he can contrast his own motivation for being involved in the UFF with those of the current leadership:

> My prison sentences were for shooting Sinn Feiners, for guns, for directing terrorism, for hijackings, but there was no extortions or bank robberies or drug dealings. Compared to the current UDA leadership now, all these men ever went to jail for is either extortion or drugs and criminality. I was there for fighting the war, and engaging with the enemy.

I asked Doug to elaborate on this point. Given the pride he takes in setting the record straight about his own motivational sources, and given the way in which he constantly contrasted his own decisions with those of others in the UDA, I asked him if he accepted the widespread belief that the entire Loyalist movement was steeped in criminal activity. Doug accepted this, and his involvement in criminal fundraising he puts down to 'the need to finance operations': 'Of course [crime] had to go on to finance the operations. I mean the organisation that I headed, we weren't getting no hand-downs from church leaders, or businesspeople, I mean, it was, it was . . . you had to engage in criminality to finance your activities.' The difference Doug points to between his involvement in crime and the UDA leadership's involvement in crime is that the leaders that Doug despises 'were only interested in lining their own pockets. I was fighting a war.'

In his defence of this, Doug points to the cost of operations and in further acknowledging the compromises necessary for a 'political movement' to engage in crime, deflects attention onto his former enemies in the IRA:

> Look, the activities that in particular the UFF were doing, they didn't come cheap. I mean to put in plan an operation cost a lotta, lotta money. But that's Northern Ireland for you. Even the IRA, who grudgingly I would respect, and I would say they were a disciplined organisation, even they were well involved in criminality. But they had a structure for it. They had a whole section of people and that was their only job. A lot of members of the IRA would never have known that that stuff was going on.

A key difference, he argues, was in the UDA's 'lack of discipline' and what he sees as a movement that is 'criminal by nature' rather than by necessity:

> Sadly the UDA was just born a criminal organisation. And, it will die a criminal organisation. Albeit that there's a Red Hand of Ulster smack bang in the middle of the UDA badge. And their motto is 'Quis Separabit' – none shall divide us. And the meaning of the organisation is Ulster *Defence* Association but to be honest and to be fair, in recent years the UDA has done more on their own people, their own community than they have done on the Republican enemies. There's no justified Loyalist

cause. The IRA, as much as I hated them, I grudgingly respected them. They've gone away. They've decommissioned their weapons, therefore there's no need for the UDA, the UVF to be there. In recent years, the only people that the UDA have used their guns on has been their own. The IRA hasn't killed people the last number of years. The only people dying over there now are at the hands of their own people, namely the UDA and the UVF.

Being involved

In an attempt to maintain a sense of focus on his own specific involvement, I asked Doug to elaborate on the role he played in the UFF and what his daily involvement entailed. At this point, Doug's demeanour changed, and the nature of his answers also changed. He paused after hearing my questions and giving his answers. He spoke more slowly, noticeably chose his words carefully and was reluctant to speak about his own personal experiences in much detail. Doug's answers reflected a sense of seniority even throughout the interview and most of his answers came from the perspective of UFF commander rather than former member. Rather than speak about the nature of his own initial involvement, Doug emphasised his one-time role as commander and gave answers to reflect that position.

Doug explains that his role as leader meant that a prominent function was in 'screening' potential recruits to his 'Company'. I asked him how he was able to identify potential recruits: 'Well to be honest with you, I was looking just for someone who had the balls to f****** kill someone. That's it in a nutshell. There's no real training, basic training needed. A man that volunteered to put his life on the line, and prepare to take life for, for the cause that he believed in and the boys that he believed in.' 'Belief' in the cause was highly valued by Doug, so much so that he recognised this as an element in his 'grudging respect' for his enemies in the IRA:

> My time in the movement, I actually adopted IRA tactics. These people are no different from us. They live a mile up the road. They've the same education. The only difference is they've 'RC' [Roman Catholic] on their birth certificate, and we've Presbyterian on ours. Can we not do what they're doing? If they're coming in, sitting in houses on the Shankill, then so can we. If they come in, and can do under-car booby-trap bombs, so can we. My methods worked. And a lot of my tactics, I just borrowed from the IRA. But they were good. Some of them were f****** brilliant.

Doug's respect and admiration for the IRA is in stark contrast to how he now views the UDA. The difference, Doug asserts, is that:

> At the end of the day, they [the IRA] *believed* in what they were fighting for. This is how you know if someone believes. Go out and rob a bank

and get a few thousand pounds. If you get caught, you spend a few years in jail. Go out and kill someone, go out and take a life, and how much do you get for that? Not a fucking penny. So that's dedication. Someone who's prepared to go out and kill someone. And remember, the easy part is pulling the trigger. That's easy.

The difficulty, Doug explains, and what he regards as 'the true test', is in what happens after the event:

> Coping with it for the rest of your life. Learning to live with it for the rest of your life. And gearing yourself up for the eventuality that you might get caught, and charged, and get life in prison. At the end of the day, nobody twists their arm to do what they're doing. They're Volunteers, that's what it is. A Volunteer. I *volunteer* to join. I *volunteer* to kill him. I *volunteer* to put that bomb down. They don't come in, twist your arm, and say, right put that bomb down.

Doug describes part of his daily routine was to screen different people for potentially different roles:

> It was my job. I was a one-time leader. I was a one-time headmaster. And it's the headmaster's job to see the weakness and strength of his pupils. It's the headmaster's job to find out who's good at maths, who's poor at English, who's good at . . . So it was my job to find out. *I think he'll be good, I think he can keep his mouth shut, I think he's got it in him,* do you understand what I mean? I would have selected guys, and I would have tested them and tried them.

Similar to Michael's experience (Chapter 6) of the IRA leadership's adeptness in matching people to specific roles, Doug explains:

> I would have tested them for specific operations, roles, and you can tell. If you've military experience, I can tell, you can just sense it, if you've been there for such a long time, without even being . . . If you've been there for such a long time, and I had been there for such a long time. And you can see it in a guy's eyes. You can see it in their heart, and you can feel it in them, if they're up for it. And nine times out of ten, the judgement was right.

I asked Doug to explain what the other 'one' time out of ten would have involved:

> The *one* time would have been the time I woulda put my trust in a Volunteer, who further down the line, had turned into an informant. Every time I opened my eyes in the morning I looked around me. The

first fight, the first battle that I had was the battle *within*. The enemy within. Not the IRA. It was a question of: *Is my right-hand man an informant? Is my third man down an informant? Is one of my footsoldiers an informant?* That was my fight. I had to put trust in the men but I also knew it was the British Intelligence's job to recruit these men. It was my job to realise that one of these men could be very well recruited today, tonight, tomorrow . . .

Doug was never charged with murdering UFF informers, but acknowledges his role in the internal operations to discover informers within his movement. He is cautious in his response:

All I can say, and speaking for myself, [my] company in the past have unearthed and uprooted informers and executed them. And I myself have been implicated in a lot of . . . so-called executions of informers. I've been questioned, about a number of them. I've actually been named in those cases, but what I mean is . . . well, they have been without any evidence. I have been questioned and released due to insignificant evidence.

Throughout the interview Doug gave the impression that he has not been found guilty for particular activities while involved in the UFF.

Speaking about his role as commander, Doug describes his unit of the UFF as highly disciplined, tightly structured and highly cohesive. When asked if members could ever leave the movement, his reply was initially a very brief: 'No.' I asked him to explain:

Well, no! Because it's an organisation where you take an oath, and you swore allegiance to your boss, and your country. It's not like the Boy Scout movement where you join one week and leave the next week. Once you're committed, once you take that oath, you're there until obviously, you're dead, or you're released on special grounds, which is very rare.

Doug explains the basis of being 'released on special grounds':

On the rare occasion, I think, my experiences of the guys I've come across that the only ones that have been ah, allowed to leave have been people that sorta turned and put their faith in God. Genuinely. And for me, as a one-time leader, I would have released people like that from the movement. But . . . or if someone was in bad health. But if someone had found God . . . I'm a great believer in God, although I don't practise it, I don't practise the Christian faith, but if someone came, a volunteer came and told me that he'd found Jesus, and was no longer wanting to be a member of the movement, if I felt that he was sincere . . . obviously he'll be monitored, for a time, but I'd let him go if he was sincere. Because obviously there's no place in an illegal organisation for someone who's practising religion. A bible in one hand and gun in the other, it just wouldn't work.

Doug acknowledged there being one more reason for allowing a member to leave the movement, and in the same answer tied the inability to disengage with the continued involvement in criminal activity by the UDA:

Well again, there's also the fact that the older the member, you . . . you just let him go. With the peace process obviously because there's no need for him, there's no more war going on. And the only reason why the UDA would hold on to its massive membership now would be the sole interest in the dues that they pay every week. The members have to pay money to be part of that organisation every week, so that would be money into the coffers of the top men. It's all geared around money with the UDA, it's just . . . Not every single member, but there is a small number of very dedicated members, but the majority are just . . . especially at leadership level.

Doug painted a picture of the UDA more generally as a movement that did not tolerate dissent and explained this with reference to the particular role or function held by members:

Well, no. If you don't agree with them, you'll be sidelined. And look what happened to myself. I can only speak for [my] brigade, and we were all as *one*. The band of men that I controlled was just all dedicated men. The majority of men that I had were in the military wing, the Ulster Freedom Fighters, and they were all for what we were doing. And if they weren't [in support of] that [violence] they just stayed in the UDA.

He explains the key distinctions:

The UDA basically comprises of two organisations. The UDA, who are non-activists, and you've the Ulster Freedom Fighters who were involved in the guns, and the bombs, the military side of it. And if you wanted to be military, you swore to the UFF, and then you became military, and that meant that you'd be involved in fighting with the enemy. And if you were UDA, that just meant that you weren't involved in military, you just went to your meetings and went to functions, and went to dances and whatever.

Involvement in the UFF meant that members kept away from UDA social functions and were generally not associable with the Loyalist movement.

Disengaging

By all accounts, Doug could be said to have been a successful terrorist. He rose to prominence as 'an effective military leader' and was highly respected by his followers. The process of his disengagement is both long and complex, the roots of which can be traced to the inception of the peace process in Northern Ireland and the onset of the 1994 ceasefires. In October 1994, less than two months after the Provisional IRA declared its 'complete cessation of military operations', the UDA/UFF and the UVF called their own ceasefires. For the first time the residents of Northern Ireland were given the hope of peace whilst the contending sides of the conflict engaged in dialogue rather than fighting with each other and the British Government. While much of the commentary surrounding the ceasefire period at the time might be characterised as both naïve and premature, there were some overlooked developments within Loyalism that remain unexplored.

At the time of the 1994 ceasefires, the Loyalist position was that much of the political change in Northern Ireland seemed to have been at their expense. Loyalist marginalisation had been a deliberate policy of the then leading Nationalist movement, the Social, Democratic and Labour Party (SDLP) that sought to go directly to the Irish or British Government motivated by a concern to limit and perhaps abolish the historical 'Unionist veto'. However, for the first time in many years, political initiatives after the ceasefire offered (and even guaranteed) the Loyalist community a voice in the political process and the future shape of Northern Ireland. That the Loyalist paramilitaries enthusiastically participated and remained in this process despite the collapse of the PIRA ceasefire is worthy of note. And while the process would go on to expose the rivalries between the paramilitary and constitutional Loyalist political parties, by at least recognising the voice of Unionism, the ceasefire discussions guaranteed an outcome of compromise rather than a complete victory.

As the process developed, however, so too did it become clear that Unionism, far from being marginalised, was being brought to centre stage. Juxtaposed against this development, the ruling Conservative Party's weaknesses forced a greater dependence on the Unionist vote in Parliament, further strengthening the Unionist's bargaining position.

Just over one year into the ceasefire, the collapse of which would be heralded by a massive Provisional IRA bomb in London, former Northern Ireland Secretary of State Mo Mowlam took the unprecedented (and risky) step of acknowledging the critical role of the prisoners in supporting the peace initiative when she visited the notorious Maze Prison in Belfast. Among those she met was Doug, who was to play a critical role in the collective disengagement of the Ulster Freedom Fighters. I asked Doug, who had been imprisoned in 1995, to explain the context to the visit by the Secretary of State:

Well, it was in a time when we Loyalist UDA prisoners felt that the

Republicans were getting all the concessions, and we were getting nothing. So we felt, if it isn't going to be level balanced here, that we were gonna withdraw our support for the peace talks, for the peace process. And we relayed this message through our political party . . . and then turned on panic stations, because without us, there would have been no peace process. As a result Mo Mowlam took a big risk. She gambled coming into the prison. Against all odds. She met us face to face, and as a result of that meeting, and her eyeballing us, myself, Michael Stone and the rest of the camp leadership, she convinced us that what we were doing was wrong. She convinced us that *yous have got it wrong, it's not the case, the peace process is going on, it's not just gonna happen overnight, it's gonna take time, there's things that they have to do to keep one side happy, there's things that they have to do that are gonna upset* . . . do you understand? *Just bear with us*, she says, *and we'll get there, and we'll all be treated equal*, and she was true, she was right.

I asked Doug to explain how the Secretary of State was able to specifically convince the UFF leadership through the prison negotiation process:

It was her desire and will against all odds to come in, and face people like myself and Michael Stone, who were angry at the fact that we felt that the Labour Government was giving concession after concession to the Republicans . . . and we Loyalists who were supporting the peace talks were being good boys, and using our influence to keep people on track, and we were just being sidelined. When someone's sitting talking to you like this, you can get more meaning, you can feel it, you understand what I mean? If you did a story about [me], you'd just guess what kinda guy he is, but if you're sitting here you can sense what kinda guy I am. You can look me in the eyes, you can feel me, you know? You can understand, you can judge me for yourself. Whereas when she came in, they could have just issued a statement through our [political party] then, to come in and just relay to us. But there wouldn't have been any substance to it. When someone comes in from the top, who was instrumental in all what was going on, and sitting, eyeballing, convincing you that this is not the case, just bear it, I mean . . . you get a feeling, and on the other hand, if I felt that she was bluffing us, well, I would have told her to f*** off. But we got that sense that she wasn't, but we realised that she had a hard job to do, and we realised that it was patience. That's what the peace process was all about.

A few months after this visit, Doug was set to be released from prison under the terms of the Good Friday Agreement, but following a short and highly publicised release, was sent back: 'Before I even got out, I was the only one prisoner that the British Government said "no, don't let him out, he's a danger." And they let me sweat for six weeks. And they referred to the

Secretary of State, it was her decision. Even before I was released they weren't letting me out.'

Doug was even asked to engage in a risk assessment process, however basic: 'I had to write a statement on a page of paper explaining why I wasn't a threat to society.' He regarded this as little more than a meaningless gesture that he says heralded 'a return' to prison. Doug described this as part of a move to keep him from public view due to fears of him undermining the peace process:

> The reasons for returning me . . . was for procuring weapons for distrib-
> uting weapons, membership, drug dealing. It's just a load of nonsense.
> But they were getting their so-called intelligence from informants. They
> couldn't bring these informants as witnesses, so therefore the intelligence
> that they had against me to show to the Commission was held *in camera*.
> I couldn't get to see it. My solicitor couldn't get to see it. So I was in a
> no-win situation. So they revoked my [release] licence. It was just another
> form of illegal internment, but it was part of the Good Friday Agreement.
> I was 100% behind the peace process. And I knew then it was only
> someone 'mixing'.

Doug steadfastly believes that a conspiracy, this 'mixing', was constructed to keep him 'off the streets and locked up in jail':

> Someone was pretending that I wanted to wreck the peace process. Just
> to get me kept in jail, so it had to be either a very, very high, well-placed
> informant, or someone on the outside who didn't want me released. And
> whose word was gospel to the security forces, who, when he spoke, he
> spoke with authority. If you know what I mean. His words were taken as
> gospel. But I wasn't against the peace process; I was 100% for it. The
> Chief Constable needs intelligence. The Chief Constable can't just wake
> up and say, *you know what, Doug's gonna do this*. It could be informants,
> it could be listening devices, it could be a combination of anything, but
> the fact that it's held in camera proves to me that it's informants, that
> they can't bring them out, they can't reveal their identity, for their own
> safety. And things have been said . . . Remember the Chief Constable
> also said after the Omagh bomb, *intelligence is not evidence*. And I also
> threw that back to them, when they were holding me. *I remind you, Chief
> Constable, what you said during the aftermath of the Omagh bombing.
> Intelligence is not evidence. So how come you got me lying here in prison,
> and yet of all, you don't have the Omagh bombers? And yet you're saying to
> the public, you know who they are? But intelligence is not evidence.*

The high-placed informant Doug believes spoke 'with authority' to the police was a man who would subsequently become a UDA leader and Doug believes 'wanted me out of the way'.

In order to appreciate the context of Doug's return to prison, it is important to understand developments within the UDA at the time of his re-imprisonment. Since 2000 the UDA degenerated into a movement torn apart by territorial jealousies, competition over the proceeds of organised crime and continued differences over political aspirations and loyalties. Jealousies, bitter rivalries and a series of personality clashes conspired to see the UDA kick Doug out in 2002 for his efforts to form an alliance with another Loyalist group, the Loyalist Volunteer Force (LVF). Some viewed Doug's efforts as an attempt to consolidate his power and influence over the combined Loyalist command.

With Doug in and out of prison during this time, the UDA began its housekeeping in earnest and the remnants of his unit were systematically dismantled. Since Doug's eventual departure to Britain, all of those who have pledged allegiance to Doug have been left alienated and at risk.

I asked Doug to explain, in his terms, the nature of the 'deep-rooted divide in the Loyalist movement' and the internecine feuding that for years had torn the UDA apart, and contributed to his isolation and disenfranchisement. He paints a picture of conspiracy, internal rivalries and intense jealousy. Specifically, the root of this he believes was the lack of shared purpose within the organisation during the peace process:

I'll tell you what I believe. During the conflict, we were all united, because there was only one common enemy. And that was all Republican. During the ceasefires, there became no common enemy. The IRA was on cease-fire, so Republicans weren't killing our people, so therefore Loyalists had no one to fight with. So as the peace sped on and on and on, and it turned to three years, four years, five years, the jealousies overtook, and that's when the infighting started. Jealousies over everything. Jealousy is a poison. It sits within every human being. If someone's good at something, other people in the movement will be jealous. When I said something, I delivered. And that just made the rest of the UDA jealous. And again, I would say that the British . . . the dirty tricks they had their fingerprints all over it too. Because British Intelligence, they want peace and they want peace to last forever. And British Intelligence used the strategy of divide and conquer. There's no more Republican and Loyalists fighting, so when you get rid of all these evil people in the paramilitaries who are running about for years killing people, saying *it's for a cause, so we need these people to go away*, and the best way of doing it is by using their own people to do it. And I've no doubt in my mind that there's informers at the highest levels of the ladder. Right down to the bottom of the ladder. And that still as we speak, there's still inform-ers at the highest levels of the UDA, UFF, IRA and have used informers to create a situation . . . to choreograph a situation which has happened in the last four or five years, which has Loyalists feuding after feuding after feuding. And one person they singled out was me. They tried to paint a picture that I was mad and they needed to get rid of this nutcase. And they done it. In a devious, treacherous way.

I asked Doug to explain the root of the perceived jealousy from the other Loyalist leaders and why this appeared to be such a strong element in his involuntary movement away from the UDA:

> During the ceasefires, the Loyalists tried to capitalise on the gains, the kinds of gains made by Sinn Fein and the Provos. They tried to, and this was one of the reasons they turned on me. I backed my colleague . . . for a meeting to go and meet with the then Lord Mayor [of Belfast], Alec Maskey, who was Sinn Fein, in the interests of peace and stability and the interfaces. They slaughtered us for doing so. I was meeting nationalists. I mean, I was reaching out and these people [the UDA leadership] didn't like it. They were jealous. And what were *they* doing? These people were wannabes. Now, they feel that they can be wannabes in the middle of a peace process, because they don't have to go to jail. They don't feel they have to take risks. And all they had to do is discredit through and through loyalists.

Doug was asked to explain how he felt at the 'betrayal' that saw 'my own movement turn its back on me' for taking such initiative. He became angry and agitated in his response:

> I never sold out. I fought *my* war, right? I fought *my* war. I took bullets in the head, bullets in the back. Sixteen years in prison. I took intimidation from the intelligence services, right through from the Special Branch to MI5, to the RUC who treated me, my family like Nazis for many, many years. But I was over 21, I knew what I was doing. Accepted it. 'Cos at the end of the day, what were these people getting? F*** all. Once the peace process came, I was saying to these people, look, listen it's people like me who've been there done it worn the t-shirt. I've seen the blood and guts. I've had friends murdered. I've had friends' legs blown to pieces. Give peace a chance for God's sake. People like myself, we're the ones saying give it a chance.

I asked Doug if, given this, he felt that there was any political voice for the UDA:

> The UDA is a criminal organisation. What direction do they have? What political brains do they have? Again jealousies . . . go back to this man [RM – the current UDA leader, and the person Doug believes is behind the alleged conspiracy to isolate him]. I truly believe he is an agent provocateur. You go back to Jimmy Craig, and the [RM] era. John McMichael had brains. Military brains. Military brains and he had

political brains. What happened to him? *Boom – get rid of him.* Set up by his own people. Now, the IRA killed him, but he was set up from within. Now, in recent years, with Davey Adams, and McMichael's son, and John White. There were the three most sensible people we had, politically, in the organisation. Where are they? Discredited. Why? Because [RM] was jealous. And that's the whole history of the UDA. Because they're that thick and daft that they can't even see what's happening. He is one jealous man.

Doug's disagreements with his former colleagues, and [RM] in particular, were acrimonious and well publicised in Northern Ireland. He remains steadfast in his belief that the senior UDA commander, the 'jealous man' is 'getting his strings pulled'.

I know this. Look, Ray Smallwoods in Belfast was murdered. He was set up. I was there. I know who does what and who did what. Jealousies. I've been there, I've seen them. If you're *good*, either the intelligence services don't like you, or the movement itself doesn't like you. Because they're jealous, and then it's *boom – you're outta here.* Six feet under or prison. [RM] was just selling us all out. Who's left there? What people . . . none of these people . . . any men that I fought alongside on the battlefield. Where are they? They're all gone, they're all stomped on, they're all treaded on. It's without a doubt a problem from within Loyalism, but it's been choreographed and controlled by British Intelligence. At the time when I was there, at the time when I was being left alone by people like [RM], look at the commitment I got from the Volunteers when I was there. 'Cos the Volunteers believed that they had a good leader. And if they didn't believe in me, we wouldn't have been as successful as we were. Look I'm not trying to blow my own trumpet, but I was the best military leader that organisation ever had. And I hate to put Big John McMichael down and all, but facts speak louder than words. And the statistics are there. I mean I fought that war. I was credited with bringing the war to the IRA. That came at a high price, but I did it. I was prepared to lead, I couldn't be bought by the Special Branch. They tried it, but it wouldn't work. I couldn't be mentally broke, and I couldn't be physically broke. I was prepared to bring in recruit after recruit after recruit, and was prepared to arm the organisation with sophisticated weaponry. Assault rifles, rocket launchers. And was prepared to lead daring attacks on Sinn Fein. Not just ordinary Catholics, but everyone, [up] to the leadership of the IRA.

Though Doug is bitter and acrimonious towards his former comrades, he displays a distinctly triumphalist view of his own achievements. Though he has been isolated, he sees enormous pride in his actions during the Troubles, and those under his command.

Fearing a Loyalist feud rising to new levels of violence, the security services in Northern Ireland successfully argued that returning Doug to prison could only be a short-term move, and that he would eventually have to be moved to England:

> I was in prison. The security forces were frightened that if I returned that obviously, trouble would brew again. So, at six o'clock one morning, they opened the prison cell. Two days before I was to get out, two days early, they came to get me. They made me put on a bulletproof jacket, they handcuffed me, made me put a big helmet on my head, and took me out into a military helicopter. They put me into a helicopter and took me to ****. I had no say in the matter. They said it was for my own safety. My intentions for the minute I got out was to go back to the Shankill. And this frightened, obviously, the UDA, and indeed the security forces, who in turn handcuffed me, flew me across the Irish Sea and put me to ****.

Now living in Scotland, Doug misses life in his former home and laments not being able to return to Northern Ireland to 'reap the benefits of peace', but acknowledges the imminent probability of risk should he return. Ever defiant, he explains that he does not fear reprisals:

> I dedicated a big part of my life to fight and maintain our Britishness, and to try and prevent the IRA from slaughtering all our people. Well, now there's peace there, I'm not getting the chance to benefit from it. I'm constantly at risk. I'm under a death threat right now from them. But I don't fear those people. Again, I was the headmaster. I know their strengths and I know their weaknesses. If the police come and tell me that my life's in danger, well I will know if someone's coming to kill me, but I don't fear death. If I had feared death, I wouldn't have been the leader I was. But my belief is, *what's for you, will not go past you*. If I was meant to die already, I'd have died a long time ago. Who knows? But if you worry about it, you won't get your job done. And had I worried about dying during the conflict, then I wouldn't have been the leader. I would have lost confidence in the men around me, so therefore I wouldn't have been as successful as I was.

Though he describes having 'settled in ok', the move has not been without challenges:

> What has happened to me in the last couple of years . . . it wasn't easy. It was a different way of life. I've been kept busy with my autobiography, and two documentaries. That's kept me really busy. But it doesn't take away from the fact that politics are ongoing back home. I've had no difficulties settling in here. I'm barred in every pub, but that's no big deal

to me. Don't get me wrong, I'd rather I wasn't barred in every pub. The cops go around and indirectly blackmail all the pub owners not to serve me. So they don't serve me. I can't force them to serve me. The drug squad have been around to my house once, ah, but they were always going to do that, just to let me know that they knew that I was here. I lost my licence for drunk driving. Well I shouldn't have been drunk driving. But other than that, there's been no problem. I've had a normal life and it's been great. And I just sit back, and there's not a day goes by that something different happens to those guys over there. I *hate* them for what they've done. I *hate* them, and they haven't gotten away with what they've gotten away with. They have caused hurt. They've killed. They've killed children. They've killed friends close to me. They've maimed, mentally scarred family and friends of mine. And I will never forget that.

Doug adamantly stressed his plan to one day return to Northern Ireland. He stresses he still enjoys 'plenty of support', but that the current UDA leadership have effectively stifled any local support for Doug and his followers:

I can tell you for a fact, if anyone came out in support of us right now in Belfast, within minutes they would be taken away and severely beaten. The Loyalist community is intimidated. They are frightened of these people. They are just bully boys and thugs. They can't speak out against them. It's mob rule, they're drunks and thugs now. The IRA are that bit more disciplined, and I think would respect their community a bit more.

Interim conclusions

Doug proved a difficult and challenging interviewee. Though nervous, he would constantly change topic and speak at literally every opportunity about his disgust towards his former colleagues in the UDA leadership. Though from a security perspective, Doug's exile has seen any potential threat from him 'contained', he remains in an unusual position. The decision to include Doug's case here, however, was due to the circumstances that surround his current situation. Having been involuntarily disengaged from the UVF through an unceremonious departure from Northern Ireland, Doug is on the one hand a former terrorist in search of a new role and a new identity. At the time of the interview, however, he remained without any such role and without a voice.

Doug's case is a striking illustration of Hirschman's[1] theory of loyalty in organisational settings. In examining exit from firms, Hirschman suggests that members with considerable attachments to the organisation will often search for 'ways to make himself influential, especially when the organisation moves in what he believes is the wrong direction' (pp77–8). Doug has struggled to do this, being 'sidelined' from the UDA upon what he argues were 'genuine' attempts to reach out to Nationalists. Though Doug emphasises the loyalty of his fellow UFF members, he has attracted followers in his place of exile only due to the fact that they themselves are exiled members of his terrorist group that would, like Doug, face persecution from former colleagues if they return to Northern Ireland.

That he held such a senior command position, in addition to the unwavering belief in his own 'loyalty' and 'successes' both in waging a terrorist campaign as well as 'doing what needed to be done to secure peace' has only contributed to Doug's anger at being isolated. Equally frustrating for Doug is the fact that he cannot channel his loyalty into anything else. There is no organisation available to him and equally no clear political role in the absence of the conflict.

He has been productive since leaving Northern Ireland and regularly appears on television and in the press media to speak about his experiences. He is exceptionally anxious to return to Northern Ireland, but finds it impossible to speak about his desire to 'reap the rewards of peace' without simultaneously (though discretely) highlighting the fact that he continues to outlive his former comrades, who he wants to see 'get what's coming to them'. On more than one occasion, Doug expresses his satisfaction that 'not a day goes that something different happens to them'. Given not only Doug's past role, but particularly given the circumstances of the internecine feuding that led to Doug fleeing Northern Ireland, it is clear that his return to Northern Ireland would raise very significant security concerns.

In speaking about the firm, Hirschman argues that a member who 'wields considerable power in an organisation and is therefore convinced he can get it "back on the track"' is likely to develop a strong affection for the organisation in which he is powerful' (p78). In some ways, this issue lies at the heart of the security concerns that surround Doug's potential return to Northern Ireland and raises the question about whether or not he would make efforts to regain some position of power in the local community in which he once reigned. Doug is explicit about his desire to return, but is unclear in what capacity:

> I just take each day as it comes. I'm an extraordinary person who's lived an extraordinary life. Why shouldn't I return? What would I do? There's no role for me but to put my feet up and enjoy the peace. There's no role in the community for me. The way I look at it, it's the politicians. It's in the hands of Paisley, McGuinness and his cohorts. Let them stick with it. They've done a good job up to now. And it's amazing how far they've come without bickering and stopping and stalling. So there's no longer room for the [Dougs] of this world.

Despite his protestations, he remains closely monitored by the security services both in Northern Ireland and in Britain. He is aware of what he feels will be a strong effort to 'put obstacles' to his return to Northern Ireland, irrespective of his public statements that his 'war is over':

I believe the IRA when they say that the war is over. Yes, absolutely I do indeed. The fact that there's no shootings and no bombings. The fact that nobody is being killed. That convinces me, 'cos that was my whole reason for being in the organisation. It was to try to prevent the IRA from killing, and bombing our people. It's not happening now. So am I convinced? Absolutely. Grudgingly I respect them, but they're sincere. And they have been for quite a number of years now. I think the IRA is a bit like me. Their war is over. I think they're clever enough to realise, that with me, there was nothing personal. It was strictly business. I was trying to do unto them as they were doing unto me. I was fighting a cause as they were fighting a cause. Their cause is over, so there's nothing in them doing anything to me. Don't get me wrong. It's still segregated over there. The most important aspect of it all is that the bomb and the bullet are now suppressed. That was the most important thing.

Doug's case raises obvious questions about the challenges posed by efforts aimed at reintegrating former terrorists into the societies that they claimed to once represent. It is unlikely that Doug would seek to return to Northern Ireland to enjoy anything less than the recognition he feels he has been deprived of and (as above) raises questions about whether or not he would be a risk to the security of Northern Ireland if allowed to return. He reiterated in detail that he is 'aware' that his disengagement served both the interests of the security services in Northern Ireland as well as the current UDA leader [RM]:

It's very simple. [RM] got rid of me at the behest of the Branch. I'm not stupid, I know how it works. I've been through it for years and years and years. I know how the dirty tricks work. I'm not the most intelligent person, but I'm streetwise and cunning. I ran that war for years and years and years. And I was up against the best. The Brits had the greatest police force in the world, and the best guerrilla terrorist organisation in the world, the IRA. And I'll still survive for many, many years. So what do they do? They bring you down. [They] knew what they were doing when they jailed me, and isolated me.

Doug is not under constant surveillance by the security forces since relocating to Scotland. He is aware that he may not be able to return to Northern Ireland for a long time and is equally aware of the perception that exists of him as having a 'score' to settle with the UDA leadership. Though insistent that he does not pose a threat to peace in the region, Doug's intentions towards his former comrades remain ambiguous.

In the following chapter, we consider a very different kind of leader, though with a striking similarity to the case of Doug. Like Doug, Omar Bakri Mohammed lives in exile, is without a clear role that he too appears to be in search of, and his case also poses difficult challenges for assessing whether or not he poses a threat to security.

8 'I don't believe in integration'

Introduction

Shortly after the Al Qaeda attacks of 11 September 2001, Britain began to face the challenge of confronting radical and extremist movements. Reaching its pinnacle with four coordinated suicide bombings on 7 July 2005, tensions between 'Islam' and 'the West' developed into a protracted and heated debate about the role of Islam in politics and society in the West. In September 2005, tensions increased further with the publication in several European newspapers of cartoons of the Prophet Mohammed. By this time, however, some of the faces of radical Islam were already public names in Britain. Among the most prominent were the former Imam of London's Finsbury Park Mosque, Egyptian-born Abu Hamza al-Masri, Jordanian Abu Qatada and Syrian-born Omar Bakri Mohammed. For many in Britain, these three individuals in particular came to represent the public face of Al Qaeda.

Omar Bakri appeared prominently in the British media, warning that Britain would face its own 9/11 if it failed to amend its destructive foreign policies. Though denying a direct Al Qaeda link, Omar Bakri has been associated in one form or another with a number of individuals charged with terrorist offences such that it is widely believed that 'every al-Qaeda operative recently arrested or identified in Europe had come into contact with Bakri at some time or other.'[1]

Though long recognised as an influential figure, Omar Bakri came to the increased attention of domestic and international security services shortly after the 1998 bombings by Al Qaeda of US embassies in Kenya and Tanzania. The bombings marked the beginning of Osama Bin Laden's shift to Al Qaeda's targeting of the 'Far Enemy'. Omar Bakri released public statements on behalf of Bin Laden shortly after the incidents.[2]

Bakri is a figure whom many associate with contradictory and exclusively self-serving views. He is also a role model for many young disaffected Muslims in search of a political identity, such that despite being exiled, he continues to attract new followers from around the globe. He has publicly declared his support for Osama Bin Laden, yet at the same time has spoken against specific incidents carried out by Al Qaeda. Speaking about the events of 9/11, Omar Bakri announced: 'If Islamists did it – and most likely it is Islamists, because of the nature of what happened – then they have fully misunderstood the teachings of Islam . . . Even the most radical of us have condemned this. I am always considered to be a radical in the Islamic world and even I condemn it.'[3] At the same time, Bakri was cited widely by the BBC for 'praising the 9/11 hijackers as the *magnificent 19.*'[4] These seeming contradictions are not unlike those expressed (though more subtly) by the other 'Omar' in Chapter 5.

To many, Bakri has 'long been regarded as little more than a loudmouth',[5] yet the perception that he ought to be categorised as either 'an irritant' or 'a threat'[6] reflects a failure to understand the significance and complexity of his unusual position. Perhaps most obviously known for helping develop Hizbut Tahrir (HT) in the United Kingdom before leaving HT to form his own movement, *Al Muhajiroun* (subsequently disbanded in 2004), Omar Bakri, not unlike Doug from our previous chapter, is an individual keen to reach a role he feels is both warranted and important. While Doug is unclear about what that role might entail, Omar Bakri is more explicit about his aspirations.

Meeting Omar Bakri Mohammed

Omar Bakri Mohammed was born Omar Bakri Fostok in 1958 in Syria.[7] Born into a wealthy family, he studied at an Islamic boarding school and joined the Syrian branch of the Muslim Brotherhood in 1972.[8] In 1977, he left Syria after being wanted for Brotherhood membership. It is believed by many that this is because of his alleged participation in a revolt against President Hafez Assad, though this, he protests, is 'completely untrue'. He moved to Beirut where he joined the Hizbut Tahrir movement. Two years later, Omar Bakri left Beirut and went to Cairo where he attended Al-Azhar University for six months. In December of that year he moved yet again, this time to Saudi Arabia, where he studied at the Islamic school of Al-Saltiyah. Hizb-ut-Tahrir did not enjoy much support in Saudi Arabia and four years later Omar Bakri established Al Muhajiroun (AM) on 3 March 1983 (the 59th anniversary of the fall of the Ottoman Caliphate) as a reaction to the lack of support for HT in the Kingdom.

Omar Bakri had by this point attracted 'about 50 followers'. In early 1984, the Saudi Arabian authorities arrested him for 'subversive activities'. Al Muhajiroun members had been distributing stickers and leaflets, denouncing the Saudi royal family. Unable to prove a direct AM link, however, Omar Bakri was released on bail. His release was short-lived. He was rearrested when the Saudi authorities ascertained that Omar Bakri was teaching from a 'subversive text' (written by HT leader Abdul Kaleem Zaloum). Omar Bakri was sent to the al-Malaz detention centre, where he was tortured for seven days.

In January 1986, Omar Bakri moved to the United Kingdom. It was there he played a major role in the development of HT in Britain. He became HT's de facto spiritual leader, following a brief sojourn to the United States where he studied English.

During the mid–late 1990s, Omar Bakri became a regular public speaker in Britain. In 1996 Omar Bakri left HT as a result of disagreements over policies, ideologies and methods. He subsequently declared 'independence' for Al Muhajiroun in the United Kingdom. He also made plans to hold a 'Rally for Islamist Revival'. The proposed meeting was expected to serve as a call to Islamic leaders, but was cancelled following intense scrutiny from the British Home Office.

Despite this, from 1996–1999, Omar Bakri rose to prominence and in his role as chief figure in the 'International Islamist Front', supported the call of Muslims to go to fight in the Balkans and in Chechnya. The Front was the political voice of the 'International Islamist Front for Jihad Against Jews and Crusaders led by Osama Bin Laden'. Bakri explains that he called on British Muslims to go to Bosnia and Kosovo for what he described as 'humanitarian reasons'. Though originally denying a link with Osama Bin Laden, Omar Bakri received a fax from Bin Laden in 1996 announcing Bin Laden's now infamous 'fatwa'. This was subsequently published in the London-based *Al Quds al Arabi* newspaper.

In 2001, following the events of 11 September, Omar Bakri became a household name in Britain. After holding a series of public meetings judged to be supportive of Al Qaeda, Bakri became a hate figure. In 2002, on the first anniversary of 9/11, he participated in a conference organised by Abu Hamza al-Masri to form the 'Islamic Council of Britain', whose stated objective was to promote the establishment of sharia law in Britain. In 2004, Omar Bakri disbanded Al Muhajiroun, declaring that all Muslims should unite as one against 'the West'.

He left the UK, taking up what he thought would be temporary residence in Lebanon shortly after it was alleged in the British press that members of AM were involved in the 7 July bombings in London. Omar Bakri was quickly refused re-entry into the United Kingdom by the Home Office, having been deemed a threat to national security. He now resides in Lebanon, from where he delivers nightly Internet broadcasts to thousands of followers around the world.

I met with Omar Bakri in Beirut and Tripoli. His life history is long and complicated and well beyond the scope of a single chapter. Though his progression into and out of several distinct Islamist movements represents an equally complicated story of disengagement and re-engagement, this case was chosen in particular because of its relevance to understanding the issue of de-radicalisation. Though a highly cooperative interviewee, interviewing Omar Bakri proved challenging. His responses to questions were very lengthy and often labyrinthine. He drew on a wide array of historical, religious and cultural references to illustrate his arguments, and many of his responses to questions, even seemingly brief questions, ran to several minutes. Additionally, and though both intellectual and lengthy, his responses were often telegraphic in nature. He would move with ease from one point to another and minutes later answer the original question.

Yet, attempting to abridge or edit his responses seems inappropriate and unfair. The semi-structured interview proved to be insufficiently structured and not formal enough to encourage the kinds of answers elicited from other interviewees. What follows, therefore, is a different kind of interview. Rather than interrupt the flow of the responses made with theme summaries, the interview is reflected upon in a section to follow at the end.

It became apparent early in the development of the Bakri case that one of the many distinguishing features is the fact that this is an individual who is heavily engaged in a variety of different kinds of activities. In some ways, it may be challenging to attribute the label of 'terrorist' to Omar Bakri – on the one hand, he is a rare case of a genuine 'true believer', a radical preacher whose activities are more appropriately characterised as subversion short of terrorism. Though his principles are consistent with Al Qaeda's global doctrine, he closely adheres to differences in interpretation in the perceived legitimacy of what is permissible in the pursuit of political Islamism. He does not condemn violence in the name of Islam, but has specific views about the appropriateness of where precisely that violence is legitimately expressed. He remains an influential figure in what he calls the 'radical Jihadi community'.

Omar Bakri cuts a defensive pose. He views himself as being unfairly expelled from the United Kingdom and was angry when recalling the circumstances that led to his expulsion. He sees himself as victimised by the British Government and a casualty of the British security services: 'My son was watched by the police for bringing me money. I cannot get a job here in Lebanon, and my supporters they raise money. I don't need a lot. They cannot send it to me, so I asked my son to bring it. He was stopped at Heathrow by the police and MI5, and they took the money. My son was allowed to come, but no money.'

He is extremely bitter about this, and offered a tentative warning to the UK authorities: 'If they harm my son, there is no limit to what I would be willing to do to them. It would break my covenant of security with them.' The event with Omar Bakri's son took place on 24 October 2006 when British police stopped him at Heathrow Airport. They seized over twelve thousand pounds under the Proceeds of Crime Act.

Throughout the interview, he claims that the reason for increased violent radicalisation in the United Kingdom is due to the actions of the British Government who, in his words, 'made them go underground'. In particular, a theme that emerges throughout the interviews is that Bakri views himself as a figure with great potential to control radicalisation among young people, and a lost 'opportunity' for the 'British community': 'I can control people. I can get into their hearts.' Similar (though slightly different in focus) to the distinctions made by the other Omar in Chapter 5, a particular distinction made by Bakri is between what he views as 'legitimate' violent Jihadist activity and 'terrorism'. The former he cites examples from Bosnia, Afghanistan and Iraq – the 'expelling of the crusaders'. While he does not provide an example of 'terrorism', he implicitly equates a negative judgement with any attempt to 'subvert the covenant of security'.

The covenant of security is a concept that is central to the way in which Omar Bakri views the world and the boundaries of social relations between Muslims and non-Muslims in particular countries. To illustrate, Omar Bakri says that he pledges allegiance to Osama Bin Laden in his 'global fight against the crusaders and enemies of Islam'. At the same time, he is explicit in his departure from any potential move by Bin Laden to subvert the 'covenant of security'. He explains: 'The covenant of security can take many forms. Visas, being a student, even having a driving licence. Even income support. How can you take income support in Britain and say there that their life has no sanctity? That's completely out of order. It is my job to condemn man-made law, but it doesn't mean something else.'

The origins of the covenant of security concept, Bakri explained, derive from a story of how the companions of the Prophet Mohammed were given protection by a country and subsequently agreed not to attack the inhabitants of the country in return. To Omar Bakri, because he availed of a 'covenant' with Britain, engaging in violent Jihad within the United Kingdom constitutes 'terrorism'. Engaging in violence to resist coalition troops in Afghanistan, however, is 'legitimate': 'I support the Taleban in their right to fight occupiers, but not their own state. That is a different story.'

The question of whether or not a breach in the covenant of security provides the automatic justification of terrorism within national borders, however, was unclear, and we return to this issue later.

On radicalisation

I began by asking Omar Bakri about how he understood the term 'radicalisation'. In his response, he was critical of the British Home Office for expelling him from the country, suggesting that: 'When I was in Britain, I was a force for stability. I was able to control the Muslim youth.' He believes that a failure to understand his 'potential' stemmed from a view in Britain that 'radicalism is bad':

> Radicalism is not something that is bad. I believe radicalism is an essential part of life. It's about going back to basics. If somebody starts to think about going back to basics, back to [exploring] the fundamental sources of his belief, I do not see anything wrong with it, especially as we see the direction the whole world is going.

The retreat to basics he describes as not 'going backward', but as a response to Western advances that threaten the security and stability of the broader Muslim world:

The Middle East in particular. The youth today, *they* see it. They hear what's going on around the world. They hear it on television, on radio. They see it on the television, on the Internet. They can really get the message clearly that there is aggression, there is oppression, there is *occupation*.

The nature and extent of this awareness, Omar Bakri argues, is significant as a risk factor in radicalisation in the context of what 'being a good Muslim' entails: 'They are part of a Muslim nation. This Muslim Brotherhood is always going to help each other. It will motivate you, and it is the driving force behind all actions, all behaviour.'

I asked Omar Bakri to explain the collective power of the *Brotherhood* and to identify how that collective power provides a source of motivation for action. He explains that this can only be understood with reference to the historical defeat of Muslims at the hands of the West. This, he argues, continues to reinforce a profound sense of humiliation and subjugation felt by Muslims:

When [Muslims] go back to find the root of these problems, and try to solve them fundamentally, this is when they become radical. The root of the problem, the root of the defeat, the root of the decline in the Muslim nation, certainly from the Golden Age of the Caliphate, the destruction of the Caliphate, 1924, the Ottoman Empire, when Muslims became fragmented into Arabs, Turks and so on. They became even more fragmented based on nationalism, based on tribalism and so on.

1924 heralded Ataturk's reforms seeing the modernisation of Turkey into a secular state. Significant for Omar Bakri is the linking of contemporary and historic events: 'There is no real difference. This is how I see it, and this is how radical Muslims will see it.' The superficial differences today, he suggests, are expressed through different crises that reflect the same underlying 'retreat' to fundamentals: 'All the issues that radicalise Muslim youth today, besides the old political issues are the hot crises. Bosnia, Kashmir, Chechnya, Palestine, then Afghanistan, then Iraq, then Somalia.'

He acknowledges, however, that being a 'radical' does not necessarily lead to violence as part of the retreat to 'fundamentals':

The question is, why do Muslims become involved in violence? This is the issue. Radicalism takes many types. When someone goes to try to find the fundamental source of Islam, and they try to find solutions [to contemporary problems], some try to preach those solutions to the people. To persuade them. I call them 'radical preachers'. They believe in *dawa*, the invitation.

Dawa is the issuance of a summons or invitation, and generally refers to the practice of encouraging Muslims to pursue piety in all aspects of their lives, basically the proselytisation of Islamic principles.

Omar Bakri draws a distinction between radical preachers who believe in *dawa* through 'persuasion' and those 'who believe in forcing others by using force'. These he terms 'radical Jihadis': 'That is the only difference between them. It looks like they both go back to the divine texts, and both of them look like they share the same beliefs, the same *rejection* of man-made law. But not the same methods. They are not the same.'

I asked Omar Bakri to explain, in his words, why the 'radical Jihadis' achieved such prominence. The answer to this, he suggests, lies with Western governments and in particular, Omar Bakri blames counter-terrorism legislation for the spread of 'radical Jihadis':

> I believe the new laws of terrorism, in Europe, were a big mistake. I am now far away from them, but I honestly believe this is the biggest mistake committed by Western powers. Before the London bombings, before the Madrid bombings, and to a certain extent before September 11, I think the strictness of the rules started to [contribute to] the uprising.

The main source of Bakri's discontent is with the Prevention of Terrorism Act 2005 (since updated to the Prevention of Terrorism Act 2006).[9] This was an Act of Parliament that formed part of rushed emergency legislation in the wake of the Al Qaeda attacks in the United States. In particular, the 2005 Act introduced the controversial 'control orders' for those suspected of involvement in terrorist activity. Essentially at the discretion of the British Home Secretary, control orders are potentially wide-ranging in scope and include provisions for placing restrictions on everything from association with particular individuals to being in a certain location, possessing specific articles (e.g. a cellphone) or access to specific facilities, such as the Internet. Control orders have been the source of intense controversy in the United Kingdom.

Omar Bakri interprets the Terrorism Act as a political attempt to stifle what he claims is genuine political dissent that the West is unable to manage: 'They [Western governments] find that there are new political parties, new parties active on university campuses, praising the ideology of Islam, calling for Islamic ideologies and for the Islamic state to be re-established, that they believe in the Islamic state, etc. etc.' In fact, Omar Bakri describes the ineffective application of the legislation as directly contributing to increased radicalisation among disaffected Muslims in the United Kingdom:

> Before 9/11 there were many restrictions being put on Islamic groups, and I [was] included in that, as I myself was Hizbut Tahrir you know, and Al Muhajiroun. However, what happened was that when they started to issue new laws of terrorism, I think that was a mistake because that will only play into the hands of Bin Laden. You have played into the hands of

Bin Laden because by radicalising, by *your* steps, and *your* policies. Remember radicalism works both ways. When *you*, the Western powers start to be more radical at home in dealing with Western youth, that will increase and increase and increase to the level where they start to become fundamentalist.

Bakri's argument raises two specific issues. He places the blame for the rise of radical Islam in the West at the doorstep of Western governments, and given this describes the emergence of fundamentalist Islam as an inevitable consequence. In addition, he implicitly suggests a distancing between himself and Osama Bin Laden, at least in this context. I asked Omar Bakri to explain the significance of referring to Bin Laden in this way, and particularly in light of what I suggested was an 'assumed view' that Bakri was a supporter of Bin Laden:

> Well, I am a radical preacher who is on the one hand pro-Mujahidin. I do look up to Sheikh Osama Bin Laden as a great leader. I do praise his activity. But I believe his role is to fight there [in Afghanistan]. But my role here is to struggle for the word of Islam. So we have two different battlefields. A *dawa* battlefield, the intellectual battlefield, and the violent battlefield. But to bring [violence] into *our* own battlefield is wrong. Because there is no way, Islamically, Osama Bin Laden can ever say to Muslim Britain, or to the West: *Fight!* Did you ever see Bin Laden do that? He can't. It is strictly forbidden to say *all people of the West, fight!* 'Go to your own people', 'pressure your own government', yes, but to all Muslims in Britain he never said *fight.*

The distinctions made by Omar Bakri might appear both self-serving and an attempt to harness support by positioning himself in a way that reflects the inability of Al Qaeda to harness its own desired level of support in the United Kingdom. In addition, given what Omar Bakri sees as oppression and subjugation of Islam by Western powers, however, it might be expected that turning from being a 'radical' to being violent is inevitable. He asserts a critical distinction here and returns to the concept of the covenant of security: 'Yes, they [Britain] reject our views, and they use the law against us, but I say *ok, we can live with it. We don't fight, we don't attack. We live under a covenant of security, Islam forbids us*, but I will still condemn British foreign policy.'

The 'covenant of security' is a concept that is critical to the extensive discourse around Britain's management of radical Islamists. Again, Omar Bakri reiterates: 'I support the Taleban in their right to fight occupiers, but not their own state. That is a different story.' In the period leading up to 2005, the British Government has been accused of being a soft touch in the management of radical preachers. The criticism has been that Britain believed that by granting a certain degree of public freedom to radical Islamic voices in the UK (e.g. supporting violent acts 'abroad') that this would prevent terrorist attacks from happening within the UK. If that assumption ever existed, it disappeared after the first Al Qaeda attacks in London in 2005.

Bakri was keen to make what he felt was an important distinction in order to clarify his position. He acknowledges explicitly that he pledges allegiance to Osama Bin Laden in his 'global fight against the crusaders and enemies of Islam', but explicitly disagrees with any move by Bin Laden to subvert the 'covenant of security'. According to Bakri, undermining the covenant of security is what will lead to terrorism within the UK.

Again, Bakri suggests that the covenant of security has been undermined by what he views as the British Government's attempt to stifle his attempts at engaging in 'dialogue': 'I think after these new laws, these new restrictions, there was an element in the Muslim community in Britain that devoted themselves to becoming radical Jihadis.' Bakri, defensively, states that he has been unfairly categorised in the same and resists an effort to conflate identities:

> But these people [the 'radical Jihadis'] always have Omar Bakri as a problem, I can tell you. Omar Bakri's groups are [seen as] a problem because Omar Bakri comes out with radical preachings. We call the Queen to Islam, openly, publicly, loudly proud. But we do so *without* fighting. You may say he's a dreamer, but this is not a problem as long as he doesn't use violence, correct? When I spoke with the youth, I used to be able to control them, to hold them back. You see, don't listen to what people say, or how we are portrayed. They [radical Jihadis] call on people to attack, to start a fight. *I* say, you cannot. Nobody is attacking you, you are here in Britain you can get income support, you can have a family here, so if you are arrested in a demonstration, it does not mean that there is a breach in your covenant of security. But those people do not believe that there is a covenant of security any more. They say it cannot exist because there is no Islamic state. *These* people are the most dangerous people living in the Islamic community.

In speaking about how he feels he was 'misunderstood', Bakri laments his exile and suggests that were he allowed return to the UK, that he would effectively be able to channel dissent away from violence. In speaking of would-be recruits to violent 'radical Jihadism', he explains:

> Obviously we don't know, ourselves, what they are planning. Where they are, what they are planning to do. But when they meet us in meetings . . . you know, from time to time, some individuals come into meetings and put their own ideas across. And obviously it's easy for us to answer them and explain to them rationally. And we can do this without labelling them, like *oh you are takfiri, oh you are this, oh you are that*. We explain to him rationally that he is wrong. And there is some very hot debate. He may issue a press release, he may label us in his own circuit. But when the

law started to be backdated, I think that is when the violation of the covenant of security started. I don't mind if they issue a new law and they say to me, *oh, Omar Bakri, you need to reform your speech now, you need to reform your stance, the law does not permit you blah blah blah*. I don't mind. I can deal with that. I can live with it. But when you start to say that this free speech is incitement of religious hatred, glorifying terrorism, I say *ok I can stop*.

The suggestion that Bakri would be able to effectively manage radical voices reflects an ongoing heated debate in the counter-terrorism community about how to engage radical Islamists and whether or not this can effectively undermine the nature and extent of violent radicalisation, rather than merely displace it.

Following the events of 7 July, such an approach with a figure like Omar Bakri would hardly find favour in the United Kingdom. Long before his departure from London, his actions there brought him to the attention of the security services. After the events of 9/11, his role in organising a series in particular brought him to the glare of the security services and the public at large. Advertising a meeting entitled 'The Magnificent 19', Bakri was accused of glorifying the 9/11 hijackers. He protests this and claims that the title 'Magnificent 19' was a ploy to draw in 'radical Jihadis' for debate:

My tactic was, on the second anniversary of 9/11, I held a conference about the ideas of history. I did something called 'The Magnificent 19'. In my conference a lot of people came. Even MI5 came to see what I said. All that happened was that I wanted people to come for me to speak about the causes of 9/11 and the effects. The causes and the effects. So the whole purpose of this advertising like this, is to make you come. And when I came there, in the end, at the end of the conference and I said, *by the way, Islam forbids operations like 9/11. Islam forbids that. It is an act of terrorism*.

Given the widespread notion that the event simply served to glorify terrorism, Bakri blames the media for their inability to 'carry the whole story and explain it':

MI5 was there, the police was there. I spoke to 2,000 people. That's why I have never been arrested. Because all that I did was advertise *The Magnificent 19*. Just like Robin Hood. He is still a thief in the end. The Magnificent 19 are terrorists, and I said in the end it is *not* allowed to happen. The Magnificent 19, the Fantastic 4 [referring to the 7 July 2005 bombings], this is a *technique*. This is a way of advertising to attract people to come. I was the biggest obstacle in the way of the radical Jihadis. I was the biggest stone in front of them. But when they started to backdate the laws, we were never going to be safe. I don't mind if they make a new law. I will reform my speech, but you don't tell me, *by the way, you said so and so two years ago. It is illegal and we are going to arrest you for it.*

Omar Bakri is aware of and knowledgeable about attempts at creating 'voice' within the broader Islamic community in the context of condemning terrorism, but is suspicious of efforts to engage young disaffected radicals through the widespread efforts to empower 'moderate Muslims'. The problem, he argues, is that the wrong people were chosen for this role:

> I think [the government]. I think they were convinced that the British moderate Muslims are really more in control of the youth. But later they will only discover that these people control nothing more than their own business, their own pockets. They are just businessmen. The Muslim Council of Britain, they are a bunch of businessmen. A bunch of old men. I think it was a big mistake of the Security Service not to invest in radical preachers, to keep their functions.

Naturally, Omar Bakri views himself as one of the radical preachers he feels should have seen such 'investment'. The rationale he offers is attractive. On the one hand, his assertion speaks to a similar sentiment as expressed by Chapter 5's 'Omar'. Having been radicalised to the point of imminent engagement in terrorist activity, Chapter 5's Omar feels that this has given him the credibility needed to reach 'the youth'.

It is difficult to see, however, a similar role for Omar Bakri Mohammed given the widespread condemnation he has received from his proclamations in Britain. I asked him to elaborate on what kind of role, in specific terms, he would be able to offer and what function this role would have in helping solve the problem of violent radicalisation. He suggests he would:

> Keep the wheel turning, keep, you know, watching them. I could have defused many of the plots that could have existed. I channelled my own anger in talks, in demonstrations, in circles. But the media always put me on the defensive position. You see, what they say, *you're either with us or you are with them.* And now I can't be independent? *No, you can't be independent.* The youth get radicalised anyway. Not just by the pictures, by the media, but by the Internet. They have no other mechanism to turn to. So now they turn to *Sheikh Google, Sheikh Yahoo.* They find a Fatwa, they find a verdict suitable for Iraq and Afghanistan and believe it to be true for it to apply to Britain also. They don't trust moderate Muslims. My own humble analysis is that the youth have been turned away. They have been turned away from demonstrations, away from picketing, speaking out, and coming out. So they go underground, they start to plot things, and this last thing I was shocked to hear. Shocked. The doctors. That is serious business, serious business. I was surprised. They tried to

link them to Al Muhajiroun, but I think the British intelligence are bigger than that.

'The doctors' refers to the attempted suicide car bombing attack on Glasgow Airport as well as the attempted bombing of a London nightclub in June 2007. Omar Bakri recalls being 'shocked' and 'surprised' at the attempted bombings. I suggested to him that this seemed at odds with his belief that Al Qaeda was attracting more and more followers in the United Kingdom, and (in his words), because of the 'drastic' legislation aimed at curbing 'the right to speak'. In responding, Bakri explains that the root of his surprise is reflected in what he calls a change in the radical Jihad scene in the UK. Unlike previous plots, where individual members were traced back to one or more radical movements in the UK:

> The men as far as I know were not members of any radical organisation. The media portrayed us all that we were one big radical bogeyman. Now it's someone else who is the bogeyman. But *how* were they recruited? *How* were they convinced about it? We don't know. It's not about just going to some trip, to a picnic. It's about blowing themselves up, attacking the centre of London. How did this happen? There is no way to get that kind of training [in the UK]. [The media] said that they learn from the alternative media, the Internet, how to do a bombing and so on. I don't believe so. You can watch a hundred tapes on how to do a bombing on the Internet, but you never attempt to do it yourself. There is *always* somebody who is well trained who will pass it on. So that is the big question, *how* these people came to be. They must be either trained [abroad] at least one of them, to do everything for the others, because the others don't do anything. The others just press a button, do you understand? But definitely they have the zeal, the will, the concept, the conviction.

Bakri explains that one role for him as a legitimate radical preacher is broader than providing an 'angry' voice for disaffected Muslim youth, thereby displacing an attempt to walk towards terrorism. He spoke at length of his ability to provide an 'ability to reform', and emphasised how political attempts to address the causes of Muslim disaffection in Britain have not only failed, but provided a further impetus for violent radicalisation. A major force for this, he argued, is in a misguided debate about 'integration':

> I can't declare I could have stopped [the airport plot]. Because I was there and I could not stop 7/7. Some things are beyond anybody's capability to stop, but reforming the youth is easy. *But* you must be honest. You [must] keep telling them Islam forbids evil. But look, you must realise that we do *not* integrate. This is impossible. [The West] will lose because every single verse of the Qu'uran speaks about living, co-existing, but not integrating.

> We are never going to believe in isolationism, but we are never also going to believe in integration. I believe in interaction. Co-existing. Live and let other people live. Discuss, debate, condemn, contest. Intellectually, rationally. Debate. Sometimes Islamic speech has different styles of communication. It could be in the form of condemnation, in demonstrations, in university campuses, in relationships, in having food together. But if you say to them *integrate*, you are going to find people going underground.

Differences in terminology here reflect a critical issue and one that has escaped analysis in the context of involvement in violent political activity. The use of language remains poorly understood, particularly in light of how ideologies essentially provide a framework for viewing the world and a context to one's own actions. Engaging in debate about ideological issues, however, and the recognition of the use of language as a mobilising tool for violent radicalisation lies at the heart of a variety of 'dialogue' initiatives. Perhaps the most obvious parallel to Omar Bakri's claim to effect 'reform' are similar efforts via Yemen's Committee for Dialogue initiative. Bakri acknowledges the Yemeni efforts but offers a familiar warning about the appropriateness of those who 'run' such programmes:

> In order to be successful, you have got to have the right people. People who can enter the heart of the youth. The elders in Britain, I can tell you. They used to condemn extremism publicly but they also used to support us. They call us extremist in the media, in spite of the support we have. When they put us in prison they create heroes for us. They create martyrs for us. You create people that are going to come out from prison that are going to be the future leaders. Before it is too late, those youths should not in any way be squeezed. *Let* them come out. *Let* them speak out. *Monitor* them. Let them always abide by law and order, but do *not* tell them, they are allowed to do so and so and *then* charge them for it.

Bakri acknowledged that there are ongoing attempts to challenge the legitimacy of 'terrorists' and to provide alternative, competing voices of authority to divert violent radical sentiments. In particular, he acknowledges the role of former members of Al Muhajiroun and Hizbut Tahrir. These groups have seen a number of former members publicly declare a role for themselves in countering violent radicalisation. Of these individuals, however, Omar Bakri is dismissive and cites what he views as problems with their 'personal ambition'.

The problem of who precisely constitutes 'the right people' is an issue that arose time and time again. I asked Bakri about one self-proclaimed former Jihadist from Hizbut Tahrir in particular:

> [He] is a bluffer. I remember every single man from Hizbut Tahrir, but

[this man] does not know me. He *says* he knows me. He makes his name off the back of our movement. In the last few months before I left, the level of radicalisation from preaching and *dawa* to go forward to jihad and fighting became widespread. It really became widespread in the Muhajiroun organisation.

I asked Omar Bakri about his understanding of the term de-radicalisation, and he responded with a reference to his earlier thoughts about his potential role:

Reformation is a better term. Our job is to bring them back and reform them. Get them back to being a good Muslim, reform them about how to address Islam with non-Muslims. You may be offended, for them directly speaking out, and they may use strong words in the place of violence.

The alternative, Bakri explains, is illustrated through the attempted bombings in 2007:

If you are really a terrorist, you know, I don't think you are going to go to demonstrations. The last thing you see in demonstrations are terrorists. It's impossible. I strongly believe the cell who was functioning in Britain now [2007] are existing since a long time ago. A *long* time ago. There are well-established cells operating in the UK. But they are not Hizbut Tahrir. They are not Al Muhajiroun. We do not know them. These people exist, I believe, since even before 9/11. I believe they existed still before the Tanzania and Kenya bombings. Libyans, Algerians, Iraqis ... They have been there, doing a lot. Raising funds, helping from abroad. And for them, *we* ourselves were the obstacle.

Bakri is under no illusions as to the difficulty in him being accepted as a 'reformer'. In this context, I asked him to explain the basis of his credibility to 'radical Jihadis'. He argues that his legitimacy within the radical community derives from remaining steadfast on the very issues he claims have caused his expulsion from Britain:

For me, I condemn killing innocent people in general. I can't condemn the four men [the 7 July bombers], do you understand? Because they have their own interpretation, and they are entitled to that interpretation. If I brought myself to condemn other people's *interpretations*, I'm just firing on myself. How can I reform the youth of radical jihad if I condemn them? I condemn the *act* of terrorism, killing innocents. Islam forbids that. But, full stop. Any more than that is not my business. They say, *oh you should report this to the police.* No! I will never report anyone to the police. How can I do that? How dare I? Another principle of Islam – *do not betray Muslims and give them to non-Muslims*. If I know him, I will stop him. I say that. I will never *let* him do it. I will call my community to stop him. But I will never work to lead the British police to him. I will not condemn him to hellfire. You do your homework. You are not my business.

Though it might appear an unusual analogy, a striking parallel is found in Irish terrorism. Gerry Adams, the leader of Sinn Fein, was regularly demonised in the Irish and British media for failing to condemn IRA atrocities. Adams was criticised in particular for failing to use his influence in the IRA to assist in the apprehension of the Real IRA perpetrators of the Omagh bombing in August 1998. The reasons behind this, as well as why Adams and fellow Sinn Fein figures were able to simultaneously engage in the peace process while failing to condemn atrocities, are on the one hand a reflection of there being a deeply divided and volatile movement in which dual roles carry immense challenges and give rise to a host of paradoxical views. Despite a commitment to a peace process, for Adams to publicly condemn IRA activities, would mean he would lose internal credibility. We return to these notions in Chapter 9.

Bakri does not shy away from acknowledging the limitations of such a 'reformer' position. He accepts that an effort to reform violent youth may simply displace the focus and location of violent expression. In elaborating on what a potential counter-radicalisation role might imply for Bakri, he asserts:

> It will be nothing more than talk, propaganda, leaflet, support abroad, but at least [it] will guarantee no attacks inside. But if the radical Jihadis take over, I think we could have chaos. This is where they will have youth, they will have heart, they really strongly believe against the West. They may believe it's ok to die and go up to Heaven, they may practise it, they may sloganise it, but *someone* has put them on the track. They will feel bad if they do not do anything. They feel that they have to do *something*. Plus, the radical Jihadi is young. Usually when you fear death, it is when you are older, not when you are younger. But they are not becoming short in number. Cell after cell they go. One of them may be a *life cell*. A cell that recruits other cells to go abroad.

To appreciate Omar Bakri's sentiments about wanting to develop a role as a type of qualified subversive – i.e. social and political subversion short of terrorism – we need to consider some examples of events surrounding the Al Muhajiroun (AM) movement. I asked Omar Bakri to explain what kinds of people were attracted to AM during his time in the movement, and how disengagement from that movement came about. In providing some context to membership, he expands on the differentiated style of membership in AM:

> One is the intellectual type. They study 12 pages, or 12 books. Dogma. That's all. They sometimes just appear spontaneously. Some people just

join us in our public circles and they 'become' Al Muhajiroun. [HA] was one of them. He wanted to do this, do that, make a big fuss. He was talking, *blah blah blah, I want to go to Pakistan*. He said he wanted to be a leader in Al Muhajiroun. So I said, *ok you want to be a leader? You want to be responsible in an area. Ok, you go to Dundee*. We used to say that to people who wanted to be leaders. *Ok if you really want it, you go there*. Of course he didn't go. He went to Pakistan. But there was somebody there already in charge. He joined them, and also tried to have his own project under them. This is why he is ashamed to speak with us. *Don't inflict your own projects on us, you fool*. He tried to convince the other Brothers that I was a British agent. I said *what are you talking about? That's childish*. And we just all laughed at him.

Bakri painted a picture of Al Muhajiroun as comprising a variety of different kinds of members who became involved and belonged in different ways. Some leave because of an ability to reach a particular role (as in the case of [HA]) or reach their own personal objectives as a member. Others leave because, Bakri explains, Al Muhajiroun did not provide an outlet for being violent enough:

Those who affiliate intellectually do not leave. Those who do not affiliate intellectually, they will leave because they don't really have the same culture that determines their behaviour and actions, like Hizbut Tahrir members. All affiliate intellectually. Now you've got huge numbers in Hizbut Tahrir, but some of them are only students. They are students who are affiliated but have not yet taken an oath. Al Muhajiroun has similar such arrangements. Sometimes people leave not in terms of culture and thought but because of *ability*. They do not have the ability any more. So these people still sympathise with us. But then you have ... there is a certain element in Muhajiroun, members who are cases of intellectually affiliated members who start to believe in radical jihad operations. But to go abroad. And to do something. I threw them out. I threw them out because it is against our constitutions. We are an ideological, political party, you see. We believe in Islam, our job is to carry out good, forbid evil. It's not our job in any way to train, to go fighting and so on.

Bakri describes the case of a member who tried to engage in 'radical Jihad operations' while at the same time 'intellectually affiliate' with AM:

One man studied with us, and then he went to [AZ] to get some training. I was shocked that he did that. He affiliated with Al Muhajiroun. He was a convert to Islam. He used to train with people at the [FY] Mosque. Martial arts training or something like that. Suddenly he tries with these other men to form another organisation. A security-something ... I was so upset I asked for a meeting. I said to [JL] *Brother what are you doing? You went to the [SA] organisation. Did you ever think about the consequences to being a member of the two organisations at the same time? I can't let you continue with us. You need to decide. You are either with Al Muhajiroun or you are with [SL].* And he left. This is the only case I can tell you about.

One other case, however, is of particular interest and provides support for Bakri's claim of 'knowing' where to look for 'radical Jihadis'. Bakri describes the case of an American Muslim who came to the UK with the expectation that Al Muhajiroun in the UK would provide him with an attractive outlet for involvement:

People come to us, they want to affiliate with us. Strange people. Even this man [BR], the North American, he was never Al Muhajiroun, never Hizbut Tahrir at all. He came to Britain. After 9/11, I receive this phone call from a woman. She said *Sheikh Omar Bakri please help me. My son ran away from home.* I said *who's your son?* She said to me *[BR].* I said *I don't know him. Who is this man?* She said *he likes you a lot. He watches you on the Internet. He has all your CDs. He's from New York.* I said *ok if he comes to London, I will . . . give me your number and I will let you call him.* So I forgot her, but her number stayed on my desk. After a few days, this man entered our school. He says *Sheikh Omar, how are you?* And I looked at him. He speaks with an American accent, but he looks Pakistani. A young man. I said *what's your name? is it [BR]?* He said *yes.* I said *here, please speak with your mother.* He said *no, please Sheikh, I don't want to. Why are you chasing me to do this?* I said *because this is your mother.* He said *I don't want to. Sheikh I came here to study Arabic, and study Islam. I want to study here. I want to be active. I want to be closer to dawa.* I said *ok.* He said *my mother, she used to work at the World Trade Center, and she left one minute before* [the attacks on 9/11]. I said, *ok [BR]. You are so young. You must go to school. I will help you. When you go back to New York, contact Brother [AR]. He will help you.* He said *but I don't like it. There aren't many activities in New York.* Anyway, I ask the brothers to buy him a plane ticket. We gave him £200 to buy a ticket and go back to New York. And Brother [SL] took him to the airport. As far as we were aware, he went back to New York.

Bakri describes, how, several days later: 'We were watching Sky News. There was an interview with Al Muhajiroun office in Lahore. I saw [BR] sitting inside, saying *I'm American. I've come here to Pakistan. I'm going to kill Americans. I'm going to slaughter American soldiers.*' Bakri recalls being outraged, and explains that he contacted the Al Muhajiroun office in Pakistan to find out why this had happened:

I can't believe it. What is he doing in our centre there? I phone and I asked [SE]. He said *he came here and he claimed he knew [HN]*. I said *why are you allowing him to do that? He is bluffing you, [HN] is also bluffing you. He is spoiling everything, what is he doing?* So we discovered later on, when he left us, he did not get on the airplane. He missed the flight. He went to Abu Hamza. Abu Hamza called me later. Told me that somebody came to him, that he asked for money to help him go to Pakistan. I knew then there was never going to be a real Al Muhajiroun in Pakistan.

This was not the last time that Omar Bakri would meet [BR], however. Bakri explains that both [BR] and [HN – another individual Omar Bakri describes as having 'his own agenda'] came back from Pakistan after they realised the failure of their attempt to establish their own branch of Al Muhajiroun:

It was not about Al Muhajiroun, and it did not work. They distributed leaflets, issued press releases, saying *don't trust Omar Bakri, join us,* all this rubbish. And in the end it was all bluffing. Why? Because they spent two years there. Two or three years I think, and [BR] came back again to Britain and came into the same office and said *salaam alaykum Sheikh.* I said *I've seen you before.* He said *I'm [BR]. I saw you two years ago. I came here . . .* I said *oh . . . [BR]. I remember you. You issued CDs everywhere. You said you were here with wahabbis, you challenged me.* He said *oh Sheikh, I was so upset. I was frustrated.* Liars, bluffers. We don't give them any attention. They play games. But we know them and we know who they are.

Interim conclusions

Omar Bakri Mohammed is a complex individual who defies easy description or categorisation. He is not a terrorist, though is certainly what would be described as an extremist, or radical Jihadist. He is more than marginally involved in the global Jihadist movement. He continues to command significant influence in that community and takes immense care to articulate his intellectual position and views. Much of the simplistic stereotyping of him in part reflects his failed attempts to engage the British media on his own terms. He concedes: 'I am good at the sound bite, but they don't print all what I say.'

One of the most prominent themes of the interviews with Omar Bakri is his effort to portray himself as someone who can develop a controlling influence in the process of violent radicalisation. A critical point made by Sageman is that the ability of the Al Qaeda social movement to survive will depend on its ability to continue to attract young Muslims and converts alike to its ranks.[10] One question that arises from Omar Bakri's sentiments is whether engaging somebody like him offers a means of countering violent radicalisation in an effective and meaningful way. At the outset, we can at least say with certainty that critical to influencing radical youth are those who can command influence. One view of this is that such influence is the product of religious training, but such credibility may also reflect the kind of influence that Chapter 5's 'Omar' can offer. As far as the public are concerned, there is probably no doubt that the 'Omar' of the previous chapter offers a more attractive alternative to Omar Bakri in that there is far less room for the kind of ambiguity that may be more potent in the influence of Omar Bakri. Omar Bakri does not shy away from accepting that counter-radicalisation in the sense that it would involve a role for him in 'reforming the youth' may continue to yield displacement effects as opposed to true prevention of violent radicalisation.

In one way the case of Omar Bakri reflects just how the threat from the global Jihadist social movement continues to change. Al Qaeda has evolved from a centralised movement to a global social movement. The current reality is a 'multitude of informal local groups trying to emulate their predecessors by conceiving and executing operations from the bottom up'.[11] His credibility and influence while in the United Kingdom were illustrated through the regular flow of individuals who sought him out for involvement in some way. Omar Bakri himself moved in and out of a variety of different movements over the years and his efforts to maintain a tight monopoly over an increasingly diverse group of individuals has proven difficult. He described several examples of would-be followers who came to Bakri with a particular expectation of engagement in violent radical activity and found themselves disappointed with their lot. The fact that this has emerged, according to Omar Bakri, is one indicator of how he has attempted to displace violent intent. To categorise Omar Bakri as 'non-violent' however may miss the point.

Though Omar Bakri presents an account of himself as someone who has been unfairly 'viewed', the internal splitting he alludes to (both in terms of his own differences with Osama Bin Laden as well as the abundance of splitting within Al Muhajiroun and Hizbut Tahrir) is not about legitimacy of the use of violence *per se*, but about the appropriateness of its use and expression in particular settings. The way in which Omar Bakri distinguishes himself from Bin Laden reflects both an ideological and intellectual difference but simultaneously a tool for enhancing a potential union between Bakri and 'radical Jihadis' who simply have not found access to an opportunity to engage in terrorism.

Of relevance here is a careful consideration of the concept of the *covenant of security*, a notion that Omar Bakri continues to be identified with. Repeated references to it suggest that, on the one hand, there is a more diverse and nuanced view within the Jihadist community that publicly condemns 'terrorism' about when and where violence is permitted. Omar Bakri's potential, he argues, is that he is a force not for prevention of radicalisation, but for containment of violence. To assume momentarily that this can somehow be proved valid, the promotion of such a figure could be argued by some as leading to a greater protection within domestic borders. However, promoting initiatives that claim adherence to a covenant of security concept may prove not so much a containment influence, but a force for displacement, giving direction and focus to a different battleground and operational theatre. A similar criticism could be levelled at the Committee for Dialogue initiative in Yemen.

Interestingly, Omar Bakri asserts that the scale of those 'radical Jihadis' compared to regular 'radicals' is overblown: 'I do believe every single Muslim has the potential to be recruited by Al Qaeda. Potentially. At some time, at some point in his life. The potential is there. But for what percentage could this really happen? I believe it's very, very small.' At the same time, however, he is acutely sensitive to the dynamics that give rise to and sustain the search for involvement in violent radical activity:

> Most people do it out of curiosity. Some of them, they do it to show off. They show off, *look at us, we are really tough, look at us, we know what's going on, I'm the big man.* They claim to have the contacts. A lot of it is childish, but what we must not do is give them the fuel. Stop giving them the fuel because they will increase even more. When they are oppressed, other people start to sympathise with them. Don't oppress them by saying *stop dawa, let's be moderate.* This will make them more radical.

Ultimately, therefore, the question of whether or not a figure such as Omar Bakri Mohammed could realistically reform radical Muslims raises a question of what constitutes 'reform'. To describe Omar Bakri as an extremist may be redundant, but it is clear that his views betray significant challenges for Western governments. In particular, a challenge in engaging radical preachers such as Bakri is one of engaging in dialogue without further sustaining the conspiracies that sustain violent radicalisation. To many, Omar Bakri's assertions about his potential role represent the one of a series of unwise (or no) options. It may be premature to characterise Omar Bakri as a true 'dissident', but the disjuncture between his views on political violence and those of Bin Laden deserves further consideration. Because Omar Bakri's views are consistent with Al Qaeda's grand doctrine, he will remain a role model for young disaffected Muslims in search of both a role and identity. Engaging Omar Bakri in the way that he aspires to (i.e. reformer) will never result in de-radicalisation of those he attracts. The very idea runs contrary to his own personal beliefs about there being 'nothing wrong with radicalism'. But while the expectation that engaging with Omar Bakri (as with any influential radical preacher) would lead to such an outcome is naïve and reflects unrealistic expectations and false hopes about what is possible, we should be mindful before dismissing the idea of engaging radical preachers – one problem may be a limitation in viewing de-radicalisation as an all or nothing outcome from such engagement. In particular, and in addition to exploring the consequences of a covenant of security concept, it may well be worth exploring how we can better distinguish, to paraphrase Omar Bakri's original sentiments, 'interpretations' from 'acts'. This will be a major challenge for any practical initiative aimed at countering radicalisation or the far more ambitious de-radicalisation.

9 Conclusions

Introduction

Following the discussions in Chapters 1 and 2, and after having presented a sample of the interview accounts, the groundwork is now set for a more substantive discussion of disengagement. In this chapter, I do not simply summarise the interim conclusions from the case studies, but reflect on several important points as a way forward, as well as consider some of the broader conclusions that collectively emerge from the case studies.

A major concern of this chapter is to examine the tentative findings from the case studies against Taylor and Horgan's conceptual model of psychological process in the development of the terrorist.[1] This will clarify and make explicit the value of the individual perspective in the study of the terrorist. Knowledge of disengagement carries with it a multitude of implications for operational applications, but before we can begin to develop these, it is essential that we work towards greater conceptual and definitional clarity. This is especially salient with respect to the current emphasis on de-radicalisation.

The emergent findings from the case studies point to disengagement encompassing as complex a process as becoming involved in the first place. This chapter explores involvement in, and disengagement from, terrorism in the context of a 'community of practice' metaphor. Finally, we will explore how developments in criminology and the notion of 'secondary desistance' offers potential for ascertaining the validity of the de-radicalisation construct for risk assessment initiatives aimed at promoting effective disengagement.

The case studies

What we know about the process of individual disengagement is probably best characterised by a series of idiosyncratic, complex accounts that appear diverse and unconnected. For the individual, terrorism can have as many different potential endings as it can have potential beginnings. Where significant differences exist in terms of ideological content, backgrounds, aims and aspirations, enough comparative analyses will likely reveal valuable similarities in patterns and processes. Some of the case studies highlight those similarities more obviously than others, but there is much to be done to establish their greater validity and reliability across and within movements. The case studies presented here are part of a larger data set that will require further detailed analysis. And although the disengagement dimensions iden-tified in Chapter 2 remain exploratory, thinking about disengagement in this way offers useful starting points. It is probably clear by now that while it is analytically useful to delineate these issues, the reality of individual accounts is such that physical, psychological, voluntary, involuntary issues and experi-ences can appear complex even within one case.

The reasons for disengagement can be numerous, conflicting, competing and seemingly contradictory. Lars' case is relatively clear-cut, with a dramatic example of disengagement that has proven permanent. The case of Omar Bakri, however, reflects an ongoing process of engagement and disengage-ment, moving from role to role and from movement to movement. Dis-engagement from one role or activity, in his case, gives rise to another elsewhere.

Just as the phase of becoming involved cannot be understood through a process of linear, discrete progression, so too does the process of disengage-ment defy any linear or deterministic notion of progression. That said, it would be premature to try to generalise from such a small sample, and the examples and illustrations provided in the case studies lack the broader evi-dential support required for fuller theoretical and conceptual development. Though useful in illustrating the complexity of the issues at stake when we consider what is meant (and implied) by 'disengagement', we must be mindful of their limitations.

We begin our reflection on the significance of the cases by reiterating that there has been a failure to grasp an obvious role for analyses of the individual in counter-terrorism strategies. Solutions proposed continue to reflect a cat-egorical error. The War on Terror exemplifies this in the sense that counter-terrorism discussions since 2001 have focused significantly on attempts to win the war in Iraq. These concerns relate not to how counter-terrorism should develop, but how one army can beat another. In this sense, much of the policy debates about counter-terrorism reflect a preoccupation about large-scale issues. These have related to a repositioning of armed forces, concerns about transnational linkages and conspiracies, to name but a few. Additionally, there appears to be a natural attraction to automated solutions, whether it is automatic image identification, bio-sensor detection, or some other effort.

What remains a striking feature about non-state terrorism is that it is characterised by smaller, more discrete issues the significance of which we fail to appreciate. While a reliance on automated operations as opposed to a reliance on people has stemmed from an attempt to reduce personal error through technology, operational counter-terrorism initiatives would benefit from a greater consideration of individual microanalyses. I made the point in Chapter 1 that while terrorism may bring with it large-scale consequences, it remains relatively low volume, perpetrated by relatively few individuals.

Consequently our understanding of those individuals remains equally asymmetric.[2] We must find a role for the individual perspective as quickly as possible.

Considering the disengagement process may provide us with such an opportunity. First, let us reiterate some important points. In developing the case studies, I decided to deliberately interview former members of as many different terrorist movements as possible. Despite this being an exploratory pilot study, it is unclear whether many such comparisons would eventually result in a 'magic bullet' formula or a list of steps to promote individual disengagement from terrorism. One of the unwavering characteristics of terrorism is its heterogeneity, not only across the broad spectrum of movements but even within specific terrorist groups. The accounts presented here offer another set of starting points, using one of several potential methods that may serve to uncover the complexity of the disengagement process.

The value of detailed case studies like these is that they offer insight into the development of complex behaviour like involvement in, and disengagement from, terrorism. The kind of idiographic analysis that would follow from such interviews would allow for a contextualisation of the decisions made by individuals that would be difficult to obtain using traditional screening or assessment tools.[3] Detailed and intricate case studies of individual terrorists can be useful in tracing the pathways and involvement process of a given individual. It is probably redundant to suggest that we should be mindful of interview limitations. The novelty of interview data in this context cannot render the interview as superior in any way to other research methods, but higher-level analyses would, in this case, seem unsuitable for exploring these issues, as the complexity of the cases would not emerge in any other way.

On a broad level, the detail from such interviews challenges a range of simplistic stereotypes, not only about the individuals involved in terrorism, but about the ways in which they make decisions and reflect on their experiences of being part of a terrorist movement. As the case studies illustrate, while an awareness of broad social and political conditions may be present in accounts of individual involvement, involvement reflects meaningful choices made by an individual. More specifically, we can say the following about the disengagement phase:

- Disengagement from terrorism can be as gradual as the process of initially becoming involved.
- Disengagement implies and results in different things for different people (even within the same movement).
- Disengagement does not necessarily result in a total break from the movement.
- Disengagement does not necessarily bring with it a fundamental change in attitudes and values that played a strong role in the process of initially becoming involved (what is loosely conceptualised as 'de-radicalisation');

in other words, it does not necessarily result in the assumption that once disengaged, there is no future risk of re-engaging.

These basic primary assertions need expansion. First, I revisit the original three-stage model from my previous book, as well as the more detailed version of that model presented by Taylor and Horgan[4] in their revision of that concept. Second, from this, I develop a way of promoting disengagement from terrorism from the perspective of a 'community of practice'. Third, I develop operational definitions of disengagement and a proposed operational definition of de-radicalisation. And finally, in light of the cases presented here, I revisit the notion of 'de-radicalisation', contrasting it with disengagement, and propose a variety of issues for exploring how de-radicalisation can be ascertained and assessed.

Revisiting Taylor and Horgan's 2006 process model

In 2005, I presented the outline of a basic model of terrorist psychology.[5] The basis of that model is the assertion that involvement in terrorism can be understood with reference to three distinct stages:

- initially becoming involved in a terrorist organisation
- continuing that involvement, which for the most part brings with it an engagement in terrorist activity and events
- and finally, disengaging.

Consistent with the 'rational choice' perspective in criminology[6] was the assertion that the factors that relate to each of these phases may not necessarily relate to either or both of the others. In other words, the factors that relate to how and why people initially become involved in a terrorist group do not necessarily have a bearing on what they subsequently do as terrorists. Additionally, the factors that relate to how and why people become involved in the first place are not necessarily helpful in understanding why the person remains or eventually disengages.

By making such distinctions, we consequently begin to develop phase-specific counter-terrorism initiatives, depending on what is the most effective intervention point: i.e. whether it is a) initial prevention of involvement, b) subsequent disruption of engagement, or c) eventual facilitation of disengagement.

From the case studies presented in this volume, and despite the fact that the disengagement phase remains the most poorly understood and least researched, ironically it would appear that practical counter-terrorism initiatives aimed not only at facilitation of disengagement but also at prevention of initial involvement may actually become more apparent during this phase. This does not negate the validity of the distinctions made in the original model, but reinforces the need to invest in the development of phase-*specific* knowledge and understanding to appreciate the nature of the relationship between the individual's experiences of involvement in the terrorist movement and the qualities associated with that involvement (for example, ascription to and immersion in an ideology and its associated social and psychological qualities).

To strengthen the case for this, it is useful to reflect upon the case study data against a more fully developed model of psychological development in the terrorist – that of Taylor and Horgan[7] – and the data presented in the interviews can be used to illustrate aspects of that process. As explained in Chapter 1, viewing involvement in terrorism as a process implies a move away from focusing on the presumed individual qualities of the terrorist to a focus on process variables. This includes the changing context in which the terrorist operates, as well as the nature of the relationships between the individual and the events he or she experiences at all stages of the process.

In our 2006 article, Max Taylor and I made some core assertions:

- Terrorists are indistinguishable from the general population except by what they do through continued engagement in terrorist activity.
- The choices made by an individual are meaningful to him or her.
- The individual has to have the opportunity to engage in terrorism.
- The individual has to have the capacity to make an informed choice about involvement.

The answer to why one person becomes involved in terrorism while others from the same background do not is not something we sought to hide behind some obscure psychological or technical issue – and we made that very explicit in the original paper. Rather, we suggested that the answer lies within the 'psychological and emotional context of the individual on which the bigger and essentially non-psychological forces of opportunity and context operate' (p588). To make the case for this, we identified three simple critical process variables that relate to the development of the terrorist. These are:

- personal factors
- setting events
- the social, political and organisational context.

Personal factors are those that relate to the psychological factors as experienced by the individual at any stage of the process. These include the risk factors identified in Chapter 1 (emotional states, a dampening of moral restraints about the use of violence, immediate experiences, peer pressure, etc.). Again, these vary from individual to individual – both in terms of the pre-involvement experiences and experiences as a *result* of continued involvement and engagement. We acknowledged in the model that while there may be some overlap, personal factors can be distinguished from *setting events* in terms of 'immediacy and salience' (p592). Chapter 1 showed that personal factors do not 'cause' choices to be made, rather they act as pre-cursors and contribute to the way in which particular choices are made.

Setting events, we argue, relate to past contextual influence. In other words, these are the kinds of experiences that are unchangeable because they have already happened to an individual as part of their socialisation through friends, family, society, culture, religion and so on. These represent a broad context. They are often the kinds of setting variables that are identified as 'root causes' and are the basis for the kinds of factors we identify through survey responses. While setting events alone 'tend to be so general as to have little predictive value' (p592), they can still contribute to the behavioural choices made by an individual by providing critical direction and motivation. As above, however, they do not 'cause' choices to be made.

Finally, the article discussed the *social, political and organisational context*. This encompasses the terrorist's 'external social context that is specifically concerned with political expression and ideology, and/or the organisational expression of that ideology' (p592). One of the major ways in which terrorism can be distinguished from other forms of instrumental violence (such as crime) is via the political, ideological and organisational array of influences that shape individual decision-making. They impinge upon the personal factors at stake – for example, becoming involved because of the perceived status in an organisational role.

Understanding the interrelationship between all three is relevant for understanding any aspect of involvement for the individual – becoming, remaining or disengaging. The way in which individuals make choices about their involvement in, and disengagement from, terrorism is complex and not reducible to single behavioural dimensions.[8] We further acknowledge that the relative weighting of these factors will always vary between individuals. Additionally, they will fluctuate for the same individual as a result of continued involvement on their own individual pathway.

The Taylor and Horgan model provides a focus on the *individual in context*. As explained in Chapter 1, the focus is on the experiences of individuals as they are impacted and shaped by the process in which they engage. But one of the core features of the model is that while personal factors are by definition resistant to change, there is great potential in effecting change upon individual decision-making. While setting events provide the context to choices already made in terms of involvement, the critical element that distinguishes a person who engages actively with terrorism relates to the personal context in which they find themselves. The interaction of that with the *social, political and organisational context* provides us with the basis for identifying some potential rate-limiting qualities – i.e. the basis for the development of operational interventions.

The accounts presented in the interviews here illustrate some basic tenets of Taylor and Horgan's process model and lend support to it:

- Terrorists do not just appear 'fully fledged': they become terrorists through involvement and engagement. They have to learn and be trained, make sense of what they learn and express that learning in various ways. They may engage in technical learning, but may also engage in ideological learning. Evidence of that learning process (through 'talking' or 'doing') can enhance loyalty and commitment to the group and/or ideology.

- Involvement in terrorism can take multiple forms and be expressed through a variety of activities and behaviours.
- The relationship between individuals and roles may be complex and multifaceted; an individual may not necessarily achieve the role they expected, nor may they necessarily occupy only one role – and that role will likely change over time.
- The aspiring terrorist is rooted in a social context that is removed from the social, organisational and political qualities of being a terrorist.
- The engaged or 'committed' terrorist has crossed a boundary; they have acquired skills and knowledge that binds them closer to the organisation. Engaging in illegal acts offers further evidence of loyalty and sustains commitment.
- There is neither one route to terrorism, one route *through* terrorism, nor one route *away* from terrorism; there are individual routes and progression though those routes as experienced by individuals changes over time.
- The significant element in strengthening engagement and giving it direction is the increased role of the *social, political and organisational context* in exerting control over behaviour as the individual becomes increasingly involved and engaged.
- Because there is no obvious route out of terrorism (rather there are multiple pathways), there are multifaceted consequences for the individual that in turn affect disengagement.

In the specific context of disengagement, we have seen how this process developed through a lessening of control in different circumstances. Though different in terms of individual content and focus, there are similarities between the disengagement as experienced by Michael, Omar (of Chapter 5) and Alan. In each case, the supportive qualities shaping their initial involvement were clear and explicit. Social, political and organisational factors facilitated their initial involvement, yet some of the problems in their commitment and sustained involvement grew from issues that stemmed from major conflict with these contexts to their activities.

Relevant to this, a critical rate-limiting factor identified by Taylor and Horgan was emotional arousal. This has the power to impede or otherwise affect decision-making that may be relevant to understanding the way in which pressures operate on the individual at any point in the process. Though we addressed the pressure towards violence in the immediate decisions made before an individual becomes involved in terrorism, this pressure is relevant to how disengagement occurs. Michael's case is illustrative. There may be specific factors that alter the intensity and expressiveness of that arousal (roles, activities and perceived responsibilities for example), but psychological disengagement can be enhanced by changes in emotional arousal in this context.

There is explicit potential to modelling events and their relationships as they relate to involvement in, and disengagement from, terrorism. At present, we do not have anything close to the kinds of requirements necessary to inform a mathematical model of the relationship between individuals and events, but we are able to express a conceptual structure in terms of hypothetical constructs. In the original paper, we acknowledged (p587) that the true development of such a process model would involve a complex, multi-layered analysis. This is well beyond the scope of the evidence currently available in terrorism studies. It also remains beyond the scope of this book, but the kinds of case studies developed here provide us with a valuable empirical base needed to embark upon a systematic research agenda to provide such data.

What is clear, however, is that while an aggregation of case studies may be a logical and tempting path to take, what is needed is that the subjects of case studies need to illustrate broader kinds of involvement than just leadership or active violent roles. While individuals like Doug and Michael represent the traditional role of 'the terrorist', this contrasts with the more fluid role held by Omar Bakri Mohammed. Omar Bakri does not engage in violence, yet the degree of ideological control over his beliefs places him in a category of the 'fully committed'. Furthermore, the credibility he sustains is sufficient to attract potential members unaware of the nuanced views he describes in his accounts. In order to understand how we can effect change in the *social, political and organisational context* (as it impacts upon the individual); however, we need to integrate this approach with concepts from communities of practice. If successful, this may offer a structured way of conceptualising and promoting disengagement.

Extending the process model: terrorism as community of practice

Community of practice (CoP) refers to the shared exercise of social learning and the related social and cultural practices that develop between and within a group. That group shares a common purpose that binds it together and requires the development of social learning to further its goals. CoP offers us a structure to understand how the individual's decisions can be affected by ideological and social control, even in the absence of a face-to-face meeting (e.g. with a terrorist leader). It allows us to understand how ideological content can impinge upon the individual as well as how ideological process exercises control over the individual's decisions.[9]

The original concept of CoP was based on the way in which learning develops as part of apprenticeship.[10] Progressing as an apprentice involves moving from some kind of peripheral membership to being a 'full member', a committed insider, complete with the status that brings. One way of developing the CoP metaphor is to consider a greater role for psychological processes. Hundeide[11] presents a stage model of becoming an insider in counter-culture groups. He examines the concept of CoP in a case study of underage soldiers in Angola and identifies the following features of involvement and engagement:

- positive rewarding contact with leading charismatic members
- joining as a form of peripheral apprenticeship
- process of redefinition of the past (sometimes a destruction of past values and an introduction to new values, styles and new promising futures)
- further demonstrations of loyalty as a test of commitment
- tacit code of loyal participation in daily collective practices and rituals with reciprocal confirmation of new values, new conceptions and new competencies
- final test of loyalty through 'committed actions' – extreme actions that undermine one's previous beliefs, values and way of life that make a return to one's previous contacts very difficult
- new status and role inside the community (a product of the movement from apprentice to full member).

According to Lave and Wenger,[12] 'legitimate peripheral participation' provides a way to speak about the relations between newcomers and old-timers ... It concerns the processes by which newcomers become part of a community of practice' (p8). In this sense, Hundeide's model involves a 'conversion', increasing the emotional commitment to being a committed insider. The apprentice's commitment to the group has to be substantiated through tests of commitment and through participation in ideological and expressive acts. This entails a gradual process of step-by-step habituation to new boundaries or standards. As part of the acquisition of a new 'mentality, and new standards of conduct', there is an equally gradual process of desensitisation that involves the blocking of normal empathic reactions towards the other.

Hundeide acknowledges that not everyone 'converts' and characterises cases of escalating involvement as a form of 'deep commitment'. This, he says, occurs when the negotiation of participation requires sacrifice of a nature that involves a radical adaptation or accommodations of one's cognitive and motivational system. It may involve a lessening of contact with pre-existing social bonds (friends, family, etc.) and foregoing one's previous image with the public identification of a new one (e.g. wearing a uniform, going on a march, etc.). Hundeide explains that the member can also commit 'actions' that 'express and confirm one's status as an insider in conflict with public morality and usually in conflict with one's previous values and moral codes' (p112).

Deep commitment, Hundeide argues, reflects a 'road of step-by-step commitment so that the way of return will be prevented and blocked by incongruent and conflicting actions and beliefs that may be impossible to face without personal crisis and personal danger' (p112). Deeply committed members have 'moved so far away into an alternative reality that they have problems adapting and finding their way back to the old values and practices that apply outside the closed world of military order and practices' (pp120–21).

In the context of terrorism, CoP extends our knowledge about how people become involved in terrorism, how that involvement is sustained and how disengagement can come about. The process model fits with Hundeide's CoP concept. However, the potential for notions of CoP extend beyond conceptualising involvement to actually suggesting (in the context of the process model) a structure for the promotion of disengagement. Critical to the success of any counter-terrorism initiative is a clearer understanding of the role of community and how the individual terrorist engages with their community. Since the events of 9/11, Western governments have failed to appreciate the reasons for one of the longstanding dynamics relevant to terrorism support – that is, that while an individual community that is 'represented' by a terrorist movement may condemn and reject an atrocity that is conducted in its name, members of that community may still remain *broadly* supportive of the terrorist group. One way of promoting disengagement from terrorism is to explore how to promote the development of *competing* communities of practice. A major goal will be to provide a challenge to the identity to those committed members. An example will help to illustrate.[13]

The movie *Paradise Now*[14] tells the story of two suicide bombers from the West Bank. The film shows the roots of the individuals' frustration, giving a human face to the bombers while simultaneously refusing to condone the violence the audience believes they are about to perpetrate. The film also provides an insight into some of the personal incentives for involvement, similar to those laid out in Chapter 1, such as direct and indirect experiences of violence and the broader theme of victimisation. Scenes from the film involve the men questioning themselves, their decisions and the usefulness of suicide bombing. Its director, Hany Abu-Assad, studied interrogations of failed suicide bombers and spoke with their families in order to provide as 'realistic' a portrayal of the protagonists as possible.

On a broader level (and perhaps more significantly) the film raises questions about the alternatives to violence and terrorism and perhaps its ultimate contribution may be that it creates a space, through mass appeal, for the discussion and debate of such issues. Before the film was released, however, concerns from various quarters about its likely impact were raised in dramatic ways. During the filming, a Palestinian militant group kidnapped the location manager while seeking reassurances that the film would not 'denigrate its cause'.[15] This was then followed by a bomb attack on the crew, which resulted in the deaths of three bystanders.[16]

The importance of a propaganda campaign for any terrorist movement is undeniable, but there is little current focus on the potential role that counter-narratives may have in redirecting or displacing cognitions and behaviours for budding recruits or 'committed insiders' – in other words, for promoting psychological disengagement. Given Omar's experiences (Chapter 5) as well as Michael's, this cannot be underestimated. The role of civil society as the 'arena of uncoerced collective action around shared interests, purposes and values'[17] and the media is worth highlighting. Collective action against the use of terrorism and the use of non-violent means of dissent can be actively encouraged and made acceptable. The mass media, both journalistic and popular (as in films), have an underdeveloped but potentially significant role to play in attempts to alter the *social, political and organisational context* in which terrorism (and support for it) thrives and simultaneously in which the attraction to involvement (and sustained involvement) in terrorism may be undermined. Realistic challenges to the myths and attractiveness of terrorism can be achieved, but are only realistic and meaningful when directed at specific populations.

The effectiveness of any form of 'counter-narratives' in terms of its effects on the individual *already involved* may appear limited at the outset, primarily because alternate views (particularly those identified as belonging to the 'enemy') are considered unacceptable to those involved, and are frequently interpreted within the framework of a conspiracy. Hundeide[18] distinguishes apprentices from those who display 'deep commitment'. However, the experiences of Michael and Alan suggest that despite being deeply committed, the seeds of psychological disengagement may already have been set in motion. It may be premature therefore to describe the 'deeply committed' as insensitive to such approaches. In addition, the effectiveness of any counter-narrative will rely heavily on the credibility and relevant expertise of the communicator. While notions of trust are also significant, the effectiveness of the communicator to persuade will be influenced of the communicator's *intention*. Therefore, people generally tend to be more trusting of the communicator if they do not perceive that the communicator has something to gain or has the explicit intention to persuade. The effectiveness of the perception of expertise on the part of the communicator can often be based on factors such as similarity in social background (e.g. similar views, values and status) but also differences in age, leadership or 'experience' for example (which promote the communicator to an 'expert' status).[19] The case of Chapter 5's Omar supports this.

In applying this to operational counter-terrorism, it would seem that a critical factor influencing the potential impact and effectiveness of any communicator is in the identification of sources more credible for counter-message communication. For example, it may be useful to encourage those who have disengaged from terrorist activity to become more vocal in dispelling the attractions and lures of involvement in movements. Lars, Omar and Michael are examples of how this can be potentially effective. Omar Bakri may not be an effective example of someone who can exert influence as a force for counter-radicalisation, but does represent a good example of a competing community of practice by differentiating himself (e.g. through greater distinctions about the covenant of security). If adequately managed, the expression of such dissent may displace otherwise violent activity. The long-term effectiveness of this as a countermeasure, however, is questionable.

Furthermore, and though it would *initially* seem that this type of counter-narrative would remain resisted by what Hundeide calls the 'deeply committed', it may not only have a real impact on those at the initial stages of involvement. It may also act as a catalyst for emotional arousal in deeply committed members experiencing the seeds of psychological disengagement. It emerges from the case of Michael, for instance, that individuals may remain involved and seem committed to continued involvement despite being deeply disillusioned. But given the social and organisational context to Michael's disengagement, to suggest that deeply committed members are impervious to counter-narrative is incorrect – what may be incorrect is how 'committed' the 'deeply committed' actually are. It may be that deeply *engaged* (in physical or role terms) rather than deeply *committed* (in psychological terms) may be a more realistic and appropriate concept in the context of terrorism.

Even the beliefs of deeply committed extremists may be subject to more change than we have expected. Although this may appear to be contradictory to the function of terrorist ideology itself, it is worthwhile to explore in relation to the role of the individual as a 'consumer' of narratives. It is also a major function of terrorist leaders to encourage changes in political and religious beliefs, even minute changes for those already deemed to be more or less converted while at the peripheral stages of involvement. This encourages the individual recruit towards a sense of accommodation in accepting involvement in terrorism as *legitimate* but also attractive, important and timely.

I recommend a multi-track strategy of making known the negative consequences of terrorism, challenging its legitimacy through the appropriate channels and encouraging a displacement of activity that would result in either a) greater involvement in a terrorist movement for a potential recruit or b) the reduction in the perceived sense of the effectiveness of terrorism itself for existing 'already involved' members. A systematic consideration of these issues could prove immensely valuable and notions of 'competing' communities of practice are relevant. Promoting effective competition in a terrorism CoP ecosystem (e.g. the broad Jihadist community), however, will require clear goals and realistic expectations. Though he poses an interesting example of an 'anomalous' source of competition, the case of Omar Bakri illustrates just how difficult subversion short of terrorism may be to reach in reality as well as remaining a socially acceptable and desirable option.

Promoting disengagement 1: establishing terminology

A limiting factor in ascertaining the validity of dimensions to disengagement lies in a lack of empirical data. Taylor and Horgan explain that while considerable effort has gone into the development of chronologies and in the construction of general case studies, neither yield the information that illustrates the issues of concern here. This does not imply that the process model is unrealistic – on the contrary the purpose of developing these dimensions is to provide a basis for modelling. Despite what appears to be a mounting series of obstacles in promoting disengagement from terrorism, however, there are grounds for a more positive outlook. The case studies offer valuable material for hypothesis development. One of the first things we can do is to extend the original three-stage process approach (becoming, remaining, disengaging) to a more detailed pathway arc into and out of terrorism (see Figure 1).

These expanded steps maintain the core dimensions of becoming, remaining and leaving, but make explicit the distinction between radicalisation and violent radicalisation, as well as a distinction between disengagement and de-radicalisation. Progression through these stages is not necessarily linear – not everyone experiences the same pathway, and as illustrated by the case studies, the disengaged terrorist may not necessarily be de-radicalised. It would seem, however, from some of the accounts presented here, that there is actually a greater link between the disengagement phase and the phase of becoming involved. A common theme throughout these diverse interviews from equally diverse movements is that there is a discrepancy between the expectations that influenced initially becoming involved and the seeds of disillusionment that played a role in the disengagement. This process is reflected in other areas. In a major study of desistance from gang activity, Decker and Van Winkle[20] found that the primary motivation for leaving was 'their experience with violence'. The authors describe the difference between 'mythic violence' of inter-gang rivalry and 'real' violence, which is far less romantic.

Evident from the beginning of this book, and in the original 2003 article *Leaving Terrorism Behind*,[21] the term *disengagement* was deliberately adopted as a term to replace *leaving*. Disengagement does not necessarily imply leaving the group, but more often than not changing roles of one kind or another. Disengagement also captures the complexity of that process more effectively than 'leaving'. We can achieve a greater distinction between the various

Figure 1 Pathway into, through and out of terrorism.

components of disengagement. Disengagement may be expressed via, and develop from, *physical* issues (e.g. role change) as well as *psychological* (e.g. disillusionment). Though either can lead to a reduction in engagement in terrorism, it is also the case that both are intertwined – physical role change can bring with it psychological change, while psychological change can lead to switching roles altogether.

Disengagement may be voluntary or involuntary; it may develop from different perceptions about the availability of pathways out of involvement, or different perceptions about what a change of role may entail. Furthermore, the disengaged terrorist may be either repentant or unrepentant. This goes to the heart of the confusion around what 'de-radicalised' means. On one level, it reflects a cognitive versus behavioural distinction (the former viewed as synonymous with de-radicalisation) yet, as explained by Bjørgo and Horgan,[22] the relationship is far more complex.

This point has not been acknowledged in terrorist risk assessment. Being physically distanced from a specific role, or from the movement, may result in a cognitive change, but not necessarily. An individual may leave a movement, but may express the same cognitions that suggest a close commitment to the *social, political and organisational context* to terrorist activity. There may still be a risk posed by the individual, but the question arises as to what exactly that risk entails.

In order to find greater conceptual and operational clarity between the various terms, I suggest the following distinctions by way of definitions:

- **Radicalisation**: the social and psychological process of incrementally experienced commitment to extremist political or religious ideology. Radicalisation may not necessarily lead to violence, but is one of several risk factors required for this.
- **Violent radicalisation**: the social and psychological process of *increased* and *focused* radicalisation through involvement with a violent non-state movement. Violent radicalisation encompasses the phases of a) becoming involved with a terrorist group and b) remaining involved and engaging in terrorist activity; it involves a process of pre-involvement searching for the opportunity to engage in violence and the exploration of competing alternatives; the individual must have both the opportunity for engagement as well as the capacity to make a decision about that engagement.
- **Disengagement**: the process whereby an individual experiences a change in role or function that is usually associated with a reduction of violent participation. It may not necessarily involve leaving the movement, but is most frequently associated with significant temporary or permanent role change. Additionally, while disengagement may stem from role change, that role change may be influenced by psychological factors such as disillusionment, burnout or the failure to reach the expectations that influenced initial involvement. This can lead to a member seeking out a different role within the movement.

- **De-radicalisation:** the social and psychological process whereby an individual's commitment to, and involvement in, violent radicalisation is reduced to the extent that they are no longer at risk of involvement and engagement in violent activity. De-radicalisation may also refer to any initiative that tries to achieve a reduction of risk of re-offending through addressing the specific and relevant disengagement issues.
- **Counter-radicalisation** should be used to refer to efforts aimed at preventing violent radicalisation or disrupting the continued involvement in terrorism of those already radicalised. It can also relate to any initiative aimed at preventing social and political radicalisation more generally (not just violent).

On this last point, 'countering' and 'preventing' may seem at opposite ends of the spectrum, but what is currently expressed in counter-radicalisation strategies and counter-terrorism policies more generally are attempts at preventing radicalisation. This may help clear the confusion between disengagement and de-radicalisation.

Though we know little about the process of disengagement, the idea of de-radicalisation remains less developed. The term carries with it a connotation of a quick fix, the idea that terrorists can be 'turned'. In the absence of specific objectives, however, it may be practically beneficial to root the concept of de-radicalisation in a specific objective of establishing whether or not a person is at risk of re-engaging in violent activity. Additionally, and a caution about assuming linearity in the development of the terrorist, we should not assume that de-radicalisation assumes a return to some 'pre-radicalisation' phase. Successful de-radicalisation may be equated with the minimisation of risk of recidivism, but for someone who has engaged in the violent radicalisation process, there can be no returning to that original phase. It does not necessarily mean that there is a heightened risk of re-engaging simply because one has already engaged. In fact, negative experiences inside the group would mitigate against this re-engagement.

De-radicalisation, in whatever future conception is developed therefore, should not be equated with some kind of 'de-programming', which for some implies a return to some pre-existing state. There is one sense in which the confusion between disengagement and de-radicalisation is not a reflection of any discussion in the literature, but rather is a reflection that assumptions that exist in practical initiatives influence the choice of terms to conceptually develop our knowledge of the area.

Finally, these definitions may not be satisfactory to all. With an emphasis on *violence*, a distinction emerges between involvement in terrorist activity and involvement in subversion short of terrorism. However, a change in focus from 'prevention' to management and control may carry with it significant political cost. We should at least make explicit the fact that interventions will need to be cognisant of there being multiple possible intervention points for disruption and prevention, depending on what the specific objectives and expectations actually are.

Promoting disengagement 2: policy recommendations

What can we do about disengagement? As Cronin asserts, 'a universal strategy for ending terrorism is by definition impossible' (p8). She adds: 'When a campaign is already under way, it becomes imperative for policymakers to be aware of the give-and-take, to recognize their part in it, adapt to it and focus on a conclusion' (p26). Cronin argues that 'in ending terrorism, a government's top priority should be not to win people's hearts and minds, but rather to amplify the natural tendency of violent groups to *lose* them' (p27). There is no reason to suggest that we cannot pursue both objectives simultaneously.

One of the first efforts to achieve this occurred on 8–11 March 2005, when over 200 terrorism experts met at the invitation of the Club de Madrid, in commemoration of the victims of the Madrid bombings. The Working Group on Individual Causes of Terrorism[23] produced several recommendations to identify potential intervention points:

- Inhibit potential recruits from joining terrorist organisations in the first place.
- Produce dissension within existing groups.
- Facilitate exit from groups.
- Reduce support for the group and subvert the legitimacy of its leadership.
- Increase societal resilience and reduce societal vulnerability to the effects of terrorism.

Issues from the case studies represent the basis of these intervention points. These would include (but not be limited to):

- the discrepancy between the public image of the movement and the activities engaged in, often exposed only to 'insiders'; this can provide a major source of psychological disengagement despite continuing commitment to a role; related to this
- the recognition that the *deeply engaged* may not necessarily be as *deeply committed* as one assumes
- the presence of power struggles, bitter rivalries and jealousies within the movement
- the acknowledgement that there are many and varied kinds of membership
- the acknowledgement that different members may merit different kinds of interventions (e.g. the imported versus local terrorist).

It is absolutely critical that we are clear about what we can and cannot achieve, and what our expectations are in promoting disengagement. Attempts to identify active individuals likely to disengage or attempts to implant disillusionment within the movement represent achievable objectives. However, attempting to *prevent* radicalisation, broadly speaking, may be both unrealistic and unfeasible. A major problem in recent years has been that we have allowed much of the discourse on counter-terrorism to be influenced by language that reflects unrealistic goals. *Radicalisation* is perceived as the major problem, not *violent radicalisation*, which is synonymous with becoming involved in terrorism. There remains a critical failure to acknowledge that the vast majority of those who identify themselves as 'radical' do not engage in violent activity. A strategy for managing and responding to subversion short of terrorism ought to be part of a broader counter-terrorism strategy that acknowledges a realistic sense of what is achievable.

Following from the conclusions of the Club de Madrid working group, in early 2008 a group of international experts addressed issues of disengagement and de-radicalisation from terrorism. The results of that collaboration were published in a book, *Leaving Terrorism Behind: Individual and Collective Disengagement*.[24] The background to the project lay with the realisation that (as explained in Chapter 2) the academic community needed to engage much more in the area of disengagement. We also realised that there was an increasing emphasis in counter-terrorism strategies to prevent radicalisation and we suggested that disengagement and de-radicalisation (understood broadly) should be part of the counter-terrorism toolbox (pp247–50). We reasoned:

- If the terrorist believes that there is no possibility of exit, they may remain involved despite being disillusioned with the movement.
- Defectors may serve as credible opinion-builders to counter violent radicalisation.
- Defectors may also provide intelligence about other terrorists in the group.
- Individual disengagement may reduce the number of active terrorists and the overall size of the network.
- Individual and collective disengagement may reduce the human, social and economic costs associated with terrorism.
- Promoting collective disengagement may help end terrorist campaigns.
- Preventing violent radicalisation is easier (though potentially more difficult to assess) earlier rather than later in process.

At the same time, it was apparent to us that several countries had started to explore ways of managing and controlling radicalisation in various settings. These ranged from preventing radicalisation in prison to establishing public counter-radicalisation strategies aimed at discouraging potential recruits to terrorist movements. Upon closer inspection, it became clear that 'de-radicalisation' was a term to encompass a variety of programmes, each of which had context-specific objectives with subjective criteria for participation and with equally context-dependent expectations of what was both desirable and possible.

An interesting feature of these programmes is the extraordinary range of terminology used in the development and implementation of these programmes. 'Desertion', 'demobilisation', 'defection', 'de-escalation' and others, while essentially implying a move away from involvement in terrorism, they carried different, quite nuanced, assumptions about how such initiatives should develop and be assessed. For example, efforts aimed at demobilising and reintegrating into society members of the Colombian FARC organisation differed from the ways in which the Yemen Committee for Dialogue sought to 'rehabilitate' young Jihadists. A striking feature of many programmes has been in their claims for success. The Saudi Arabian counselling programme has claimed over 90% success in rehabilitating former Jihadists, yet the criteria for establishing such 'success' remain obscure.[25]

It is too difficult to draw anything more than generalisations from these initiatives. From early (though promising) schemes, there can be no ideal template for what would be involved in 'reinsertion' or 'reintegration' of former terrorists. If the development of terrorism is a product of its own time and place, it follows that issues of disengagement will also be context-specific and necessarily nuanced in terms of how the programmes are constructed, implemented and promoted. Different perceptions about broader issues of disengagement will exist between and within the individual terrorist group. However, the issue may be differentially perceived within the constituent population that is represented (or otherwise) by the terrorist movement. During the 1994 ceasefires in Northern Ireland, both Republican and Loyalist communities respectively claimed victory, while large sections of both communities engaged in triumphant displays of celebration. Bjørgo and Horgan identified a need for evaluating claims for success and for establishing reliable and valid criteria for establishing that success (or failure).

A more basic question that the project did not yet answer was whether or not 'de-radicalisation' could be held up as a valid concept. Despite the claims for success in the various programmes, there was (and remains) little clarity about what de-radicalisation implies. Given that, there is even less sense in which we can effectively assess claims for the success of such initiatives. One way forward here (and perhaps one answer to both problems) is found in criminology.

Secondary desistance as de-radicalisation

In addressing desistance from criminal activity, David Gadd argues that while desistance may be influenced by an event or events, it is 'inadequately theorized by a singular moment'.[26] For the most part, and except for cases of involuntary physical disengagement because of peace agreements or ceasefires, disengagement from terrorism can be characterised in a similar way. Furthermore, criminal desistance does not refer to a termination *event* that takes place at the time of a last offence. Desistance, Maruna argues, is a process of refraining or abstaining, in this case from illegal behaviour.[27]

Desistance from terrorism also reflects a process rather than a singular event and accordingly effective desistance from terrorism is not simply stopping terrorist behaviour, but desisting from a wide array of behaviours aimed at subverting the authority and legitimacy of the state. Whether that represents a realistic objective is another issue, but of interest here is how Maruna and Farrall[28] distinguish *primary* desistance from *secondary* desistance.

Primary desistance refers to a temporary state of affairs, a sort of 'crime-free' phase for the individual. Secondary desistance signifies a more lasting long-term shift. In addition to non-offending, they argue that: 'long term desistance does involve identifiable and measurable changes at the level of personal identity' (pp174–5). Closely related to this, Gadd[29] highlights the development of identity and identification in this process and raises questions about what kinds of change we can expect from desisting offenders. He explores desistance from hate crimes in a detailed case study of a former far-right activist. A key psychological component in hate crimes, he argues, involves a significant effort to separate oneself from the symbolic 'other'. Gadd draws on similar research to suggest that successful desistance from crime requires an ability to reconstruct one's past as part of a 'generative script', and the belief of significant others, contributing to a feeling of 'earned redemption'. He acknowledges that change may be very gradual, piecemeal, sometimes contradictory, and that 'desistance from crime can often mean the resumption of other forms of behaviour that are no less problematic, dangerous and destructive' (p196). He concludes that this 'may be as good as it gets for many reforming offenders' (p196). Gadd asserts here that primary desistance does not automatically imply secondary desistance – i.e. 'those who undergo crime-free gaps are set on a pathway between primary and secondary desistance' (p196).

These issues are attractive for thinking about both the disengagement process as well as the development of de-radicalisation. Yet it is unclear just how the establishment of this new identity is necessary for long-term 'desistance' from terrorism. One possibility is to examine the ways in which changes in terrorist language reflect a lessening of ideological control and whether or not that represents a valid risk indicator. Maruna[30] discovered that active criminal offenders and desisting ex-offenders differ in terms of *explanatory styles*. Explanatory styles are essentially the ways in which people offer similar kinds of explanations for what happens to them throughout their lives. In clinical settings, psychologists work on redressing explanatory styles that may have 'trapped' an individual into a pattern of behaviour (e.g. depression). Compared to desisting ex-offenders, active offenders tend to interpret negative events in their lives as being the product of internal, stable and global forces. On the other hand, active offenders were more likely to believe that the good events in their lives were the product of external, unstable and specific causes. These other dimensions of offender cognitions may be useful in understanding the psychological aspects of desistance from crime. To illustrate Maruna's concept with examples from terrorism:

- EVENT: I went to join Al Qaeda.
- EXPLANATION: Because I was misled by my peers.
- EVENT: I escaped capture by the security forces.
- EXPLANATION: Because I worked hard to make it happen.

Maruna makes the critical assertion that the explanations may not necessarily be true, but that such 'self-narratives seem to be the most supportive of efforts to maintain desistance from crime'. He acknowledges that they could be viewed as 'positive illusions' that serve to sustain abstinence.

If we are to effectively explore the feasibility of terrorist de-radicalisation, we would do well to explore how explanatory styles develop and change. One issue would be to compare explanatory styles in members of the same movement who are at different phases of their involvement (becoming radicalised, disengaged, etc.), as well as to correlate specific ideological narratives associated with terrorist groups with the explanatory styles of its members. This would be an enormously complex undertaking, but offers us an interesting research agenda for ascertaining the validity of terrorist de-radicalisation as a type of secondary desistance. Smith et al.[31] have already demonstrated, through thematic content analysis of documentation, differences between terrorist and non-terrorist groups. It would be useful to consider whether linguistic change for the terrorist represents a promising indicator for risk assessment.

There are some conceptual limitations to the applicability of such notions to terrorism and political violence, and certainly the concept of 'abstinence' raises questions around the basic assumptions that underpin how to understand human motivation. Terrorists view their activity within some ideological frame and as such, analogies with criminal behaviour are difficult. Terrorists themselves take great effort to explain why they are different from 'ordinary criminals' and reject any attempt at comparison. 'Abstaining' from terrorism suggests that engagement in terrorist activity signifies a loss of control and raises implicit assumptions about impulsivity. Once involved and committed to a terrorist movement, only in a limited sense does an *individual* take responsibility for terrorist action – in some cases, there is a command and control function, while in others, relative autonomy exists for the individual to source targets and engage in localised operations. In any case, the reality is more complex and diffuse. Thinking about 'abstaining' from terrorism would seem to be at odds with the sense of personal agency in the decision to become involved that is repeated throughout the case studies.

However, the issue deserves further exploration, and perhaps the main challenge to this analogy is in fact a lack of clarity about what the focus would be in the context of terrorism. We should ask if success is to be measured in terms of reducing engagement in terrorist activity or is it 'being rehabilitated'? For example, comparing the Saudi Arabian counselling programme to, say, that of the Colombian reintegration programme, rehabilitation and reformation may imply different things, none of which may necessarily be related to risk. Despite innovative approaches by criminologists Maruna and Gadd, there is little relevant conceptual development in the criminological literature – there is no evidence thus far of satisfactory progress in assessing the meaningfulness of effective desistance. In studying self-help groups established to promote and sustain desistance from crime, Maruna et al.[32] explain: 'Neither the clients nor the counselors we interviewed had an agreed upon standard for determining whether a person has "rehabilitated" or "reformed" ' (p276). '. . . Ironically, we found that while clients often looked to counselors to know when the recovery was complete, the counselors often told clients to look within themselves' (p277).

A major finding from the Bjørgo and Horgan project was that the term 'de-radicalisation' appeared to be 'understood as *any* effort aimed at preventing radicalisation from taking place' (p3; my emphasis). Unless we develop much clearer terminology here, we will continue to face this unsatisfactory state of affairs. Additionally, Bjørgo and Horgan describe how the challenges to ascertaining successful disengagement should include (but not be limited to):

- screening out insincere participants through some selection process
- influencing their values and behaviour
- monitoring ex-militants after their release, with severe sanctions for breaching conditions
- providing the necessary skills, resources and social networks to enable them to reintegrate into society.

Issues of amnesty and successful reintegration posed immense social and political challenges. Success in Northern Ireland, Saudi Arabia, Colombia and South Africa, however, reveals promise. Critical to the effective evaluation of such initiatives, however, will be step 3 above. Regrettably, we know very little about recidivism and terrorism.

In a 2008 article in *Studies in Conflict and Terrorism*, Pluchinsky[33] estimated there to be approximately 5,000 imprisoned global Jihadists (outside of detainees held in Iraq and Afghanistan). He explains that while approximately 15% of those imprisoned received death sentences or life sentences, the majority of judgments were for sentences of less than 20 years (p183). Given that 'even terrorists receive sentence reductions for good behavior . . . it is unlikely that many global jihadists will serve out their full prison terms' (ibid.). Pluchinsky consults recidivism rates for the general population and argues: 'There is a tendency of released criminals . . . to return to crime. Thus, it can be assumed that this would be a logical tendency of [terrorists]' (p184). Furthermore, Pluchinsky argues 'terrorists with a secular motivation and goal are more likely to be reformed in prison than terrorists who are driven by religious grievances' (p187). He suggests that religious terrorists are more difficult to 'reform' because they operate according to 'God's word' (p187). His concern is merited, but it is incorrect to state that the secular terrorist is likely to be reformed more easily. It is likely that this argument stems from a limited view about the nature of ideological control.

The IRA member, for example, not only believes that he or she represents the interests of a large community of followers, but that he or she is engaged in a legitimate struggle against a corrupt and illegitimate government. Furthermore, that IRA member is able to draw on hundreds of years of militant Republican tradition and history, continuous reinforcement for which is found every day in the community in which that IRA member operates. For the IRA volunteer, the foundations of his or her belief, and the sanctity of it, may be no less significant than those of the religious 'true believer'. As explained in Chapter 2, secular terrorists are likely to have command structures and informal movements inside prisons. While the secular terrorist may be involuntarily disengaged, his or her continued involvement through another role even while in prison is common. In the context of so-called 'religious terrorism', it is highly likely that those who truly believe they are following the word of God are exceptionally few in number. The Al Qaeda social movement, as described by Sageman,[34] comprises a diverse and heterogeneous sample many members of which are unlikely to even have the ability to engage in theological debate. Even in a movement such as Al Qaeda, true believers (in a religious or ideological sense) are likely to be very few and far between.

Final thoughts

Disengagement and its related processes represent a serious gap in our knowledge and understanding of the terrorist. Far more work is now needed on these issues to reach full potential. The case studies presented in this book, as well as the broader sample from which they were extracted, represent one tentative step towards this. It may appear that in attempting to provide answers about disengagement from terrorism, more questions than answers have been produced. This may be disappointing to some but reflects the current state of affairs.

To reiterate a point made in Chapter 1, one of the most positive ways in which we can establish a psychological approach within the study of terrorism is to find an unambiguous sense of what is meant by an *individual perspective* in terrorism studies. The process approach taken by Taylor and Horgan recognises that individual experiences may be unique, but offers a framework for understanding that uniqueness within a broader context.

What is even more promising is that by improving our understanding of these processes, we may have at our disposal the basis for changing the perceived *effects* of that process as they impinge upon the individual. We are not likely to effectively change personal factors, but we can effect change at the level of the *social, political and organisational context*. Moving our level of analysis from properties to processes, and thus from profiles to pathways, seems to offer tangible rewards beyond just conceptual adequacy to the development of operational counter-terrorism initiatives.

This is especially relevant in terms of the ways in which the dimensions identified above may form the basis of a psychological operations counter-terrorism initiative. Drawing on the potential offered by community of practice notions, we have one very powerful framework from which to launch targeted interventions to affect the influence of social, political and organisational context as it exercises influence on the individual terrorist at all stages of his or her involvement.

While research on ascertaining the effectiveness of de-radicalisation programmes has already begun, an issue that deserves further systematic and comparative analysis relates to the roles of ex-militants in countering violent radicalisation. Some of these examples (e.g. that of Nasir Bin Abbas, Dr Fadl, etc.) were detailed in Chapter 2, but some of the case studies contained in this volume illustrate the extraordinary potential former terrorists may have in countering radicalisation into violence.

An urgent need is for greater clarity in terminology. Radicalisation, violent radicalisation, disengagement and de-radicalisation represent unique phases in the psychological development of the terrorist, and it is critical that we have explicit operational definitions. Without such clarity, practical initiatives aimed at either preventing initial violent radicalisation or promoting subsequent disengagement may suffer from a lack of clarity and an unrealistic sense of what is achievable through the promotion of such initiatives.

To help in developing a clearer role for the individual perspective in the study of terrorism, we need to understand individual–group dynamics. A sole emphasis either on individual factors or on collective disengagement will not reveal everything about the risk of recidivism. While the Early Release Scheme as part of the Good Friday Agreement in Northern Ireland saw a major release of terrorist prisoners, some re-engaged in high-profile terrorist activity. This offers a warning against the use of untested assumptions about how risk is conceptualised.

The criminology literature on desistance offers useful insights into how we can begin to conceptualise de-radicalisation, though there are distinctions between the politically motivated offender and the ordinary criminal. Successful de-radicalisation, however we choose to conceive it, may not necessarily require a fundamental change in individual identity. A more realistic objective is for us to develop a sense of the issues that reduce the risk of engaging in violence. Furthermore, the concept of secondary desistance comes close to our expectations of what successful de-radicalisation may bring.

Absent from discussions about communities of practice as well as from much of the literature on desistance is the specific role of language and how language (as part of ideology) exerts control over an individual. Maruna's work on explanatory styles offers a promising area for exploration in the context of assessing the feasibility of the terrorist equivalent of secondary desistance. The idiographic method of collecting narratives and analysing accounts of former terrorists represents a valuable first step in this. Indeed, and more broadly, a major benefit from drawing on the work of criminologists is that, as Bjørgo and Horgan illustrate, our knowledge and understanding of these processes as they relate to terrorism may well be informed by studying disengagement from youth gangs, racist and right-wing movements, and criminal lifestyles more generally (pp7–8).

Thinking about disengagement more broadly, it also follows that the promotion of disengagement will necessarily have to be tailor-made to the specific movement in question. It also will need to be carefully positioned within the context of the specific socio-political or other issues experienced by the group or the host government at any particular moment in time. As above, disengagement from terrorism, because of the broad factors that facilitate it from an individual perspective, may not necessarily result in the emergence of a 'repentant community' nor the successful reintegration of that community into the larger community it previously claimed to represent. While some minor efforts have developed in Northern Ireland to initiate restorative justice programmes between terrorists and families of their victims, these have been largely unsuccessful and, in some cases, have led to the development of significant tensions.

Finally, given the lack of conceptual development around disengagement issues, and on involvement in terrorism more generally, it is both naïve and premature at this point to draw general conclusions about disengagement. As the exploratory case studies and subsequent discussion have illustrated, we have valuable starting points. There is potential for tension in the promotion of disengagement initiatives, especially given renewed arguments that terrorism is not a problem that has a military solution. We may not overcome this tension any time soon, but at its heart, terrorism will continue to be a social problem and previously untested initiatives as well as previously underdeveloped perspectives may ultimately warrant much greater consideration in the future. Greater knowledge of the disengagement process plays a critical first step in this.

Notes

Foreword

1 Jerrold M. Post, M.D. is Professor of Psychiatry, Political Psychology and International Affairs, and Director of the Political Psychology Program, at the George Washington University. He is the author of *The Mind of the Terrorist: The Psychology of Terrorism from the IRA to al-Qaeda* (New York: Palgrave-MacMillan, 2007).
2 Post, J., E. Sprinzak and L. Denny, 'The Terrorists in their Own Words: Interviews with 35 Incarcerated Middle Eastern Terrorists,' *Terrorism and Political Violence*, *15* (1), 171–184, Spring 2003.
3 Post, J. (2000) 'Murder in a Political Context: Profile of an Abu Nidal Terrorist' *Bulletin of the Academy of Psychiatry and the Law* (Spring, 2000).
4 Horgan, J. (2005). *The Psychology of Terrorism*. New York: Routledge.
5 Post, J. (2005) 'The Psychological Causes of Terrorism', pp. 7–12 in *Addressing the Causes of Terrorism*, Vol. 1, The Club de Madrid Series on Democracy and Terrorism. Madrid: the Club de Madrid.
6 Post, J. (2005) 'Psychological Operations and Counter-terrorism'. *Joint Force Quarterly*, 37, 105–10.

Preface

1 Shrouded in mystery, conspiracy and omnipresent suspicion of internal collusion in Lebanon, *Fatah Al Islam* (FAI), a Sunni Islamist movement and *Al Qaeda* progeny, had set about trying to execute 'Operation 755' – its plan to establish an emirate in north Lebanon. It would try to do this firstly by imposing Islamic law, or *Sharia*, at Nar-el Bared. Secondly, it would use Nar-el Bared as a launch pad for terrorist operations organised against Israel. The 'emirate' would also serve as safe haven for Islamists in the region, particularly those seeking exit from Iraq. Led by Palestinian Shaker al-Abssi, FAI had sought refuge in Nar-el Bared, with cadres and their families being shipped inside in small groups over time. The PLO, Hamas and other Palestinian movements in the camp realised, far too late, what FAI's intentions entailed. An organised, disciplined movement, FAI members only came out at night, and viewed Palestinians within the camp as hostile and not to be trusted. Seizing existing weapons from PLO stashes within the camp, the movement began preparations for what would be its eventual, bloody showdown with the Lebanese army. In the spring of 2007, several FAI members became cornered in an apartment complex in Tripoli following a bank robbery in Amyoun, a small nearby town. A tense stand-off followed, with the subsequent gun battle leaving only one FAI member alive. Rather than face imminent capture by the closing army, he decided to blow himself up.

2 Sageman, M. (2008). *Leaderless Jihad*. Philadelphia: University of Pennsylvania Press.

3 Reich, W. (1990). 'Understanding Terrorist Behavior: The Limits and Opportunities of Psychological Inquiry'. In W. Reich (ed.) *Origins of Terrorism: Psychologies, Ideologies, Theologies, States of Mind*. New Jersey: Woodrow Wilson Center Press.

4 Jamieson, A. (1989). *The Heart Attacked*. London: Marion Boyars.

5 Horgan, J. (2005). *The Psychology of Terrorism*. Oxon: Routledge.

1 Qualities are not causes

1 BBC News Online (2008). *BBC Special Reports – In Depth: The London Attacks*. http://news.bbc.co.uk/2/hi/in_depth/uk/2005/london_explosions/default.stm

2 *Report of the Official Account of the Bombings in London on 7th July 2005, to the House of Commons*. 11 May 2006 (London: Stationery Office).

3 Macintyre, B. (2006). ' "Insignificant, shabby, miserable" – the banal stamp of the terrorist'. *The Times Comment*, 13 May, 21.

4 Silke, A. (1998). 'Cheshire Cat Logic: The Recurring Theme of Terrorist Abnormality in Psychological Research'. *Psychology, Crime and Law*, *4*, 51–69; also see J. Victoroff (2005). 'The Mind of the Terrorist: A Review and Critique of Psychological Approaches'. *The Journal of Conflict Resolution*, *49*, 3–42.

5 Hoffman, B. (2001). 'All You Need Is Love: How The Terrorists Stopped Terrorism'. *The Atlantic Monthly*, September.

6 Bjørgo, T. (ed.) (2005). *Root Causes of Terrorism*. Oxon: Routledge.

7 See for example, the edited collections by Reich and Silke: Reich, W. (ed.) (1990). *Origins of Terrorism: Psychologies, Ideologies, Theologies, States of Mind*. NJ: Woodrow Wilson Center Press; Silke, A. (ed.) (2003). Terrorists, Victims and Society: *Psychological Perspectives on Terrorism and Its Consequences* (Wiley Series in Psychology of Crime, Policing and Law). London: Wiley Blackwell.

8 I am grateful to Ariel Merari for making this key distinction.

9 Horgan, J. (2005). *The Psychology of Terrorism*. Oxon: Routledge.

10 Taylor, M. (1988). *The Terrorist*. London: Brassey's.

11 Arendt, H. (1969). *On Violence*. New York: Harvest, p3.

12 Jamieson, A. (1989). *The Heart Attacked*. London: Marion Boyars, pp267–8.

13 This is despite partially encouraging progress since Reich's (note 7) path-breaking collection from 1990. A recent excellent collection was produced by Bruce Bongar and colleagues: Bongar, B., Brown, L.M., Beutler, L.E., Breckenridge, J.N. & Zimbardo, P.G. (eds) (2007). *Psychology of Terrorism*. New York: Oxford University Press.

14 Taylor (note 10).

15 Interview conducted by the author, Cork, 1999.

16 CNN (2008). 'US Military: Al Qaeda in Iraq seeks female patients as bombers'. http://edition.cnn.com/2008/WORLD/meast/02/14/iraq.main/

17 Interviewed by the author, London, 2006.

18 Eysenck, H. (1957). *The Dynamics of Anxiety and Hysteria*. London: Routlege, p13.

19 Silke, A. (ed.) (2004). *Researching Terrorism: Trends, Successes, Failures*. London: Frank Cass.

20 See, for example, the critique of much of the psychological literature by Silke (note 7); Silke (note 4) and Horgan, J. (2003). 'The search for the terrorist personality', in Silke, A. (ed.) (2003). *Terrorist, Victims, and Society: Psychological Perspectives on Terrorism and its Consequences* (pp3–27). London: Wiley. For early prescient examples: Corrado, R.A. (1981). 'A critique of the mental disorder perspective of political terrorism'. *International Journal of Law and Psychiatry*, *4* (3–4), 293–309.

21 Hoffman, B. (2008). 'The Myth of Grass-Roots Terrorism: Why Osama Bin

Laden Still Matters'. *Foreign Affairs*, May/June; also Marc Sageman and Bruce Hoffman, 'Does Osama Still Call the Shots? Debating the Containment of al-Qaeda's Leadership'. *Foreign Affairs*, July/August 2008.

22 See Reich (note 7), especially the final chapter in this collection, by Reich himself.
23 For two good examples, see: Post, J.M., Sprinzak, E. and Denny, L.M. (2003). 'The Terrorists in their Own Words: Interviews with Thirty-Five Incarcerated Middle Eastern Terrorists'. *Terrorism and Political Violence*, *15*, 171–84; Crawford, C. (2003). *Inside the UDA: Volunteers and Violence*. Dublin: Pluto.
24 For an early promising example of this see Cordes, B. (1987). 'Euroterrorists Talk About Themselves: A Look at the Literature', in P. Wilkinson & A.M. Stewart (eds) *Contemporary Research on Terrorism* (pp318–36). Aberdeen: Aberdeen University Press.
25 Macintyre (note 3).
26 Paterson, L. (2007). *U-Boat Combat Missions – The Pursuers and the Pursued – First-Hand Accounts of U-Boat Life and Operations*. New York: Barnes and Noble, p27.
27 Macintyre (note 3).
28 Taylor, M. & Horgan, J. (2006). 'A Conceptual Framework for Addressing Psychological Process in the Development of the Terrorist'. *Terrorism and Political Violence*, *18* (4), 585–601.
29 Ibid., p586.
30 For a greater and more detailed consideration of this, see Taylor and Horgan (note 28).
31 Presentation delivered by the author at the Center for the Study of Terrorism and Political Violence, University of St Andrews.
32 Sageman, M. (2008). *Leaderless Jihad*. University of Pennsylvania: University of Pennsylvania Press.
33 BBC News Online. (2005). 'London bomber video aired on TV'. http://news.bbc.co.uk/2/hi/uk_news/4206708.stm
34 Bassiouni's 'profile' of the terrorist contains not dissimilar elements, although they are identified in a different context – see Bassiouni, M.C. (1987). *Legal Responses to International Terrorism*. Boston, MA: Martinus Nijhoof.
35 Roberts, K. & Horgan, J. (2008). 'Risk Assessment and the Terrorist'. *Perspectives on Terrorism*, *2*, 6, March, 3–9.
36 BBC News Online. (2007). 'UK Fertilizer Bomb Plot'. http://news.bbc.co.uk/2/shared/spl/hi/guides/457000/457032/html/nn1page6.stm (see especially the section on '7/7 Links').
37 'Student Guilty of Terrorism Charge for Altered 9/11 Poster'. *The Scotsman*, 26 July 2007.
38 Kalyvas, S.N. (2003). 'The Ontology of "Political Violence": Action and Identity in Civil Wars'. *Perspectives on Politics*, *1*(3), 475–94.
39 Post, J. (2008). *The Mind of the Terrorist: The Psychology of Terrorism from the IRA to Al Qaeda*. New York: Palgrave Macmillan, p9.
40 Gadd, D. (2006). 'The Role of Recognition in the Desistance Process: A Case Analysis of a Former Far-right Activist'. *Theoretical Criminology*, *10*(2), 179–202.
41 Ibid., p179.
42 Clark, R.P. (1983). 'Patterns in the Lives of ETA Members'. *Terrorism*, *6* (3), pp423–54; also see Clark, R.P. (1983). *The Basque Insurgents: ETA 1952–1980*. Madison: University of Wisconsin Press.
43 Reich, W. (ed.) (1990). *Origins of Terrorism: Ideologies, Psychologies, Theologies, States of Mind*. Princeton, NJ: Woodrow Wilson Center Press.
44 Hoffman, B. (1998). *Inside Terrorism*. New York: Colombia.
45 Alonso, R. (2006). *The IRA and Armed Struggle*. Oxon: Routledge.
46 Miller, A.H. (1989). 'Book Review'. *Terrorism and Political Violence*, *1* (3), 391–6.

47 de Cataldo Neuburger, L. & Valentini, T. (1996). *Women and Terrorism*. Hampshire: Macmillan.
48 Harnden, T. & Jones, G. (1999). 'Early Release of Terrorists Under Attack'. *Daily Telegraph*, 4 February.

2 How, when and why terrorism ends

1 See Taylor, M. & Horgan, J. (2006). 'A Conceptual Framework for Addressing Psychological Process in the Development of the Terrorist'. *Terrorism and Political Violence, 18* (4), 585–601.
2 See Horgan, J. (2005). 'Psychological Factors Related to Disengaging from Terrorism: Some Preliminary Assumptions and Assertions', in C. Benard (ed.) *A Future for the Young: Options For Helping Middle Eastern Youth Escape the Trap of Radicalization*. Washington DC: Rand Working Paper WR-354 (also see chapters by Bjørgo, and Taarnby, in the same volume).
3 Horgan, J. (2006). 'Disengaging from Terrorism'. *Jane's Intelligence Review, 18* (12), 34–7.
4 Rapoport, D.C. (1992). 'Terrorism', in M.E. Hawkesworth & M. Kogan (eds) *Routledge Encyclopedia of Government and Politics. Vol. 2*. London: Routledge.
5 Wilkinson, P. (1987). 'Pathways out of Terrorism for Democratic Societies', in Paul Wilkinson & A.M. Stewart (eds) *Contemporary Research on Terrorism*. Aberdeen: Aberdeen University Press, pp453–65.
6 Horchem, H.J. (1991). 'The Decline of the Red Army Faction'. *Terrorism and Political Violence, 3* (2), 61–74.
7 Jamieson, A. (1990). 'Entry, Discipline and Exit in the Italian Red Brigades'. *Terrorism and Political Violence, 2* (1), 1–20.
8 Weinberg, L. & Eubank, W.L. (1987). *The Rise and Fall of Italian Terrorism*. London: Westview; also for a more recent examination of the decline of the 'formation' of terrorist movements, see Pedahzur, A., Eubank, W. & Weinberg, L. (2002). 'The War on Terrorism and the Decline of Terrorist Group Formation: A Research Note'. *Terrorism and Political Violence, 14* (3), 141–7.
9 Alonso, R. (2004). 'Pathways Out of Terrorism in Northern Ireland and the Basque Country: The Misrepresentation of the Irish Model'. *Terrorism and Political Violence, 16* (4), 695–713; also see Barros, C.P. & Gil-Alana, L.A. (2006). 'ETA: A Persistent Phenomenon'. *Defence and Peace Economics, 17* (2), 95–116; and Moore, M. (2005). 'End of Terrorism? ETA and the Efforts for Peace'. *Harvard International Review, 27* (2), 12.
10 Gerges, F. (1999). 'The Decline of Revolutionary Islam in Algeria and Egypt'. *Survival, 41* (1), 113–25.
11 Kassimeris, G. (2005). 'Urban Guerrilla or Revolutionary Fantasist? Dimitris Koufodinas and the Revolutionary Organization 17 November'. *Studies in Conflict and Terrorism, 28* (1), 21–31.
12 Lopez-Alves, F. (1989). 'Political Crises, Strategic Choices and Terrorism: The Rise and Fall of the Uruguayan Tupamoros'. *Terrorism and Political Violence, 1* (2), 202–41.
13 Cronin, A.K. (2008). *Ending Terrorism: Lessons for Defeating Al-Qaeda. International Institute for Strategic Studies Adelphi Paper 394*. Oxon: Routledge.
14 See in particular, Mueller, J. (2006). *Overblown: How Politicians and the Terrorism Industry Inflate National Security Threats and Why We Believe Them*. New York: Free Press.
15 Crenshaw, M. (1987). 'How Terrorism Ends'. Paper Presented at the Annual meeting of the American Political Science Association, Chicago, IL, September. Also see Cronin, A.K. (2006). 'How Al-Qaida Ends: The Decline and Demise of Terrorist Groups'. *International Security, 31* (1), 7–48; Crenshaw, M. (1991). 'How

Terrorism Declines'. *Terrorism and Political Violence*, *3* (1), 69–87. Crenshaw is one of a number of authors who contributed to a multi-authored report of United States Institute of Peace (1999). *How Terrorism Ends*. Special Report, No.48. Washington DC: U.S. Institute of Peace: http://purl.access.gpo.gov/GPO/LPS14739

16 Gupta, D. (2008). *Understanding Terrorism and Political Violence: The Life Cycle of Birth, Growth, Transformation and Demise*. Oxon: Routledge, p161.

17 Cronin (note 13) p28.

18 The same argument applies to issues relevant to explaining organisational decline in businesses and non-illegal organisations. See for example: Whetten, D.A. (1980). 'Organizational Decline: A Neglected Topic in Organizational Science'. *The Academy of Management Review*, *5* (4), 577–88; Wilkinson, A. & Mellahi, K. (2005). 'Organisational Failure: Introduction to the Special Issue'. *Long Range Planning – International Journal of Strategic Management*, *38* (3), 233–8.

19 See Adair, J. with McKendry, G. (2007). *Mad Dog*. London: Blake.

20 First Report of the Independent Monitoring Commission, Presented to the Government of the United Kingdom and the Government of Ireland under Articles 4 and 7 of the International Agreement establishing the Independent Monitoring Commission, April 2004 (Section 3.13).

21 Ibid., section 4.10.

22 Ibid.

23 Ibid., section 5.20.

24 Third Report of the Independent Monitoring Commission. Presented to the Government of the United Kingdom and the Government of Ireland under Articles 4 and 7 of the International Agreement establishing the Independent Monitoring Commission, November 2004.

25 Ross, J.I. & Gurr, T.R. (1989). 'Why Terrorism Subsides: A Comparative Study of Canada and the United States'. *Comparative Politics*, *21* (4), 405–26.

26 Oots, K.L. (1989). 'Organizational Perspectives on the Formation and Disintegration of Terrorist Groups'. *Terrorism*, *12*, 139–52. On the broader organisational issues related to terrorism, see Crenshaw, M. (1985). 'An Organisational Political Approach to the Analysis of Political Terrorism'. *Orbis*, *29* (3), 465–89; and in particular the essential collection of contributions contained in Rapoport, D.C. (ed.) (1988). *Inside Terrorist Organisations*. London: Frank Cass.

27 Oots, K.L. (1989). 'Bargaining With Terrorists: Organisational Considerations'. *Terrorism*, *13*, 145–58.

28 Hirschman, A.O. (1970). *Exit, Voice, and Loyalty: Responses to Decline in Firms, Organizations and States*. Cambridge, MA: Harvard University Press.

29 Bergen, P. & Cruickshank, P. (2008). 'The Unraveling: The Jihadist Revolt Against Bin Laden'. *The New Republic*, 11 June. Available at: http://www.tnr.com/politics/story.html?id=702bf6d5-a37a-4e3e-a491-fd72bf6a9da1

30 Belfast Newsletter (2006). ' "Terror convention" cancelled as finger points at the IRA'. 29 August. Available at: http://www.newsletter.co.uk/ViewArticle.aspx?SectionID=3425&ArticleID=1726257

31 Dowling, B. (2006). 'Efforts to unite North dissident groups pose "real threat". *Irish Independent*, 28 August. Available at: http://www.independent.ie/national-news/efforts-to-unite-north-dissident-groups-pose-real-threat-85137.html

32 Ibid.

33 Clarke, L. (2006). 'IRA split adds to violence worries'. *Sunday Times*. 27 August. Available at: http://www.timesonline.co.uk/tol/news/world/ireland/article620853.ece

34 Gupta (note 16), p124.

35 Ibid., citing the work of Jessica Stern, p125.

36 Also see Zirakzadeh, C.E. (2002). 'From Revolutionary Dreams to Organizational

Fragmentation: Disputes over Violence within ETA and Sendero Luminoso'. *Terrorism and Political Violence, 14* (4), 66–92.

37 Bloom, M. (2005). *Dying to Kill: The Allure of Suicide Terror.* New York: Columbia.

38 Also for one of the earliest works on this see Zawodny, J.K. (1978). 'Internal Organizational Problems and the Sources of Tensions of Terrorist Movements as Cataylsts of Violence'. *Terrorism, 1* (3–4), 277–85.

39 A fascinating revisiting of the IRA's alleged successes in Ireland is provided by Rogelio Alonso (2007) in his book *The IRA and Armed Struggle.* Oxon: Routledge.

40 Ibid. Also Abrams, M. (2007). 'Why Terrorism Does Not Work'. *International Security, 31* (2), 42–78.

41 First Report of the Independent Monitoring Commission, Presented to the Government of the United Kingdom and the Government of Ireland under Articles 4 and 7 of the International Agreement establishing the Independent Monitoring Commission, April 2004, Section 3.12.

42 Debray, R. (1967). *Revolution in the Revolution.* New York: MR Press.

43 BBC News Online. (2007). 'Sadr "freezes" militia activities'. 29 August.

44 Horgan, J. & Taylor, M. (1999). 'Playing the Green Card: Financing the Provisional IRA – Part 1'. *Terrorism and Political Violence, 11* (2), 1–60.

45 BBC News Online. (2007). 'Replica guns at march condemned'. 4 September. Available online at http://news.bbc.co.uk/1/hi/northern_ireland/6977173.stm

46 Cusack, J. & Taylor, M. (1993). 'Resurgence of a Terrorist Organisation – Part 1: The UDA, a Case Study'. *Terrorism and Political Violence, 5* (3), 1–27.

47 Some examples: Bamford, B.W.C. (2005). 'The Role and Effectiveness of Intelligence in Northern Ireland'. *Intelligence and National Security, 20* (4), 581–607; Bergen, P. (2001). 'The Bin-Laden Trial: What Did We Learn?' *Studies in Conflict and Terrorism, 24* (6), 429–34; Bonner, D. (1988). 'Combating Terrorism: Supergrass Trials in Northern Ireland.' *The Modern Law Review, 51* (1), 23–53; Cohen, H. & Dudai, R. (2005). 'Human Rights Dilemmas in Using Informers to Combat Terrorism: The Israeli-Palestinian Case.' *Terrorism and Political Violence, 17* (1–2), 229–43; Gil-Har, Y. (2003). 'British Intelligence and the Role of Jewish Informers in Palestine'. *Middle Eastern Studies,* 39 (1), 117–49; Greer, S.C. (1987). 'The Supergrass System in Northern Ireland', in P. Wilkinson & A.M. Stewart (eds) *Contemporary Research on Terrorism.* Aberdeen: Aberdeen University Press, pp510–35; Hillyard, P. & Percy-Smith, J. (1984). 'Converting Terrorists: The Use of Supergrasses in Northern Ireland'. *Journal of Law and Society, 11* (3), 335–55; Sarma, K. (2005). 'Informers and the Battle Against Republican Terrorism: A Review of 30 Years of Conflict'. *Police Practice and Research, 6* (2), 165–80; United States Congress Senate Committee of Governmental Affairs. (1992). *Terrorist defectors: are we ready? : Hearing before the Committee on Governmental Affairs, United States Senate, One Hundred Second Congress, second session, February 4, 1992.* Washington, U.S. G.P.O.; Wayne, P.J.M. & Morton, J. (1995). 'Supergrasses and Informers'. *Spectator,* 275 (8726), 47.

48 Bjørgo, T. (1998). *Recruitment and Disengagement from Extreme Groups: The Case of Racist Youth Subcultures.* Paper presented at the 7th International Seminar on Environmental Criminology and Crime Analysis, Barcelona, 21–24 June; Bjørgo, T. (1999). *How Gangs Fall Apart: Processes of Transformation and Disintegration of Gangs.* Paper presented at the 51st Annual Meeting of the American Society of Criminology, Toronto, Canada, 17–20 November; Bjørgo, T. (2006). 'Reducing Recruitment and Promoting Disengagement from Terrorist Groups: The Case of Racist Sub-Cultures', in C. Benard (ed.) *A Future for the Young: Options for helping Middle Eastern Youth Escape the Trap of Radicalisation.* Washington DC: Rand Working Paper WR-354; Bjørgo, T. & Carlsson, Y. (2005). *Early Intervention*

with Violent and Racist Youth Groups. NUPI-paper 677. Available at: http://
www.nupi.no/IPS/filestore/Paper677.pdf
49 The literature on desistance from criminal activity is substantial: Bottoms, A.,
Shapland, J., Costello, A., Holmes, D. & Muir, G. (2004). 'Towards Desistance:
Theoretical Underpinnings for an Empirical Study'. *The Howard Journal of
Criminal Justice, 43* (4), 368–89; Brame, R., Bushway, S.D. & Paternoster, R.
(2003). 'Examining the prevalence of criminal desistance'. *Criminology, 41*(2),
423–48; Bushway, S.D., Piquero, A.R., Broidy, L.M., Cauffman, E. & Mazerolle,
P. (2001). 'An Empirical Framework for Studying Desistance as a Process'. *Crim-
inology, 39* (2), 491–515; Bushway, S.D., Thornberry, T.P. & Krohn, M.D. (2003).
'Desistance as a Developmental Process: A Comparison of Static and Dynamic
Approaches'. *Journal of Quantitative Criminology, 19* (2), 129–53; Doherty, E.E.
(2006). 'Self-control, Social Bonds, and Desistance: A Test of Life-course Inter-
dependence'. *Criminology, 44* (4), 807–33; Farrall, S. (2005). 'On the Existential
Aspects of Desistance from Crime'. *Symbolic Interaction, 28* (3), 367–86; Farrall,
S. & Maruna, S. (2004). 'Desistance-Focused Criminal Justice Policy Research:
Introduction to a Special Issue on Desistance from Crime and Public Policy'. *The
Howard Journal of Criminal Justice, 43* (4), 358–67; Gadd, D. (2006). 'The Role of
Recognition in the Desistance Process – A Case Analysis of a Former Far-right
Activist'. *Theoretical Criminology, 10* (2), 179–202; Gadd, D. & Farrall, S. (2004).
'Criminal Careers, Desistance and Subjectivity: Interpreting Men's Narratives of
Change'. *Theoretical Criminology, 8* (2), 123–56; Giordano, P.C., Cernkovich, S.A.
& Holland, D.D. (2003). 'Changes in Friendship Relations over the Life Course:
Implications for Desistance from Crime'. *Criminology, 41* (2), 293–327;
Kanazawa, S. & Still, M.C. (2000). 'Why Men Commit Crimes (And Why They
Desist)'. *Sociological Theory, 18* (3), 434–47; Maruna, S. (2004). 'Desistance from
Crime and Explanatory Style: A New Direction in the Psychology of Reform'.
Journal of Contemporary Criminal Justice, 20 (2), 184–200; Mulvey, E., Steinberg,
L. & Fagan, J. (2005). 'Theory and Research on Desistance from Antisocial Activity
among Serious Adolescent Offenders'. *Youth Violence and Juvenile Justice, 2* (3),
213–36; Walters, G. (2002). 'Developmental Trajectories, Transitions, and Nonlinear Dynamical Systems: A Model of Crime Deceleration and Desistance'. *International Journal of Offender Therapy and Comparative Criminology, 46* (1), 30–44.
50 Simon, B. (2007). 'Switching Sides: Inside the Enemy Camp'. *60 Minutes*, 6 May;
also see Bergen and Cruickshank (note 29); Middle East Media Research Institute
(MEMRI), (2008). 'Report: Al Qaeda Maghreb Commander Turns Self In'.
8 June.
51 Bergen and Cruickshank (note 29).
52 For an exceptional example of the kind of research facilitated by changes since the
peace process, see Alonso, R. (2007) *The IRA and Armed Struggle*. Oxon:
Routledge.
53 For example, the Quilliam Foundation at http://www.quilliamfoundation.org. The
Quilliam Foundation is described on its website as a 'counter extremist think
thank [it was] created by former activists of radical Islamist organisations'; also
see Wright, L. (2008). 'The Rebellion Within'. *New Yorker*, 2 June; Brandon,
J. (2008) 'The UK's Experience in Counter-Radicalization'. *The Sentinel*
(Countering Terrorism Center), *1* (5).
54 Harmon, C. (2008). *Terrorism Today*. 2nd edition. Oxon: Routledge, p179.
55 Some elementary examples of statement reflecting a decision by movements to
'cease' hostilities: BBC News. (2005). 'IRA statement in full'. 28 July. Available at:
http://news.bbc.co.uk/1/hi/northern_ireland/4724599.stm; BBC News. (2006).
'Text: Eta declares ceasefire'. 23 March. Available at: http://news.bbc.co.uk/1/hi/
world/europe/4833490.stm; Red Army Faction. (1998). *Statement of the RAF* (the
1998 disbanding of the Rote Army Faction): The Final Communiqué from the

Red Army Faction. Available at: http://www.baader-meinhof.com/students/resources/communique/engrafend.html

56　Reich, W. (ed.) (1990). *Origins of Terrorism: Psychologies, Ideologies, Theologies, States of Mind*. New York: Cambridge University Press.

57　MacFarquhar, N. (2008). 'Speakers at Academy Said to Make False Claims'. *New York Times*, US Section, 7 February; Zubeck, P. (2008). 'Cadets' Guest Speaker will Focus on Christianity'. *Colorado Springs Gazette*.

58　Cordes, B. (1987). 'Euroterrorists Talk about Themselves: A Look at the Literature', in P. Wilkinson & A.M. Stewart (eds) *Contemporary Research on Terrorism* (pp318–36). Aberdeen: Aberdeen University Press. This volume remains one of the most important cornerstone texts any student of terrorism can ever read.

59　Horgan, J. (2005). 'Psychological Factors Related to Disengaging from Terrorism: Some Preliminary Assumptions and Assertions', in C. Benard (ed.) *A Future for the Young: Options For Helping Middle Eastern Youth Escape the Trap of Radicalization*. Washington DC: Rand Working Paper WR-354, 2005.

60　Garfinkel, R. (2007). 'Personal Transformations: Moving From Violence To Peace'. *United States Institute of Peace Special Report*, 186, April.

61　Ebaugh, H.R.F. (1988). *Becoming an Ex: The Process of Role Exit*. Chicago: University of Chicago Press.

62　See, for example: Horgan (notes 3, 59); Horgan, J. (2003). 'Leaving Terrorism Behind: An Individual Perspective', in A. Silke (ed.) *Terrorists, Victims and Society: Psychological Perspectives on Terrorism and its Consequences*. London: John Wiley.

63　Ibid.

64　See Ripley, A. (2008). 'Reversing Radicalism'. *TIME*.

65　This is from a translated copy of Patrizio Peci's autobiographical *I, the Contemptible One* detailing his involvement in the Red Brigades as told to Bruno Guerri, Arnoldo Mondadori, Editore S.P.A. Milano (1983, translation 1985 by the Foreign Broadcast Information Service). I am very grateful to Jerrold Post for providing me with this example.

66　Collins, E. (with M. McGovern) (1997). *Killing Rage*. Granta: London.

67　Cusack, J. & Taylor, M. (1993). 'Resurgence of a Terrorist Organisation: Part 1 – The UDA: A Case Study'. *Terrorism and Political Violence*, 5 (1993) 1–27.

68　Nasiri, O. (2006). 'Focus: My life as a spy at the heart of Al-Qaeda'. *Sunday Times*, 19 November, pp14–15.

69　O'Keefe, A. (2008). 'Jungle Fever'. *The Observer*, 24 August.

70　Ibid.

71　McDermott, J. (2008). 'Farc's female Rambo surrenders to resurgent Colombian police'. *The Scotsman*, May 20.

72　Interviewed by the author in Jakarta in 2007.

73　Bergen and Cruickshank (note 29).

74　The 9/11 Commission Report, p62.

75　Bergen and Cruickshank (note 29).

76　Horgan, J. (2003). 'Leaving Terrorism Behind: An Individual Perspective', in A. Silke (ed.) *Terrorists, Victims and Society: Psychological Perspectives on Terrorism and its Consequences*. London: John Wiley.

77　O'Keefe (note 69).

78　Ibid.

79　These examples are from J. Horgan, *The Psychology of Terrorism*.

80　Horgan (ibid). See Chapters 5 and 6 in particular.

81　Debray (note 42).

82　McDermott (note 71).

83　BBC News Online. (2007). 'Taleban sack military commander'. 29 December. Available at: http://www.bbc.co.uk/2/hi/south_asia/7164277.stm

84 Markey, P. (2007). 'Colombian warlord violates deal, faces extradition'. Reuters, 24 August. Available at: http://www.reuters.com/article/worldNews/idUSN2433300420070824

85 Ibid.

86 Interview with senior IRA member, Dublin, December 2007.

87 BBC News Online. (2007). 'NI politicians help at Iraq talks'. 3 September. Available at: http://news.bbc.co.uk/1/hi/northern_ireland/6976706.stm; to put these and related issues in context, see Byman, D. (2006). 'The Decision to Begin Talks with Terrorists: Lessons for Policymakers'. *Studies in Conflict and Terrorism*, 29 (5), 403–14.

88 Caldwell, J. (2007). 'Ex-paramilitary Tesco "superhero" '. 19 April. Available at: http://news.bbc.co.uk/1/hi/northern_ireland/6570165.stm.

89 Combating Terrorism Center. (2008). *Bombers, Bank Accounts and Bleedout: Al Qaida's Road in and Out of Iraq*. New York: CTC West Point. Available at: http://www.ctc.usma.edu/harmony/Sinjar2.asp. For an example of one of the 'Separation Contracts', see http://www.ctc.usma.edu/harmony/pdf/summaries%20in%20pdfs/Separation%20Contracts.pdf

90 CNN Larry King Live. (2002). Interview with Patty Hearst. Aired 22 January. Available at: http://transcripts.cnn.com/TRANSCRIPTS/0201/22/lkl.00.html

91 The 9/11 Commission Report; for an interesting example of a related case, see Simpson, C., Swanson, S. & Crewdson, J. (2003). '9/11 Suspect Cut Unlikely Figure in Terror Plot'. *Chicago Tribune*, 23 February.

92 This issue (in a non-terrorism context) is discussed in great detail in Albert Hirschman's (note 28) seminal study on exit from organisations and firms.

4 'I volunteered'

1 McDonald, H. and Cusack, J. (1997). *UVF*. Dublin: Poolbeg.

2 Dillon, M. (1991). *The Shankill Butchers: A Case Study of Mass Murder*. London: Arrow.

3 The UVF increasingly saw the 'Butchers' as a hindrance to their cause such that the UVF leadership actually tipped off the Provisional IRA as to Murphy's location.

5 'There is no conscious decision'

1 Sageman, M. (2008). *Leaderless Jihad*. Philadelphia: University of Pennsylvania Press.

6 'A step too far'

1 Hirschman, A.O. (1970). *Exit, Voice, and Loyalty: Responses to Decline in Firms, Organizations and States*. Cambridge, MA: Harvard University Press.

7 'They were once my people'

1 Hirschman, A.O. (1970). *Exit, Voice, and Loyalty: Responses to Decline in Firms, Organizations and States*. Cambridge, MA: Harvard University Press.

8 'I don't believe in integration'

1 CNN. (2002). 'Al Qaeda Now'. Available at: http://archives.cnn.com/2002/ALLPOLITICS/05/27/time.alqaeda/

2 Ronson, J. (2002). *Them: Adventures With Extremists*. London: Simon and Schuster.

3 *The Gazette* (Montreal, Quebec, Canada), 13 September 2001, pB6.
4 BBC News Online. (2005). 'Cleric Bakri "will return" to UK'. 9 August. Available at: http://news.bbc.co.uk/2/hi/uk_news/politics/4133150.stm
5 Fielding, N. (2005). 'Terror links of the Tottenham Ayatollah'. *Sunday Times*. 24 July. Available at: http://www.timesonline.co.uk/tol/news/uk/article547466.ece
6 Ibid.
7 For a detailed biography of Omar Bakri, see Casciani, D. (2005). 'Profile: Omar Bakri Mohammed'. BBC News Online, 12 August. Available at: http://news.bbc.co.uk/2/hi/uk_news/4144892.stm
8 The Muslim Brotherhood is perhaps the most important organisation that has provided focus and direction for the development of political Islam in over 60 countries.
9 For access to the full text of the Terrorism Act, see http://www.homeoffice.gov.uk/security/terrorism-and-the-law/terrorism-act-2006/
10 Ibid., p149.
11 Sageman, M. (2008). *Leaderless Jihad*. Philadelphia: University of Pennsylvania Press, pvii.

9 Conclusions

1 Taylor, M. & Horgan, J. (2006). 'A Conceptual Framework for Addressing Psychological Process in the Development of the Terrorist', *Terrorism and Political Violence*, *18* (4), 585–601.
2 I am grateful to Conor Lynch for discussion on this issue.
3 See the discussion in Gadd, D. (2006). 'The role of recognition in the desistance process: A case analysis of a former far-right activist'. *Theoretical Criminology*, *10* (2), 179–202.
4 Taylor and Horgan (note 1).
5 Horgan, J. (2005). *The Psychology of Terrorism*. Oxon: Routledge.
6 See, for example: Farrington, D. (1992). 'Explaining the Beginning, Progress and Ending of Antisocial Behaviour from Birth to Adulthood', in J. McCord (ed.) *Facts, Frameworks and Forecasts: Advances in Criminological Theory, Volume 3*. New Brunswick: Transactional Publishers; Clarke, R.V.G. & Cornish, D.B. (1985). 'Modeling Offenders' Decisions: A Framework for Research and Policy', in M. Tonry and N. Morris (eds) *Crime and Justice: An Annual Review of Research, Volume 6*. Chicago: University of Chicago Press; Cusson, M. (1993). 'A Strategic Analysis of Crime: Criminal Tactics as Responses to Precriminal Situations', in R.V. Clarke & M. Felson (eds.) *Routine Activity and Rational Choice: Volume 5*. New Brunswick, NJ: Transaction; Fattah, E.A. (1993). 'The Rational Choice/ Opportunity Perspectives as a Vehicle for Integrating Criminological and Victimological Theories'. In R.V. Clarke & M. Felson (eds) *Routine Activity and Rational Choice: Volume 5*. New Brunswick, NJ: Transaction.
7 Taylor and Horgan (note 1).
8 Taylor and Horgan (p591).
9 Hall, S. (1985). 'Signification, Representation, Ideology: Althusser and the Post-Structuralist Debates'. *Critical Studies in Mass Communication*, *2*, 535–62.
10 Wenger, E. (1998). *Communities of Practice: Learning, Meaning, and Identity*. Cambridge: Cambridge University Press.
11 Hundeide, K. (2003). 'Becoming a Committed Insider'. *Culture and Psychology*, *9* (2), 107–27.
12 Lave, J. & Wenger, E. (1991). *Situated Learning*. Cambridge: Cambridge University Press.
13 I am grateful to Dr Lorraine Bowman for her research assistance with this example.

14 Abu-Assad, H. (Director). (2005). *Paradise Now*. Augustus Film.
15 Walt, V. (2005). 'Ordinary People', *Time*, 10 October.
16 Ibid.
17 Shulman, M.R. (2004). *Civil Society's Response to the Challenges of Terrorism: A Conference Report*. From a Meeting held at the Luso-American Foundation, Lisbon, Portugal, 7–8 June.
18 Hundeide (note 11).
19 Hovland, C.I., Janis, I.L. & Kelley, H.H. (1953). *Communication and Persuasion: Psychological Studies of Opinion Change*. New Haven: Yale University Press.
20 Decker, S.H. & Van Winkle, B. (1996). *Life in a Gang: Family, Friends and Violence*. New York: Cambridge University Press.
21 Horgan, J. (2003) 'Leaving Terrorism Behind', in Silke, A. (ed.) *Terrorists, Victims and Society: Psychological Perspectives on Terrorism and its Consequences*. London: John Wiley; also Horgan, J. (2006). 'Disengaging from Terrorism', *Jane's Intelligence Review*, December, 34–7.
22 Bjørgo, T. & Horgan, J. (eds) (2009). *Leaving Terrorism Behind: Individual and Collective Disengagement*. Oxon: Routledge.
23 Of which I was a member.
24 Ibid.
25 Ibid. See Christopher Boucek's chapter in the volume.
26 Gadd (note 3).
27 Maruna, S. (2004). 'Desistance from Crime and Explanatory Style: A New Direction in the Psychology of Reform'. *Journal of Contemporary Criminal Justice, 20* (2), 184–200.
28 Maruna, S. & Farrall, S. (2004) 'Desistance from Crime: A Theoretical Reformulation', in D. Oberwittler and S. Karstedt (eds) *Kolner Zeitschrift fur Soziologie und Sozialpsychologie, 43*, pp171–94. Soziologie der Kriminalitaet Koelner Zeitschrift fuer Soziologie und Sozialpsychologie, VS Verlag fuer Sozialwissenschaften, Wiesbaden.
29 Gadd (note 3).
30 Maruna (note 27).
31 Smith, A.G., Suedfelt, P., Conway III, L.G. & Winter, D.G. (2008). 'The Language of Violence: Distinguishing Terrorist from Nonterrorist Groups by Thematic Content Analysis.' *Dynamics of Asymmetric Conflict, 1* (2), 142–63.
32 Maruna, S., LeBel, T., Mitchel, N. & Naples, M. (2004). 'Pygmalion in the Reintegration Process: Desistance from Crime through the Looking Glass'. *Psychology, Crime and Law, 10* (3), 271–81.
33 Pluchinsky, D.A. (2008). 'Global Jihadist Recidivism: A Red Flag'. *Studies in Conflict and Terrorism, 31* (3), 182–200.
34 Sageman, M. (2008). *Leaderless Jihad*. University of Pennsylvania: University of Pennsylvania Press.

Bibliography

Abrams, M. (2007). 'Why Terrorism Does Not Work'. *International Security*, *31* (2), 42–78.

Abu-Assad, H. (2005). *Paradise Now*. Augustus Film.

Adair, J. (with McKendry, G.). (2007). *Mad Dog*. London: Blake.

Alonso, R. (2004). 'Pathways Out of Terrorism in Northern Ireland and the Basque Country: The Misrepresentation of the Irish Model'. *Terrorism and Political Violence*, *16* (4), 695–713.

Alonso, R. (2006). *The IRA and Armed Struggle*. Oxon: Routledge.

Arendt, H. (1969). *On Violence*. New York: Harvest.

Bamford, B.W.C. (2005). 'The Role and Effectiveness of Intelligence in Northern Ireland'. *Intelligence and National Security*, *20* (4), 581–607.

Barros, C.P. & Gil-Alana, L.A. (2006). 'ETA: A Persistent Phenomenon'. *Defence and Peace Economics*, *17* (2), 95–116.

Bassiouni, M.C. (1987). *Legal Responses to International Terrorism*. Boston, MA: Martinus Nijhoof.

BBC News Online. (2005a). 'London bomber video aired on TV'. 2 September. Available at: http://news.bbc.co.uk/2/hi/uk_news/4206708.stm

BBC News Online. (2005b). 'IRA statement in full'. 28 July. Available at: http://news.bbc.co.uk/1/hi/northern_ireland/4724599.stm

BBC News Online. (2005c). 'Cleric Bakri "will return" to UK'. 9 August. Available at: http://news.bbc.co.uk/2/hi/uk_news/politics/4133150.stm

BBC News Online. (2006). 'Text: ETA declares ceasefire'. 23 March. Available at: http://news.bbc.co.uk/1/hi/world/europe/4833490.stm

BBC News Online. (2007a). 'UK fertilizer bomb plot'. Available at: http://news.bbc.co.uk/2/shared/spl/hi/guides/457000/457032/html/nn1page6.stm

BBC News Online. (2007b). 'NI politicians help at Iraq talks'. 3 September. Available at: http://news.bbc.co.uk/1/hi/northern_ireland/6976706.stm

BBC News Online. (2007c). 'Replica guns at march condemned'. 4 September. Available at: http://news.bbc.co.uk/1/hi/northern_ireland/6977173.stm

BBC News Online. (2007d). 'Sadr "freezes" militia activities'. 29 August. Available at: http://news.bbc.co.uk/2/hi/middle_east/6968720.stm

BBC News Online. (2007e). 'Taleban sack military commander'. 29 December. Available at: http://www.bbc.co.uk/2/hi/south_asia/7164277.stm

BBC News Online. (2008). *BBC Special Reports – In Depth: The London Attacks*. Available at: http://news.bbc.co.uk/2/hi/in_depth/uk/2005/london_explosions/default.stm

Belfast Newsletter. (2006). ' "Terror convention" cancelled as finger points at the IRA'. 29 August. Available at: http://www.newsletter.co.uk/ViewArticle.aspx? SectionID=3425&ArticleID=1726257

Bergen, P. (2001). 'The Bin-Laden Trial: What Did We Learn?'. *Studies in Conflict and Terrorism*, *24* (6), 429–34.

Bergen, P. & Cruickshank, P. (2008). 'The Unraveling: The Jihadist Revolt Against Bin Laden'. *The New Republic*, 11 June. Available at: http://www.tnr.com/politics/ story.html?id=702bf6d5-a37a-4e3e-a491-fd72bf6a9da1.

Bjørgo, T. (1998). *Recruitment and Disengagement from Extreme Groups: The Case of Racist Youth Subcultures*. Paper presented at the 7th International Seminar on Environmental Criminology and Crime Analysis, Barcelona, 21–24 June.

Bjørgo, T. (1999). *How Gangs Fall Apart: Processes of Transformation and Disintegration of Gangs*. Paper presented at the 51st Annual Meeting of the American Society of Criminology, Toronto, Canada, 17–20 November.

Bjørgo, T. (2006). 'Reducing Recruitment and Promoting Disengagement from Terrorist Groups: The Case of Racist Sub-Cultures'. In C. Benard (ed.) *A Future for the Young: Options for helping Middle Eastern Youth Escape the Trap of Radicalization*. Washington DC: Rand Working Paper WR-354.

Bjørgo, T. (ed.) (2005). *Root Causes of Terrorism*. Oxon: Routledge.

Bjørgo, T. & Carlsson, Y. (2005). *Early Intervention with Violent and Racist Youth Groups*. NUPI-paper 677. Available at: http://www.nupi.no/IPS/filestore/ Paper677.pdf

Bjørgo, T. & Horgan, J. (eds) (2009). *Leaving Terrorism Behind: Individual and Collective Disengagement*. Oxon: Routledge.

Bloom, M. (2005). *Dying to Kill: The Allure of Suicide Terror*. New York: Columbia.

Bongar, B., Brown, L.M., Beutler, L.E., Breckenridge, J.N. & Zimbardo, P.G. (eds) (2007). *Psychology of Terrorism*. New York: Oxford University Press.

Bonner, D. (1988). 'Combating Terrorism: Supergrass Trials in Northern Ireland'. *Modern Law Review*, *51* (1), 23–53.

Bottoms, A., Shapland, J., Costello, A., Holmes, D. & Muir, G. (2004). 'Towards Desistance: Theoretical Underpinnings for an Empirical Study'. *The Howard Journal of Criminal Justice*, *43* (4), 368–89.

Brame, R., Bushway, S.D. & Paternoster, R. (2003). 'Examining the Prevalence of Criminal Desistance'. *Criminology*, *41* (2), 423–48.

Brandon, J. (2008) 'The UK's Experience in Counter-Radicalization'. *The Sentinel* (Countering Terrorism Center), *1* (5).

Bushway, S.D., Piquero, A.R., Broidy, L.M., Cauffman, E. & Mazerolle, P. (2001). 'An Empirical Framework for Studying Desistance as a Process'. *Criminology*, *39* (2), 491–515.

Bushway, S.D., Thornberry, T.P. & Krohn, M.D. (2003). 'Desistance as a Developmental Process: A Comparison of Static and Dynamic Approaches'. *Journal of Quantitative Criminology*, *19* (2), 129–53.

Byman, D. (2006). 'The Decision to Begin Talks with Terrorists: Lessons for Policymakers'. *Studies in Conflict and Terrorism*, *29* (5), 403–14.

Caldwell, J. (2007). 'Ex-paramilitary Tesco "superhero" '. 19 April. Available at: http:// news.bbc.co.uk/1/hi/northern_ireland/6570165.stm

Casciani, D. (2005). 'Profile: Omar Bakri Mohammed'. 12 August. Available at: http:// news.bbc.co.uk/2/hi/uk_news/4144892.stm

Clarke, L. (2006). 'IRA split adds to violence worries'. *Sunday Times*. 27 August.

Available at: http://www.timesonline.co.uk/tol/news/world/ireland/article620853.ece

Clark, R.P. (1983a). 'Patterns in the Lives of ETA Members', *Terrorism*, 6 (3), 423–54.

Clark, R.P. (1983b). *The Basque Insurgents: ETA 1952–1980*. Madison: University of Wisconsin Press.

Clarke, R.V.G. & Cornish, D.B. (1985). 'Modeling Offenders' Decisions: A Framework for Research and Policy', in M. Tonry & N. Morris (eds). *Crime and Justice: An Annual Review of Research, Volume 6*. Chicago: University of Chicago Press.

CNN. (2002). 'Al Qaeda now'. 27 May. Available at: http://archives.cnn.com/2002/ALLPOLITICS/05/27/time.alqaeda/

CNN. (2008). 'US Military: Al Qaeda in Iraq seeks female patients as bombers'. 14 February. Available at: http://edition.cnn.com/2008/WORLD/meast/02/14/iraq.main/

CNN Larry King Live. (2002). Interview with Patty Hearst. 22 January. Available at: http://transcripts.cnn.com/TRANSCRIPTS/0201/22/lkl.00.html

Cohen, H. & Dudai, R. (2005). 'Human Rights Dilemmas in Using Informers to Combat Terrorism: The Israeli-Palestinian Case'. *Terrorism and Political Violence*, 17 (1–2), 229–43.

Collins, E. (with M. McGovern) (1997). *Killing Rage*. Granta: London.

Combating Terrorism Center. (2008). *Bombers, Bank Accounts and Bleedout: Al Qaida's Road in and Out of Iraq*. New York: CTC West Point. Available at: http://www.ctc.usma.edu/harmony/Sinjar2.asp.

Cordes, B. (1987). 'Euroterrorists Talk about Themselves: A Look at the Literature', in P. Wilkinson & A.M. Stewart (eds) *Contemporary Research on Terrorism* (pp318–36). Aberdeen: Aberdeen University Press.

Corrado, R.A. (1981). 'A critique of the mental disorder perspective of political terrorism'. *International Journal of Law and Psychiatry*, 4 (3–4), 293–309.

Crawford, C. (2003). *Inside the UDA: Volunteers and Violence*. Dublin: Pluto.

Crenshaw, M. (1985). 'An Organisational Political Approach to the Analysis of Political Terrorism'. *Orbis*, 29 (3), 465–89.

Crenshaw, M. (1987). 'How Terrorism Ends'. Paper Presented at the annual meeting of the American Political Science Association, Chicago, IL, September.

Crenshaw, M. (1991). 'How Terrorism Declines'. *Terrorism and Political Violence*, 3 (1), 69–87.

Cronin, A.K. (2006). 'How Al-Qaida Ends: The Decline and Demise of Terrorist Groups'. *International Security*, 31 (1), 7–48.

Cronin, A.K. (2008). *Ending Terrorism: Lessons for Defeating Al-Qaeda. International Institute for Strategic Studies Adelphi Paper 394*. Oxon: Routledge.

Cusack, J. & Taylor, M. (1993). 'Resurgence of a Terrorist Organisation – Part 1: The UDA, A Case Study'. *Terrorism and Political Violence*, 5 (3), 1–27.

Cusson, M. (1993). 'A Strategic Analysis of Crime: Criminal Tactics as Responses to Precriminal Situations', in R.V. Clarke & M. Felson (eds) *Routine Activity and Rational Choice: Volume 5*. New Brunswick, NJ: Transaction.

Debray, R. (1967). *Revolution in the Revolution*. New York: MR Press.

De Cataldo Neuburger, L. & Velentini, T. (1996). *Women and Terrorism*. Hampshire: Macmillan.

Decker, S.H. & Van Winkle, B. (1996). *Life in a Gang: Family, Friends and Violence*. New York: Cambridge University Press.

Dillon, M. (1991). *The Shankill Butchers: A Case Study of Mass Murder*. London: Arrow.

Doherty, E.E. (2006). 'Self-control, Social Bonds, and Desistance: A Test of Life-course Interdependence'. *Criminology*, *44* (4), 807–33.

Dowling, B. (2006). 'Efforts to unite North dissident groups pose "real threat" '. *Irish Independent*. 28 August. Available at: http://www.independent.ie/national-news/efforts-to-unite-north-dissident-groups-pose-real-threat-85137.html

Ebaugh, H.R.F. (1988). *Becoming an Ex: The Process of Role Exit*. Chicago: University of Chicago Press.

Eysenck, H. (1957). *The Dynamics of Anxiety and Hysteria*. London: Routledge.

Farrall, S. (2005). 'On the Existential Aspects of Desistance from Crime'. *Symbolic Interaction*, *28* (3), 367–86.

Farrall, S. & Maruna, S. (2004). 'Desistance-focused Criminal Justice Policy Research: Introduction to a Special Issue on Desistance from Crime and Public Policy'. *The Howard Journal of Criminal Justice*, *43* (4), 358–67.

Farrington, D. (1992). 'Explaining the Beginning, Progress and Ending of Antisocial Behaviour from Birth to Adulthood', in J. McCord (ed.) *Facts, Frameworks and Forecasts: Advances in Criminological Theory, Volume 3*. New Brunswick, NJ: Transactional Publishers.

Fattah, E.A. (1993). 'The Rational Choice/Opportunity Perspectives as a Vehicle for Integrating Criminological and Victimological Theories', in R.V. Clarke & M. Felson (eds) *Routine Activity and Rational Choice: Volume 5*. New Brunswick, NJ: Transaction.

Fielding, N. (2005). 'Terror links of the Tottenham Ayatollah'. *Sunday Times*. 24 July. Available at: http://www.timesonline.co.uk/tol/news/uk/article547466.ece

Gadd, D. (2006). 'The Role of Recognition in the Desistance Process: A Case Analysis of A Former Far-right Activist'. *Theoretical Criminology*, *10* (2), 179–202.

Gadd, D. & Farrall, S. (2004). 'Criminal Careers, Desistance and Subjectivity: Interpreting Men's Narratives of Change'. *Theoretical Criminology*, *8*(2), 123–56.

Garfinkel, R. (2007). 'Personal Transformations: Moving From Violence To Peace', *United States Institute of Peace Special Report*, *186*, April.

Gerges, F. (1999). 'The Decline of Revolutionary Islam in Algeria and Egypt'. *Survival*, *41* (1), 113–25.

Gil-Har, Y. (2003). 'British Intelligence and the Role of Jewish Informers in Palestine'. *Middle Eastern Studies*, *39* (1), 117–49.

Giordano, P.C., Cernkovich, S.A. & Holland, D.D. (2003). 'Changes in Friendship Relations over the Life Course: Implications for Desistance from Crime.' *Criminology*, *41* (2), 293–327.

Greer, S.C. (1987). 'The Supergrass System in Northern Ireland', in P. Wilkinson & A.M. Stewart (eds) *Contemporary Research on Terrorism* (pp510–35). Aberdeen: Aberdeen University Press.

Gupta, D. (2008). *Understanding Terrorism and Political Violence: The Life Cycle of Birth, Growth, Transformation and Demise*. Oxon: Routledge.

Hall, S. (1985). 'Signification, Representation, Ideology: Althusser and the Post-Structuralist Debates'. *Critical Studies in Mass Communication*, *2*, 535–62.

Harmon, C. (2008). *Terrorism Today*. 2nd edition. Oxon: Routledge.

Harnden, T. & Jones, G. (1999). 'Early release of terrorists under attack'. *Daily Telegraph*, 4 February.

Hillyard, P. & Percy-Smith, J. (1984). 'Converting Terrorists: The Use of Supergrasses in Northern Ireland.' *Journal of Law and Society*, *11* (3), 335–55.

Hirschman, A.O. (1970). *Exit, Voice, and Loyalty: Responses to Decline in Firms, Organizations and States*. Cambridge, MA: Harvard University Press.

Hoffman, B. (1998). *Inside Terrorism*. New York: Columbia.

Hoffman, B. (2001). 'All You Need Is Love: How The Terrorists Stopped Terrorism'. *The Atlantic Monthly*, September.

Hoffman, B. (2008). 'The Myth of Grass-Roots Terrorism: Why Osama Bin Laden Still Matters'. *Foreign Affairs*, May/June.

Horchem, H.J. (1991). 'The Decline of the Red Army Faction'. *Terrorism and Political Violence*, *3* (2), 61–74.

Horgan, J. (2003a). 'Leaving Terrorism Behind: An Individual Perspective', in A. Silke (ed.) *Terrorists, Victims and Society: Psychological Perspectives on Terrorism and its Consequences*. London: John Wiley.

Horgan, J. (2003b). 'The Search for the Terrorist Personality', in A. Silke (ed.) *Terrorist, Victims, and Society: Psychological Perspectives on Terrorism and its Consequences*. London: John Wiley.

Horgan, J. (2005a). 'Psychological Factors Related to Disengaging from Terrorism: Some Preliminary Assumptions and Assertions', in C. Benard (ed.) *A Future for the Young: Options For Helping Middle Eastern Youth Escape the Trap of Radicalization*. Washington DC: Rand Working Paper WR-354.

Horgan, J. (2005b). *The Psychology of Terrorism*. Oxon: Routledge.

Horgan, J. (2006). 'Disengaging from Terrorism'. *Jane's Intelligence Review*, *18* (12), 34–7.

Horgan, J. & Taylor, M. (1999). 'Playing the Green Card: Financing the Provisional IRA – Part 1'. *Terrorism and Political Violence*, *11* (2), 1–60.

Hovland, C.I., Janis, I.L. & Kelley, H.H. (1953). *Communication and Persuasion: Psychological Studies of Opinion Change*. New Haven: Yale University Press.

Hundeide, K. (2003). 'Becoming a Committed Insider'. *Culture and Psychology*, *9* (2), 107–27.

Independent Monitoring Commission. (2004a). *First Report of the Independent Monitoring Commission, Presented to the Government of the United Kingdom and the Government of Ireland under Articles 4 and 7 of the International Agreement establishing the Independent Monitoring Commission*. April.

Independent Monitoring Commission. (2004b). *Third Report of the Independent Monitoring Commission, Presented to the Government of the United Kingdom and the Government of Ireland under Articles 4 and 7 of the International Agreement establishing the Independent Monitoring Commission*. November.

Jamieson, A. (1989). *The Heart Attacked*. London: Marion Boyars.

Jamieson, A. (1990). 'Entry, Discipline and Exit in the Italian Red Brigades.' *Terrorism and Political Violence*, *2* (1), 1–20.

Kalyvas, S.N. (2003). 'The Ontology of "Political Violence": Action and Identity in Civil Wars'. *Perspectives on Politics*, *1* (3), 475–94.

Kanazawa, S. & Still, M.C. (2000). 'Why Men Commit Crimes (And Why They Desist)'. *Sociological Theory*, *18* (3), 434–47.

Kassimeris, G. (2005). 'Urban Guerrilla or Revolutionary Fantasist? Dimitris Koufo-dinas and the Revolutionary Organization 17 November'. *Studies in Conflict and Terrorism*, *28* (1), 21–31.

Lave, J. (1988). *Cognition in Practice*. Cambridge: Cambridge University Press.

Lave, J. & Wenger, E. (1991). *Situated Learning*. Cambridge: Cambridge University Press.

Lopez-Alves, F. (1989). 'Political Crises, Strategic Choices and Terrorism: The Rise and Fall of the Uruguayan Tupamoros'. *Terrorism and Political Violence, 1* (2), 202–41.

MacFarquhar, N. (2008). 'Speakers at Academy Said to Make False Claims'. *New York Times*, US Section, 7 February.

Macintyre, B. (2006). ' "Insignificant, shabby, miserable" – the banal stamp of the terrorist'. *The Times Comment*, 13 May, p21.

Markey, P. (2007). 'Colombian warlord violates deal, faces extradition'. *Reuters*, 24 August. Available at: http://www.reuters.com/article/worldNews/idUSN2433300420070824

Maruna, S. (2004). 'Desistance from Crime and Explanatory Style: A New Direction in the Psychology of Reform'. *Journal of Contemporary Criminal Justice, 20* (2), 184–200.

Maruna, S. & Farrall, S. (2004) 'Desistance from Crime: A Theoretical Reformulation', in D. Oberwittler & S. Karstedt (eds) *Kölner Zeitschrift für Soziologie und Sozialpsychologie, 43*, 171–94. Soziologie der Kriminalitaet Koelner Zeitschrift fuer Soziologie und Sozialpsychologie, VS Verlag fuer Sozialwissenschaften, Wiesbaden.

Maruna, S., LeBel, T., Mitchel, N. & Naples, M. (2004). 'Pygmalion in the Reintegration Process: Desistance from Crime through the Looking Glass'. *Psychology, Crime and Law, 10* (3), 271–81.

McDermott, J. (2008). 'Farc's female Rambo surrenders to resurgent Colombian police'. *The Scotsman*, May 20.

McDonald, H. & Cusack, J. (1997). *UVF*. Dublin: Poolbeg.

Middle East Media Research Institute. (2008). 'Report: Al Qaeda Maghreb Commander Turns Self In'. 8 June.

Miller, A.H. (1989). 'Book Review'. *Terrorism and Political Violence, 1* (3), 391–6.

Moore, M. (2005). 'End of Terrorism? ETA and the Efforts for Peace'. *Harvard International Review, 27* (2), 12.

Mueller, J. (2006). *Overblown: How Politicians and the Terrorism Industry Inflate National Security Threats and Why We Believe Them*. New York: Free Press.

Mulvey, E., Steinberg, L. & Fagan, J. (2005). 'Theory and Research on Desistance from Antisocial Activity among Serious Adolescent Offenders'. *Youth Violence and Juvenile Justice, 2* (3), 213–36.

Nasiri, O. (2006). 'Focus: My life as a spy at the heart of Al-Qaeda'. *Sunday Times*, 19 November.

O'Keefe, A. (2008). 'Jungle Fever'. *Observer*, 24 August.

Oots, K.L. (1989a). 'Bargaining With Terrorists: Organisational Considerations'. *Terrorism, 13*, 145–58.

Oots, K.L. (1989b). 'Organizational Perspectives on the Formation and Disintegration of Terrorist Groups'. *Terrorism, 12*, 139–52.

Paterson, L. (2007). *U-Boat Combat Missions – The Pursuers and the Pursued – First-Hand Accounts of U-Boat Life and Operations*. New York: Barnes and Noble.

Peci, P. (1985). *I, the Contemptible One* as told to Bruno Guerri, Arnoldo Mondadori, Editore S.P.A. Milano (1983, translation 1985 by the Foreign Broadcast Information Service).

Pedahzur, A., Eubank, W. & Weinberg, L. (2002). 'The War on Terrorism and the

Decline of Terrorist Group Formation: A Research Note'. *Terrorism and Political Violence, 14* (3), 141–7.

Pluchinsky, D.A. (2008). 'Global Jihadist Recidivism: A Red Flag'. *Studies in Conflict and Terrorism, 31* (3), 182–200.

Post, J. (2008). *The Mind of the Terrorist: The Psychology of Terrorism from the IRA to Al Qaeda.* New York: Palgrave Macmillan.

Post, J.M., Sprinzak, E. & Denny, L.M. (2003). 'The Terrorists in their Own Words: Interviews with Thirty-Five Incarcerated Middle Eastern Terrorists'. *Terrorism and Political Violence, 15,* 171–84.

Rapoport, D.C. (1992). 'Terrorism', in M.E. Hawkesworth & M. Kogan (eds) *Routledge Encyclopedia of Government and Politics. Vol. 2.* London: Routledge.

Rapoport, D.C. (ed.) (1988). *Inside Terrorist Organisations.* London: Frank Cass.

Red Army Faction. (1998). *Statement of the RAF* (the 1998 disbanding of the Red Army Faction): The Final Communiqué from the Red Army Faction. Available online: http://www.baader-meinhof.com/students/resources/communique/engrafend.html

Reich, W. (1990). 'Understanding Terrorist Behavior: The Limits and Opportunities of Psychological Inquiry', in W. Reich (ed.) *Origins of Terrorism: Psychologies, Ideologies, Theologies, States of Mind* (pp261–79). New Jersey: Woodrow Wilson Center Press.

Reich, W. (ed.) (1990). *Origins of Terrorism: Psychologies, Ideologies, Theologies, States of Mind.* New Jersey: Woodrow Wilson Center Press.

Report of the Official Account of the Bombings in London on 7th July 2005, to the House of Commons. (2006). London: Stationery Office.

Ripley, A. (2008). 'Reversing radicalism'. *Time.* Available at: http://www.time.com/time/specials/2007/article/0,28804,1720049_1720050_1722062,00.html

Roberts, K. & Horgan, J. (2008). 'Risk Assessment and the Terrorist'. *Perspectives on Terrorism, 2* (6), 3–9.

Ross, J.I. & Gurr, T.R. (1989). 'Why Terrorism Subsides: A Comparative Study of Canada and the United States'. *Comparative Politics, 21* (4), 405–26.

Sageman, M. (2008). *Leaderless Jihad.* Philadelphia: University of Pennsylvania Press.

Sageman, M. & Hoffman, B. (2008). 'Does Osama Still Call the Shots? Debating the Containment of al-Qaeda's Leadership'. *Foreign Affairs,* July/August.

Sarma, K. (2005). 'Informers and the Battle Against Republican Terrorism: A Review of 30 Years of Conflict'. *Police Practice and Research, 6* (2), 165–80.

Shulman, M.R. (2004). *Civil Society's Response to the Challenges of Terrorism: A Conference Report.* From a meeting held at the Luso-American Foundation, Lisbon, Portugal, 7–8 June.

Silke, A. (1998). 'Cheshire Cat Logic: The Recurring Theme of Terrorist Abnormality in Psychological Research'. *Psychology, Crime and Law, 4,* 51–69.

Silke, A. (ed.) (2003). *Terrorists, Victims and Society: Psychological Perspectives on Terrorism and Its Consequences* (Wiley Series in Psychology of Crime, Policing and Law). London: John Wiley.

Silke, A. (ed.) (2004). *Researching Terrorism: Trends, Successes, Failures.* London: Frank Cass.

Simon, B. (2007). 'Switching Sides: Inside the Enemy Camp'. *60 Minutes,* 6 May.

Simpson, C., Swanson, S. & Crewdson, J. (2003). '9/11 suspect cut unlikely figure in terror plot'. *Chicago Tribune,* 23 February.

Smith, A.G., Suedfelt, P., Conway III, L.G. & Winter, D.G. (2008). 'The Language of Violence: Distinguishing Terrorist from Nonterrorist Groups by Thematic Content Analysis'. *Dynamics of Asymmetric Conflict, 1* (2), 142–63.

Taylor, M. (1988). *The Terrorist*. London: Brassey's.

Taylor, M. & Horgan, J. (2006). 'A Conceptual Framework for Addressing Psychological Process in the Development of the Terrorist'. *Terrorism and Political Violence, 18* (4), 585–601.

United States Congress Senate Committee of Governmental Affairs (1992). *Terrorist defectors: are we ready? : Hearing before the Committee on Governmental Affairs, United States Senate, One Hundred Second Congress, second session, February 4, 1992*. Washington, U.S. G.P.O.

United States Institute of Peace (1999). *How terrorism ends*. Special Report, No.48. Washington D.C: U.S. Institute of Peace: http://purl.access.gpo.gov/GPO/LPS14739.

Victoroff, J. (2005). 'The Mind of the Terrorist: A Review and Critique of Psychological Approaches'. *The Journal of Conflict Resolution, 49*, 3–42.

Walt, V. (2005). 'Ordinary People'. *Time*, 10 October.

Walters, G. (2002). 'Developmental Trajectories, Transitions, and Nonlinear Dynamical Systems: A Model of Crime Deceleration and Desistance'. *International Journal of Offender Therapy and Comparative Criminology, 46* (1), 30–44.

Wayne, P.J.M. & Morton, J. (1995). 'Supergrasses and Informers'. *Spectator, 275*, (8726), 47.

Weinberg, L. & Eubank, W.L. (1987). *The Rise and Fall of Italian Terrorism*. London: Westview.

Wenger, E. (1998). *Communities of Practice: Learning, Meaning, and Identity*. Cambridge: Cambridge University Press.

Whetten, D.A. (1980). 'Organizational Decline: A Neglected Topic in Organizational Science'. *The Academy of Management Review, 5* (4), 577–88.

Wilkinson, A. & Mellahi, K. (2005). 'Organisational Failure: Introduction to the Special Issue'. *Long Range Planning – International Journal of Strategic Management, 38* (3), 233–8.

Wilkinson, P. (1987). 'Pathways out of Terrorism for Democratic Societies', in P. Wilkinson & A.M. Stewart (eds) *Contemporary Research on Terrorism* (pp453–65). Aberdeen: Aberdeen University Press.

Wright, L. (2008) 'The Rebellion Within'. *New Yorker*, 2 June.

Zawodny, J.K. (1978). 'Internal Organizational Problems and the Sources of Tensions of Terrorists Movements as Cataylsts of Violence'. *Terrorism, 1* (3–4), 277–85.

Zirakzadeh, C.E. (2002). 'From Revolutionary Dreams to Organizational Fragmentation: Disputes over Violence within ETA and Sendero Luminoso'. *Terrorism and Political Violence, 14* (4), 66–92.

Zubeck, P. (2008). 'Cadets' guest speaker will focus on Christianity'. *Colorado Springs Gazette*.

Index